A PRACTITIONER'S GUIDE TO PROBATE DISPUTES

A PRACTITIONER'S GUIDE TO PROBATE DISPUTES

Nasreen Pearce

Wildy, Simmonds & Hill Publishing

© Nasreen Pearce, 2016

Contains public sector information licensed under the Open Government Licence v3.0

ISBN: 9780854901371

British Library Cataloguing in Publication Data

A catalogue record for this book is available from the British Library

The right of Nasreen Pearce to be identified as the author of this Work has been asserted by her in accordance with the Copyright, Designs and Patents Act 1988.

All rights reserved. No part of this book may be reproduced, stored in a retrieval system, or transmitted, in any form or by any means, electronic, mechanical, photocopying, recording or otherwise, without the consent of the copyright owners, application for which should be addressed to the publisher. Such a written permission must also be obtained before any part of this publication is stored in a retrieval system of any nature.

All reasonable care was taken in the preparation of this book, but any person relying on any of the statements, express or implied, in this book does so entirely at his or her own risk and without liability on the part of either the author or the publisher.

First published in 2016 by

Wildy, Simmonds & Hill Publishing
58 Carey Street
London WC2A 2JF
England
www.wildy.com

Typeset by Cornubia Press Ltd, Bristol.
Printed in Great Britain by CPI Antony Rowe, Chippenham, Wiltshire.

Contents

Table of Cases	xiii
Table of Statutes	xxv
Table of Statutory Instruments	xxix
Table of Conventions	xxxiii

1 Introduction 1

1.1	Wills and codicils	2
1.2	Formalities relating to wills	2
1.3	Grounds for challenge	3
1.4	Statutory right to challenge	3
1.5	Other testamentary dispositions	4
1.6	International wills	5
1.7	Prospective reforms	5

2 Form, Content and Interpretation of a Will 7

2.1	Introduction	7
2.2	Nature and form of a will	7
2.3	Uncertainty relating to intention, subject matter or donee	8
2.4	Examples of cases of construction of wills	10
2.5	Wills where there is a foreign element	16
2.6	Requirements of international wills	17

3 Execution of a Will 19

3.1	Formal requirements	19
3.2	Will must be in writing	20
3.3	Will must be signed by the testator/testatrix or by some other person at his/her direction	20
3.4	Position of the signature	22
3.5	Execution of the wrong will	23
3.6	Acknowledgement of signature in the presence of witnesses	24
3.7	Attestation in the presence of witnesses	25
3.8	Evidence of attestation	26
3.9	Competence of witnesses	28

4 Testamentary Capacity — 31

- 4.1 Introduction — 31
- 4.2 Test of testamentary capacity under common law — 32
  - 4.2.1 Nature of the act of making a will — 32
  - 4.2.2 Effect of making a will — 33
  - 4.2.3 Nature and extent of the property being disposed of — 33
  - 4.2.4 Claims on the estate — 33
  - 4.2.5 Capricious, frivolous, mean or even bad motives — 34
- 4.3 Ascertaining testamentary capacity – the *Golden Rule* — 34
- 4.4 At what stage is assessment of capacity relevant? — 40
- 4.5 Mental Capacity Act 2005 and the test for capacity under common law — 40
  - 4.5.1 Diagnostic stage — 41
  - 4.5.2 Functional stage — 42
- 4.6 Delusions — 43
- 4.7 Senility, confusion and lucid intervals — 45
- 4.8 Drunkenness — 46
- 4.9 Language and literacy — 47
- 4.10 Medical evidence and its limitations — 47
- 4.11 Evidence and standard of proof — 50
- 4.12 Conclusion — 51

5 Knowledge and Approval — 53

- 5.1 Introduction — 53
- 5.2 Mistake — 54
- 5.3 Disability — 55
- 5.4 Lack of testamentary capacity — 55
- 5.5 Suspicious circumstances — 56
- 5.6 Standard and burden of proof — 59
- 5.7 Conclusion — 62

6 Undue Influence — 63

- 6.1 Introduction — 63
- 6.2 What constitutes undue influence — 64
- 6.3 Confidential/fiduciary relationship — 66
- 6.4 Nature of the undue influence — 67
- 6.5 Fraud — 73
- 6.6 Burden of proof — 73
- 6.7 Standard of proof — 74
- 6.8 Evidence — 74
- 6.9 Procedure — 75

7 Forgery — 77

- 7.1 Introduction — 77
- 7.2 Evidence — 77
- 7.3 Interface between civil action and forgery as a criminal offence — 80

	7.4	Burden and standard of proof			82
	7.5	Conclusion			83
8	**Burial Disputes**				**85**
	8.1	Introduction			85
	8.2	Ownership of the body			85
	8.3	Exceptions to the rule on testator/ testatrix direction over body			86
		8.3.1	Human Tissue Act 2004		86
			8.3.1.1	Authorisation of activities for scheduled purposes	86
			8.3.1.2	'Appropriate consent'	88
			8.3.1.3	Nominated representatives	89
			8.3.1.4	Qualifying relationship	89
		8.3.2	Human Fertilisation and Embryology Act 2008		90
			8.3.2.1	Posthumous use of sperm	90
	8.4	Persons who have responsibilities for the body and funeral arrangements			90
		8.4.1	Others with the right to possession and duty to dispose of a body		91
		8.4.2	Disposal of the body of a child		92
			8.4.2.1	Child in care	94
			8.4.2.2	Adopted child	94
	8.5	Impact of the European Convention on Human Rights			96
	8.6	Procedure			101
9	**Rectification**				**105**
	9.1	Introduction			105
	9.2	Section 20 of the Administration of Justice Act 1982			106
	9.3	Clerical error			107
		9.3.1	Errors made in a DIY will		112
	9.4	Failure to understand the testator's/testatrix's instructions			113
		9.4.1	Situations to which section 20(1)(b) of the Administration of Justice Act 1982 does not apply		114
	9.5	Limitation period			115
	9.6	Burden and standard of proof			117
	9.7	Procedure			117
		9.7.1	Unopposed applications where there is no other claim		117
			9.7.1.1	Venue	117
			9.7.1.2	Form	118
			9.7.1.3	Service of the application	118
			9.7.1.4	Criteria for making the order	118
		9.7.2	Procedure for opposed application		119
			9.7.2.1	Venue	119
			9.7.2.2	Form	119
			9.7.2.3	Service	119
			9.7.2.4	Defendant's response	119
			9.7.2.5	Orders	120
	9.8	Summary			120

10	**Revocation of a Will**	**121**
10.1	Introduction	121
10.2	Revocation by marriage	121
10.3	Revocation by marriage between same sex couples	122
10.4	Revocation by formation of civil partnership	124
10.5	Effect of conversion of civil partnership to same sex marriage	125
10.6	Revocation by annulment or dissolution of the testator's/testatrix's marriage	125
10.7	Revocation by annulment or dissolution of the testator's/testatrix's civil partnership	126
10.8	Revocation and execution of a subsequent will	126
	10.8.1 Presumption of revocation	129
10.9	Application for the admission to proof of a copy will or codicil where original is missing	131
10.10	Revocation by destruction	131
	10.10.1 Partial destruction	133
10.11	Conditional revocation	134
10.12	Preparation and evidence	134
11	**Lifetime Agreements and Gifts**	**137**
11.1	Introduction	137
11.2	Contracts to leave property by will	138
	11.2.1 Court's powers under the Inheritance (Provision for Family and Dependants) Act 1975 in relation to contracts to leave property by will	140
11.3	Proprietary estoppel	141
11.4	Mutual wills	147
11.5	*Donatio mortis causa*	149
11.6	Conclusion	150
12	**Jointly Owned Assets and Assets Held on Constructive Trust**	**151**
12.1	Jointly owned assets	151
	12.1.1 Introduction	151
	12.1.2 Property held as joint tenants	152
	12.1.3 Severance of joint tenancy	153
	12.1.3.1 Severance as a consequence of actions taken in proceedings	153
	12.1.3.2 Severance by the court in a claim under the Inheritance (Provision for Family and Dependants) Act 1975	154
	12.1.4 Limitation period	155
	12.1.5 Meaning of property	155
	12.1.6 Circumstances which will lead to an order being considered	156
	12.1.7 Criteria which the court will apply	156
12.2	Constructive trust	156
12.3	Conclusion	162

13 Claims under the Inheritance (Provision for Family and Dependants) Act 1975 — 163

- 13.1 Introduction — 163
- 13.2 Who may apply? — 164
  - 13.2.1 Spouse or civil partner of the deceased — 164
  - 13.2.2 Former spouse or civil partner — 165
  - 13.2.3 Person living as husband or wife or civil partner of the deceased — 166
  - 13.2.4 Child of the deceased — 167
  - 13.2.5 Child who is treated as a child of the family — 167
  - 13.2.6 Any other person who immediately before the death of the deceased was being maintained either wholly or partly by the deceased — 168
- 13.3 Time limit for making the claim — 168
  - 13.3.1 Procedure for an application out of time — 170
- 13.4 Grounds for making a claim for financial provision under the Inheritance (Provision for Family and Dependants) Act 1975 — 170
  - 13.4.1 Meaning of 'reasonable financial provision' in relation to a surviving spouse or civil partner — 171
  - 13.4.2 Meaning of 'reasonable financial provision' in relation to all other cases — 171
- 13.5 Matters which the court must take into account — 171
- 13.6 Powers of the court to make orders — 173
- 13.7 Property treated as part of the net estate and available for financial provision — 174
- 13.8 Conclusion — 175

14 Procedure — 177

- 14.1 Introduction — 177
- 14.2 Part 1 of the Civil Procedure Rules – 'the overriding objective' — 177
- 14.3 Venue — 179
- 14.4 First step to take – enter a caveat — 179
  - 14.4.1 What is a caveat? — 179
  - 14.4.2 Procedure for entering a caveat — 180
  - 14.4.3 Duration and renewal of 'caveat'/'objection' — 180
  - 14.4.4 Warning to a caveat/response to an objection — 180
  - 14.4.5 Entering an appearance — 181
  - 14.4.6 Withdrawal of caveat/objection — 181
  - 14.4.7 Powers of the court — 182
  - 14.4.8 Further caveat/objection — 182
- 14.5 Probate claims — 182
  - 14.5.1 Parties — 182
  - 14.5.2 How to start a probate claim — 183
  - 14.5.3 Venue — 183
  - 14.5.4 Contents of the claim form — 184
  - 14.5.5 Documents which must be filed with the claim form — 184
- 14.6 What the court office must do — 185

	14.7	Service	185
	14.8	Acknowledgement of service and defence	185
		14.8.1 Documents to be served with acknowledgement of service	186
	14.9	Counterclaim	186
	14.10	Contents of defence/counterclaim	187
	14.11	Failure to acknowledge service or file a defence	187
	14.12	Discontinuance or dismissal of a claim	188
	14.13	Extension of time limits	188
	14.14	Disclosure	188
		14.14.1 Pre-action disclosure	188
		14.14.2 Disclosure under the Senior Courts Act 1981	189
		14.14.3 Disclosure under Part 31 of the CPR	190
		14.14.4 Obtaining further information under Part 18 of the CPR	190
	14.15	Inspection of testamentary documents	191
	14.16	Rectification of wills	191
	14.17	Costs	192
	14.18	Conclusion	195

15 Statutory Wills — **197**

	15.1	Introduction	197
	15.2	Court's statutory powers to make a statutory will	197
	15.3	Best interests	198
	15.4	Pre-action preparation	199
	15.5	Procedure	199
		15.5.1 Who may apply	199
		15.5.2 Respondents to the application	200
		15.5.3 People who must be notified of the application	200
		15.5.4 Application form	200
		15.5.5 Information to accompany the application form	200
		15.5.6 Execution of the will	201
	15.6	Effect of execution	202
	15.7	Conclusion	202

Appendices — **203**

A	Statutory material		
	A1	Wills Act 1837	203
	A2	Administration of Justice Act 1982 (extracts)	217
B	Precedents		
	B1	Non-Contentious Probate Rules 1987 (SI 1987/2024) – First Schedule, Form 3 Caveat	221
	B2	Non-Contentious Probate Rules 1987 (SI 1987/2024) – First Schedule, Form 4 Warning to Caveator	223
	B3	Non-Contentious Probate Rules 1987 (SI 1987/2024) – First Schedule, Form 5 Appearance to Warning	225
	B4	Affidavit of Service of Warning and of Non-receipt of Summons for Directions	227
	B5	Witness Statement/Affidavit about Testamentary Documents	229

	B6	Some Examples of Undue Influence to be Set Out in the Particulars of Claim	231
	B7	Defence Limited to Putting the Personal Representative to Proof of the Will	233
	B8	Defence Alleging Want of Due Execution: Lack of Testamentary Capacity	235
C	Practice Guidance		
	C1	ACTAPS Practice Guidance for the Resolution of Probate and Trust Disputes (ACTAPS Code)	237

Index   255

Table of Cases

References are to page numbers.

A (A Child of the Family), Re [1998] 1 FLR 347, [1998] 1 FCR 458, [1998] Fam Law 14, CA	168
Adams (Deceased), Re [1990] Ch 601, [1990] 2 All ER 97, [1990] 2 WLR 924, ChD	133
Aitken's Trustees v Aitken 1927 SC 374, 1927 SLT 308, 1927 SN 26, Ct of Sess	8
Atter v Atkinson (1869) LR 1 P&D 665, 33 JP 440, 20 LT 404	60
Austin v Woodward [2011] EWHC 2458 (Ch), [2012] WTLR 559	2, 110
Banks v Goodfellow (1870) LR 5 QB 549, 39 LJQB 237, 22 LT 813, Ct of QB	32, 37, 38, 39, 42, 43, 44, 46, 47, 49, 51, 52
Barclays Bank Ltd v Quistclose Investments [1970] AC 567, [1968] 3 All ER 651, [1968] 3 WLR 1097, HL	158
Barrett v Bem & Ors [2011] EWHC 1247 (Ch), [2012] Ch 573, [2011] 3 WLR 1193, [2011] All ER (D) 182 (May)	21, 29
Barry v Butlin (1838) 2 Moo PCC 480, 163 ER 223	21, 57, 59–60
Basham (Deceased), Re [1987] 1 All ER 405, [1986] 1 WLR 1498, [1987] 2 FLR 264, ChD	142, 144–145
Battan Singh v Amirchand [1948] AC 161, [1948] 1 All ER 152, [1948] LJR 827, PC	34
Bean's Estate, Re [1944] P 83, [1944] 2 All ER 348, 113 LJP 65, PD&A	22
Bell v Georgiou [2002] EWHC 1080 (Ch), [2002] WTLR 1105, [2002] All ER (D) 433 (May)	107, 114–115, 117
Bell v Georgiou [2002] EWCA Civ 1510	114–115
Bhura v Bhura [2014] EWHC 727 (Fam), [2015] 2 FCR 353, [2015] 1 FLR 153, [2014] Fam Law 1116, FD	161
Bieber & Others v Teathers Ltd (In liquidation) [2012] EWCA Civ 1466, [2013] 1 BCLC 248, 15 ITELR 492, [2013] 1 P&CR D23	157–159
Bird v Luckie (1850) 8 Hare 301, 14 Jur 1015, 68 ER 375	34
Blewitt's Goods, Re (1880) 5 PD 116, 44 JP 768, 49 LJP 31, PD&A	20

Borrows v HM Coroner for Preston [2008] EWHC 1387 (QB), [2008] 2
FLR 1225, [2008] Fam Law 984, [2008] All ER (D) 201 (May)   86, 97–98,
99, 100, 102
Boughton v Knight. *See* Broughton v Knight
Boyle v The United Kingdom (Application 16580/90) (1994) 19 EHRR
179, [1994] 2 FCR 822, ECHR   98
Boyse v Rossborough (1857) 6 HLC 2, 3 Jur NS 373, 5 WR 414, 10 ER
1192, [1843–60] All ER Rep 610, 29 LTOS 27, HL   73
Bradshaw v Hardcastle [2002] All ER (D) 219 (Nov), ChD   68
Brassington, in the Goods of [1902] P 1, 71 LJP 9, 85 LT 644,
PD&A   132
Broughton v Knight; *sub nom* Boughton v Knight (1873) LR 3 P & D 64,
37 JP 598, 647, 42 LJP & M 25, Ct of Prob   34, 43–44
Brudenell-Bruce, Earl of Cardigan v Moore and Anor [2012] EWHC 1024
(Ch), 14 ITELR 967, [2012] NLJR 621, [2012] 2 P & CR D24   146
Buchanan v Milton [1999] 2 FLR 844, [1999] Fam Law 692, 53 BMLR
176, FD   95, 102
Buckenham v Dickinson [1997] CLY 4733, QBD   36, 45, 61

C v Advocate General for Scotland. *See* Connolly v MOD
Cant v Johnstone. *See* Ray, Re
Carr & Others v Beaven & Others [2008] EWHC 2582 (Ch), [2008] All
ER (D) 289 (Oct)   44–45
Chalcraft, Re; Chalcraft v Giles [1948] P 222, [1948] 1 All ER 700, [1948]
LJR 1111, PD&A   21
Chana (Gavinder) v Chana (Harjit Kaur) [2001] WTLR 205, ChD   47, 64
Channon v Perkins (A Firm) [2005] EWCA Civ 1808, [2006] WTLR 425,
149 Sol Jo LB 1493, [2005] All ER (D) 30 (Dec)   28
Charles v Fraser [2010] EWHC 2154 (Ch), [2010] WTLR 1489,
13 ITELR 455, 154 Sol Jo (no 32) 30, [2010] All ER (D) 68 (Aug)   148–149
Chittock v Stevens [2000] WTLR 643, ChD   108, 115–116
Clancy v Clancy [2003] EWHC 1885 (Ch), [2003] WTLR 1097, [2003] 37
LS Gaz R 32, [2003] All ER (D) 536 (Jul)   40
Clarke v Brothwood [2006] EWHC 2939 (Ch), [2006] All ER (D) 207
(Nov)   109–110, 112–113
Clarke's Goods, Re (1858) 1 SW & Tr 22, 27 LJP & M 18, 4 Jur NS 234   21
Connolly v MOD; *sub nom* C v Advocate General for Scotland [2011]
CSOH 124, 2012 SLT 103   99–100, 102
Cook's Estate, Re; Murison v Cook [1960] 1 All ER 689, [1960] 1 WLR
353, 104 Sol Jo 311, PD&A   20
Couser v Couser [1996] 3 All ER 256, [1996] 1 WLR 1301, [1996] 3 FCR
745, ChD   25
Cowderoy v Cranfield [2011] EWHC 1616 (Ch), [2011] WTLR 1699,
[2011] All ER (D) 191 (Jun)   36–37

Table of Cases

Cowenbergh v Valkova [2008] EWHC 2451 (Ch), [2008] All ER (D) 264
(Oct)   34
Craig v Lamoureux [1920] AC 349, 89 LJPC 22, 122 LT 208, PC   65, 73
Craven's Estate, Re; Lloyds Bank v Cockburn [1937] Ch 423, [1937] 3 All
ER 33, 106 LJ Ch 308, ChD   150

D, Re (Secretary of State for NI intervening); *sub nom* R (D) v Life
Sentence Review Comrs (Northern Ireland) [2008] UKHL 33, [2008]
NI 292, [2008] 4 All ER 992, [2008] 1 WLR 1499   83
Dabbs (Lawrence Stanley) (Deceased), Re. *See* Hart v Dabbs
Daniel v Drew [2005] EWCA Civ 507, [2005] 2 FCR 365, [2005] WTLR
807, [2005] All ER (D) 84 (May)   68
Davies' Estate, Re; Russell v Delaney [1951] 1 All ER 920, Assizes   25
Davis v Smith [2011] EWCA Civ 1603, [2012] 1 FLR 1177, [2012] Fam
Law 401, [2012] All ER (D) 55 (Jan)   154
Dennis (Deceased), Re; Dennis v Lloyds Bank Ltd [1981] 2 All ER 140,
124 Sol Jo 885, 131 NLJ 210, ChD   169–170
Devas & Others v Mackay [2009] EWHC 1951 (Ch), [2009] All ER (D) 09
(Aug)   83
Devillebichot (Deceased), Re; Brennan v Prior [2013] EWHC 2867 (Ch),
[2013] WTLR 1701, [2013] All ER (D) 243 (Sep)   42
D'Eye v Avery (1997) [2001] WTLR 227, COP   55
Dharamshi & Others v Velji & Others [2013] EWHC 3917 (Ch)   38, 162
Dingmar v Dingmar [2006] EWCA Civ 942, [2007] Ch 109, [2007] 2 All
ER 382, [2006] 3 WLR 1183   156
Dix, Re. *See* Gully v Dix
Dixon v Treasury Solicitor [1905] P 42, 74 LJP 33, 92 LT 427, PD&A   134
Dobson v North Tyneside Health Authority [1996] 4 All ER 474, [1997] 1
WLR 596, [1997] 2 FCR 651, CA   90
Dodsbo v Sweden [2006] ECtHR Application No 61564/00, (2006) 45
EHRR 581, ECHR   96
Doland's Will Trusts, Re; Westminster Bank Ltd v Phillips [1970] Ch 267,
[1969] 3 All ER 713, [1969] 3 WLR 614, ChD   14–15
Drakeford v Cotton [2012] EWHC 1414 (Ch), [2012] 3 All ER 1138, 15
ITELR 144, [2012] 3 FCR 464, ChD   152

Edwards v Edwards [2007] EWHC 1119 (Ch), [2007] WTLR 1387   65–66
Esson v Esson [2009] EWHC 3045 (Ch), [2010] WTLR 187   12
Evans v HSBC Trust Co (UK) Ltd [2005] WTLR 1289, ChD   142–143
Everest (Deceased), Re [1975] Fam 44, [1975] 1 All ER 672, [1975] 2
WLR 333, FD   133–134
Fessi v Whitmore [1999] 1 FLR 767, [1999] Fam
Law 221, ChD   92–93, 101–102
Finn's Estate, Re (1935) 105 LJP 36, [1935] All ER Rep 419, 80 Sol Jo 56,
PD&A   20

Fleming's Will Trusts, Re; Ennion v Hampstead Old People's Housing
Trust Ltd [1974] 3 All ER 323, [1974] 1 WLR 1552, 118 Sol Jo 850,
ChD   8
Franks v Sinclair [2006] EWHC 3365 (Ch), [2007] WTLR 439, [2006] All
ER (D) 340 (Dec)   57–58
Fuld's Estate (No 3), Re; Hartley v Fuld [1968] P 675, [1965] 3 All ER
776, [1966] 2 WLR 717, PD&A   63
Fuller v Strum [2001] EWCA Civ 1879, [2002] 2 All ER 87, [2002] 1
WLR 1097, 4 ITELR 454, CA   60-61

G (Children) (Residence: Same-sex Partner), Re [2006] UKHL 43, [2006]
4 All ER 241, [2006] 1 WLR 2305, [2006] 3 FCR 1   97
Gale v Gale [2010] EWHC 1575 (Ch), [2010] All ER (D) 234
(Jun)   83–84
Gallorotti v Sebastianelli [2012] EWCA Civ 865, 15 ITELR 277, [2013] 1
FCR 210, [2012] 2 P&CR D47   161
Garnett-Botfield v Garnett-Botfield [1901] P 335, 71 LJP 1, 85 LT 641,
PD&A   55
Gibson (Deceased), Re [1949] P 434, [1949] 2 All ER 90, [1949] LJR
1260, PD&A   29
Gill v Gill [1909] P 157, 78 LJP 60, 53 Sol Jo 359, PD&A   132
Gill v RSPCA [2009] EWHC 2990 (Ch)   67
Gill v Woodall [2010] EWCA Civ 1430, [2011] Ch 380, [2011] 3 WLR
85, [2011] WTLR 251, [2010] All ER (D) 167 (Dec)   56
Gissing v Gissing [1971] AC 886, [1970] 3 WLR 255, [1970] 2 All ER
780, 21 P & CR 702, HL   160
Goldcorp Exchange Ltd (in Receivership), Re; *sub nom* Kensington v
Unrepresented Non-allocated Claimants [1995] 1 AC 74, [1994] 3
WLR 199, [1994] 2 All ER 806, [1994] 2 BCLC 578, PC   157
Good (Deceased), Re; Carapeto v Good [2002] EWHC 640 (Ch), [2002]
WTLR 801, [2002] All ER (D) 141 (Apr)   73–74
Goodchild (Deceased), Re; Goodchild v Goodchild [1996] 1 WLR 694,
[1996] 1 All ER 670, [1997] 1 FCR 45, [1996] 1 FLR 591, ChD   147
Goodchild v Bradbury [2006] EWCA Civ 1868, [2007] WTLR 463, [2006]
All ER (D) 247 (Dec)   70
Goodman v Goodman [2006] EWHC 1757 (Ch), [2006] WTLR 1807,
[2006] All ER (D) 193 (Jul)   113
Gully v Dix; *sub nom* Dix, Re [2004] EWCA Civ 139, [2004] 1 WLR
1399, [2004] 1 FCR 453, [2004] 1 FLR 918   167
Hadler's Estate, Re; Goodall v Hadler (1960) *The Times*,
20 October   24
Hall v Hall (1868) LR 1 P&D 481, 32 JP 503, 37 LJP & M 40,
16 WR 544   64-65
Hameed v Qayyum [2009] EWCA Civ 352, [2009] 3 FCR 545, [2009] 2
FLR 962, [2009] Fam Law 811, [2009] BPIR 870   157

Table of Cases xvii

Harding (decd), Re; Gibbs v Harding [2007] EWHC 3 (Ch), [2008] Ch 235, [2007] 1 All ER 747, [2008] 2 WLR 361	10
Harnett v Elliott; Denning, Re [1958] 1 WLR 462, [1958] 2 All ER 1, 102 Sol Jo 293, PD&A	26
Harper's Will Trusts, Re; Haller v Attorney General [1962] Ch 78, [1961] 3 WLR 924, [1961] 3 All ER 588, 105 Sol Jo 609, CA	14, 15
Harris v Goddard [1983] 1 WLR 1203, [1983] 3 All ER 242, 46 P & CR 417, [1984] FLR 209, CA	153
Harrison v Gibson; Harrison, Re [2005] EWHC 2957 (Ch), [2006] 1 WLR 1212, [2006] 1 All ER 858, 8 ITELR 588, [2005] All ER (D) 345 (Dec)	13
Hart v Dabbs; *sub nom* Dabbs (Lawrence Stanley) (Deceased), Re [2001] WTLR 527, [2000] All ER (D) 934, ChD	61
Hartshorne v Gardner [2008] EWHC B3 (Ch), [2008] EWHC 3675 (Ch), [2008] 2 FLR 1681, [2008] Fam Law 985	92, 93–94
Hawes v Burgess [2013] EWCA Civ 74, [2013] WTLR 453, [2013] All ER (D) 220 (Feb)	39, 58
Healey v Brown [2002] EWHC 1405 (Ch), [2002] WTLR 849, 4 ITELR 894, [2002] All ER (D) 249 (Apr)	149
Holland v Murphy; *sub nom* Murphy v Murphy [2003] EWCA Civ 1862, [2004] WTLR 239, [2003] All ER (D) 410 (Dec)	152
Holtham v Arnold (1986) 2 BMLR 123, ChD	91, 102
Hornal v Neuberger Products Ltd [1957] 1 QB 247, [1956] 3 WLR 1034, [1956] 3 All ER 970, 100 Sol Jo 915, CA	82
Howell, Re [1955] OWN 85, Ont Sur Ct	67
Hughes v Hughes [2005] EWHC 469 (Ch), [2005] 1 FCR 679, [2005] All ER (D) 404 (Mar)	70
Hunt, The Goods of (1875) LR 3 P&D 250, 39 JP 744, 44 LJP & M 43, 23 WR 553, PD&A	54
Ibuna v Arroyo [2012] EWHC 428 (Ch), [2012] WTLR 827, [2012] 12 LS Gaz R 22, [2012] NLJR 392	98–99, 100–101
Irani v Irani & Others [2006] EWHC 1811 (Ch), [2006] WTLR 1561, [2006] All ER (D) 335 (Jul)	138–140
James's Will Trusts, Re; Peard v James [1962] Ch 226, [1960] 3 WLR 1031, [1960] 3 All ER 744, 104 Sol Jo 1077, ChD	14, 15
Jarrom v Sellars [2007] EWHC 1366 (Ch), [2007] WTLR 1219, [2007] All ER (D) 202 (Apr)	192, 194
Jessop v Jessop [1992] 1 FLR 591, [1992] 1 FCR 253, [1992] Fam Law 328, CA	156
Jones v Kernott [2011] UKSC 53, [2012] 1 AC 776, [2011] 2 WLR 1121, [2012] 1 All ER 1265, [2011] 3 FCR 495	159–161
Kennard v Adams (1975) *The Times*, 29 November	35

Kensington v Unrepresented Non-allocated Claimants. *See* Goldcorp Exchange Ltd (in Receivership), Re

Key (Deceased), Re; Key v Key & Others [2010] EWHC 408 (Ch), [2010] 1 WLR 2020, [2010] WTLR 623, [2010] All ER (D) 155 (Apr)   31, 36, 37, 38, 42, 45, 61

Killick v Pountney [2000] WTLR 41, [1999] All ER (D) 365, ChD   74

Kinane v Mackie-Conteh [2005] EWCA Civ 45, [2005] WTLR 345, [2005] 2 P&CR D9, [2005] All ER (D) 229 (May), CA   145

King v Chiltern Dog Rescue and Redwings Horse Sanctuary [2015] EWCA Civ 581, [2015] WTLR 1225, [2015] All ER (D) 105 (Jun), CA; reversing in part *sub nom* King v Dubrey [2014] EWHC 2083 (Ch), [2014] PLSCS 196, [2014] WTLR 1411, [2014] All ER (D) 24 (Jul)   150

King v Dubrey. *See* King v Chiltern Dog Rescue and Redwings Horse Sanctuary

Kostic v Chaplin [2007] EWHC 2298 (Ch), 10 ITELR 364, [2007] All ER (D) 203 (Oct)   44

Lamothe v Lamothe [2006] EWHC 1387 (Ch), [2006] WTLR 1431, [2006] All ER (D) 153 (Jun)   127, 128–129

Leeburn v Derndorfer [2004] WTLR 867, SC Vic (Aus)   91, 93

Lewisham Hospital NHS Trust v Hamuth & Others [2006] EWHC 1609 (Ch), [2007] WTLR 309, 150 Sol Jo LB 168, [2006] All ER (D) 145 (Jan)   91

Lilleyman v Lilleyman [2012] EWHC 821 (Ch), [2013] Ch 225, [2012] 3 WLR 754, [2013] 1 All ER 302, [2012] WTLR 1007   194

Lim v Thompson [2009] EWHC 3341 (Ch), [2010] WTLR 661   21, 28

Lindop v Agus, Bass and Hedley [2009] EWHC 14 (Ch), [2010] 1 FLR 631, [2009] WTLR 1175, [2009] Fam Law 808   167

Little, Re; Foster v Cooper [1960] 1 WLR 495, [1960] 1 All ER 387, 104 Sol Jo 369, PD&A   22

Lowthorpe-Lutwidge v Lowthorpe-Lutwidge [1935] P 151, 104 LJKB 71, [1935] All ER Rep 338, 153 LT 103, PD&A   127, 129

Loxton (Deceased), Re; Abbot v Richardson [2006] EWHC 1291 (Ch), [2006] WTLR 1567, [2006] All ER (D) 54 (May)   46

MacDonald v Frost [2009] EWHC 2276 (Ch), [2009] WTLR 1815, 12 ITELR 577, [2010] 1 P&CR D36, [2009] All ER (D) 55 (Oct)   145

Mann's Goods, Re [1942] P 146, [1942] 2 All ER 193, 111 JP 86, 167 LT 189, PD&A   22

Marley v Rawlings & Anor [2012] EWCA Civ 61, [2013] Ch 271, [2013] 2 WLR 205, [2012] 4 All ER 630, [2012] WTLR 639, CA   54–55, 105, 110, 111

Marley v Rawlings & Anor [2011] EWHC 161 (Ch), [2011] 1 WLR 2146, [2011] 2 All ER 103, [2011] WTLR 595, [2011] 1 FLR 2052   54–55, 105, 110, 111

Marley v Rawlings & Anor [2014] UKSC 2, [2015] AC 129, [2014] 2 WLR 213, [2014] 1 All ER 807, [2014] WTLR 1511	11, 23–24, 55, 111, 114
Marshall v Marshall [1998] EWCA Civ 1467	153
Meyer's Estate, Re [1908] P 353, 77 LJP 150, 52 Sol Jo 716, 99 LT 881, PD&A	23, 54
Minns v Foster [2002] All ER (D) 225 (Dec), ChD	56
Morris deceased, Re; Lloyds Bank Ltd v Peake (Hurdwell cited) [1971] P 62, [1970] 2 WLR 865, [1970] 1 All ER 1057, 113 Sol Jo 923, PD&A	61, 128
Mulhall v Mulhall [1936] IR 712, Ir HC	25
Murphy v Murphy. *See* Holland v Murphy	
Murrin v Matthews; Papillon (dec'd), Re [2006] EWHC 3419 (Ch), [2006] All ER (D) 297 (Dec)	28
Nicholls, Re; Hunter v Nicholls [1921] 2 Ch 11, 90 LJ Ch 379, 65 Sol Jo 533, 125 LT 55, ChD	22
NT v FS (by his litigation friend, the Official Solicitor) [2013] EWHC 684 (COP), [2013] WTLR 867, [2013] All ER (D) 292 (Mar)	198
O'Learly v Douglass (1878) 1 LR IR 45	128
Olins v Walters [2008] EWCA Civ 782, [2009] Ch 212, [2009] 2 WLR 1, [2008] All ER (D) 58 (Jul)	147–148
Oswald, Goods of (1874) LR 3 P & D 162, 38 JP 425, 43 LJP & M 24, 30 LT 344	128
Oxley v Hiscock [2004] EWCA Civ 546, [2005] Fam 211, [2004] 3 WLR 715, [2004] 3 All ER 703, [2004] 2 FCR 295	160
P, Re [2009] EWHC 163 (COP), [2010] Ch 33, [2009] 2 All ER 1198, [2009] WTLR 651, [2009] All ER (D) 160 (Feb)	197–198, 199
Parker v Felgate (1883) 8 PD 171, 47 JP 808, 52 LJP 95, 32 WR 186, PD&A	40, 46, 56, 61
Parkinson v Fawdon [2009] EWHC 1953 (Ch), [2010] WTLR 79, [2009] All ER (D) 322 (Jul)	11, 16
Parsons, Re; Borman v Lel [2002] WTLR 237, [2001] All ER (D) 94 (Jun), ChD	46
Pearce v Beverley [2013] EW Misc 10 (CC), [2014] WTLR 85, [2013] All ER (D) 159 (Aug), Leeds Cty Ct	33, 34, 51, 53, 63, 66
Pengelly v Pengelly [2007] EWHC 3227 (Ch), [2007] WTLR 1619	107, 108, 116
Perrins (Deceased), Re; Perrins v Holland & Anor [2009] EWHC 1945 (Ch), [2009] All ER (D) 30 (Aug)	39, 40, 46, 56
Perrins v Holland & Ors [2010] EWCA Civ 840, [2011] Ch 270, [2011] 2 All ER 174, [2011] 2 WLR 1086	20, 56
Pesticcio v Huet [2003] 2 P & CR D22, 73 BMLR 57, [2003] All ER (D) 237 (Apr), ChD	69

Phelan, Re [1972] Fam 33, [1971] 3 WLR 888, [1971] 3 All ER 1256, 115 Sol Jo 710	132
Pinnell v Anison [2005] EWHC 1421 (Ch), [2006] WTLR 1047, [2005] All ER (D) 458 (May)	14
Powell v Osborne [1993] 1 FLR 1001, [1993] 1 FCR 797, [1993] Fam Law 287, CA	155
Powell v Powell (1866) LR 1 P & D 209, 35 LJP & M 100, [1861–73] All ER Rep 362, 14 LT 800, Ct of Prob	134
Powell v Powell [1900] 1 Ch 243, 69 LJ Ch 164, 44 Sol Jo 134, 82 LT 84, ChD	66
Price v Craig [2006] WTLR 1873, ChD	109, 116
Q v Q [2008] EWHC 1874 (Fam), [2009] 1 FLR 935, [2009] Fam Law 17, 11 ITELR 748	157
Quigley v Masterson [2011] EWHC 2529 (Ch), [2012] 1 All ER 1224, [2012] WTLR 521, [2012] 1 FCR 541, [2011] 3 EGLR 81	154
Quistclose Investments, Re. *See* Barclays Bank Ltd v Quistclose Investments	
R (D) v Life Sentence Review Comrs (Northern Ireland). *See* D, Re (Secretary of State for NI intervening)	
R (Stevens) v Plymouth City Council & Anor [2002] EWCA Civ 388, [2002] 1 WLR 2583, [2002] 1 FLR 1177, [2002] LGR 565	50
R v Gwynedd County Council ex parte B [1992] 3 All ER 317, [1991] FCR 800, [1991] 2 FLR 365, CA	94
R v Human Fertilisation and Embryology Authority ex parte Blood [1999] Fam 151, [1997] 2 WLR 806, [1997] 2 All ER 687, [1997] 2 FLR 742	90
R v St George, Hanover Square, Overseers. *See* R v Stewart	
R v Stewart; *sub nom* R v St George, Hanover Square, Overseers (1840) 12 Ad & El 773, 4 JP 792, 10 LJMC 40	92
Randall v Randall [2014] EWHC 3134 (Ch), [2015] WTLR 99	182
Rawlinson, Re; Kayll v Rawlinson [2010] WTLR 1443, ChD	28
Rawstron and Pearce v Freud [2014] EWHC 2577 (Ch), [2014] WTLR 1453, 17 ITELR 479, [2015] 1 P & CR D13	10–11
Ray, Re; *sub nom* Cant v Johnstone [1916] 1 Ch 461, 85 LJ Ch 781, 114 LT 688, ChD	9
Resch's Will Trusts, Re; Le Cras v Perpetual Trustee Co Ltd [1969] 1 AC 514, [1968] 3 WLR 1153, [1967] 3 All ER 915, PC	12, 128
Revenue and Customs v Benchdollar Ltd [2009] EWHC 1310 (Ch), [2010] 1 All ER 174, [2009] STC 2342, 79 TC 668	144
Richards v Allan [2001] WTLR 1031, ChD	46
Ritchie (deceased), Re; Ritchie v Joslin [2009] EWHC 709 (Ch), [2009] All ER (D) 59 (Apr)	39, 44, 45, 48
Roberts' Estate, Re [1934] P 102, 103 LJP 61, [1934] All ER Rep 62, PD&A	22

Ross v Caunters [1980] Ch 297, [1979] 3 WLR 605, [1979] 3 All ER 580, 123 Sol Jo 605, ChD	51
Ross v Perrin-Hughes [2004] EWHC 2559 (Ch), [2005] WTLR 191, 7 ITELR 405, [2004] All ER (D) 159 (Nov)	14
Rowe v Clarke [2005] EWHC 3068 (Ch), [2006] WTLR 347, 149 Sol Jo LB 1450, [2005] All ER (D) 368 (Oct)	130
Rowe v Clarke (No 2) (Probate: Costs) [2006] EWHC 1292 (Ch), [2007] WTLR 373, [2006] All ER (D) 124 (May)	192, 193
Royal Bank of Scotland v Etridge (No 2) [2001] UKHL 44, [2002] 2 AC 773, [2001] 3 WLR 1021, [2001] 4 All ER 449	67–68, 73
Salmon (Deceased), Re; Coard v National Westminster Bank Ltd [1981] Ch 167, [1980] 3 WLR 748, [1980] 3 All ER 532, 124 Sol Jo 813, ChD	116, 120, 169
Savory's Goods, Re (1851) 15 Jur 1042, 18 LTOS 280	20
Scammell v Farmer [2008] EWHC 1100 (Ch), [2008] WTLR 1261, [2008] All ER (D) 296 (May)	43, 48–49
Schomberg v Taylor [2013] EWHC 2269 (Ch), [2013] WTLR 1413, [2013] All ER (D) 74 (Jan)	66
Schrader v Schrader [2013] EWHC 466 (Ch), [2013] WTLR 701, 157 Sol Jo (no 11) 31, [2013] All ER (D) 89 (Mar)	63, 66, 70–72
Scotch v Birching (2008) (unreported)	94
Segelman Deceased, Re [1996] Ch 171, [1996] 2 WLR 173, [1995] 3 All ER 676, ChD	107–108, 109, 110, 112
Sen v Headley [1991] Ch 425, [1991] 2 WLR 1308, [1991] 2 All ER 636, CA	149, 150
Sharon McGeever (AP) as legal representative of her daughter Sophie v Maureen Nicol [2012] CSOH 115	77
Sharp v Adam [2006] EWCA Civ 449, [2006] WTLR 1059, 10 ITELR 419, [2006] All ER (D) 277 (Apr)	38–39, 42, 44
Sharp v Hutchins; Estate of Ronald Hubert Butcher (Deceased), Re [2015] EWHC 1240 (Ch), [2015] WTLR 1269, [2015] All ER (D) 46 (May)	58–59
Sherrington v Sherrington [2005] EWCA Civ 326, [2005] WTLR 587, 7 ITELR 711, [2005] 3 FCR 538	27, 34
Shirt v Shirt [2012] EWCA Civ 1029, [2013] WTLR 317, [2013] 1 FLR 232, [2012] 3 FCR 304	145
Simpson, Re; Schaniel v Simpson [1977] 127 NLJ 487, (1977) 121 Sol Jo 224, [1977] LS Gaz R 187, ChD	35, 36, 45
Singellos v Singellos [2010] EWHC 2353 (Ch), [2011] Ch 324, [2011] 2 WLR 1111, [2011] WTLR 327	40
Smith v Bottomley [2013] EWCA Civ 953, [2014] 1 FLR 626, [2014] Fam Law 35, [2013] 2 P & CR D67	145–146
Solicitor for the Affairs of Her Majesty's Treasury v Doveton & Anor [2008] EWHC 2812 (Ch), [2009] BPIR 352	77–79, 83

Southwell v Blackburn [2014] EWCA Civ 1347, [2015] Fam Law 530,
    [2015] WTLR 147, [2014] HLR 736   161
Spiers v English [1907] P 122, 76 LJP 28, 96 LT 582, PD&A   75
Sprackling v Sprackling [2008] EWHC 2696 (Ch), [2009] WTLR 897,
    [2008] All ER (D) 55 (Nov)   107, 113–114, 117
Stack v Dowden [2007] UKHL 17, [2007] 2 AC 432, [2007] 2 WLR 831,
    [2007] 2 All ER 929, [2007] WTLR 1053   159, 160
Staden v Jones [2008] EWCA Civ 936, [2008] 2 FLR 1931, [2008] Fam
    Law 1000, [2008] All ER (D) 176 (Jun)   157
Stott, Re; Klouda v Lloyds Bank Ltd [1980] 1 WLR 246, [1980] 1 All ER
    259, 123 Sol Jo 422, ChD   53
Stephen Supple v Pender & Another [2007] EWHC 829 (Ch), [2007]
    WTLR 1461, [2007] All ER (D) 195 (Feb)   81–82
Synge v Synge [1894] 1 QB 466, 58 JP 396, 63 LJQB 202, CA   138

Thompson v Hurst [2012] EWCA Civ 1752, [2013] 1 FCR 522, [2014] 1
    FLR 238, [2013] Fam Law 396   161
Thorner v Major [2009] UKHL 18, [2009] 1 WLR 776, [2009] 3 All ER
    945, [2009] WTLR 713   141, 142, 143–144
Ticehurst, Re; Midland Bank Executor and Trustee Co v Hankinson (1973)
    The Times, 6 March   58
Tiverton Estates Ltd v Wearwell Ltd [1975] Ch 146, [1974] 2 WLR 176,
    [1974] 1 All ER 209, CA   140
Toovey v Milne (1819) 2 B&A 683   158
Townsend v Moore [1905] P 66, 74 LJP 17, 53 WR 338, CA   127
Turkey v Awadh [2005] EWCA Civ 382, [2005] 2 FCR 7, [2006] WTLR
    553, [2005] All ER (D) 131 (Mar)   69
Turner v Phythian; Wilson, Re [2013] EWHC 499 (Ch), [2013] All ER (D)
    154 (Mar)   42, 72
Twinsectra Ltd v Yardley [2002] UKHL 12, [2002] AC 164, [2002] 2
    WLR 802, [2002] 2 All ER 377, [2002] WTLR 423   157, 158
Tyrell v Painton [1894] P 151, 6 R 540, 42 WR 343, CA   73

Vallee v Birchwood; Bogusz (decd), Re [2013] EWHC 1449 (Ch), [2014]
    Ch 271, [2014] 2 WLR 543, [2013] WTLR 1095   150
Vann, Re; R v William Vann (1851) 169 ER 523, 2 Den 325   92
Vegetarian Society & Anor v Scott [2013] EWHC 4097 (Ch), [2014]
    WTLR 525, 164 NLJ 7593, [2014] All ER (D) 205 (Jan)   34, 51

W v Egdell [1990] Ch 359, [1990] 2 WLR 471, [1990] 1 All ER 835, CA   50
Watson, Re [1999] 1 FLR 878, [1999] 3 FCR 595, [1999] Fam Law 211,
    ChD   167
Watson v Huber [2005] All ER (D) 156 (Mar), ChD   70
Wayland's Estate, Re [1951] 2 All ER 1041, 95 Sol Jo 804, PD&A   127–128

Wayling v Jones [1995] 2 FLR 1029, [1996] 2 FCR 41, [1996] Fam Law 88, CA	145
Westendrop v Warwick [2006] EWHC 915 (Ch), [2006] All ER (D) 248 (Apr)	58
Williams v Williams (1882) 20 Ch D 659, 46 JP 726, 51 LJ Ch 385, ChD	85
Williams v Williams [2003] EWHC 742 (Ch), [2003] WTLR 1371, [2003] All ER (D) 403 (Feb), ChD	69–70
Williams (decd), Re; Wiles v Madgin [1985] 1 WLR 905, [1985] 1 All ER 964, 129 Sol Jo 469, ChD	112
Wilson v Beddard (1841) 12 Sim 28, 10 LJ Ch 305, 5 Jur 624	21
Wingrove v Wingrove (1885) 11 PD 81, 50 JP 56, 55 LJP 7, 34 WR 260, PD&A	64, 73
Wintle v Nye [1959] 1 WLR 284, [1959] 1 All ER 552, 103 Sol Jo 220, HL	58, 61, 63, 75
Wood v Smith [1993] Ch 90, [1992] 3 WLR 583, [1992] 3 All ER 556, CA	22
Wordingham v Royal Exchange Trust Co Ltd [1992] 1 Ch 412, [1992] 2 WLR 496, [1992] 3 All ER 204, ChD	107, 108, 112
Wren v Wren [2006] EWHC 2243 (Ch), [2007] WTLR 531, 9 ITELR 223, [2006] 3 FCR 18	130–131
Wright, Re; Kentfield v Wright [2010] EWHC 1607 (Ch), [2010] All ER (D) 07 (Jul)	27
Wylde v Culver [2006] EWHC 923 (Ch), [2006] 1 WLR 2674, [2006] 4 All ER 345, [2006] WTLR 931	192, 193
Wyniczenko v Plucinska-Surowka [2005] EWHC 2794 (Ch), 8 ITELR 385, [2005] All ER (D) 245 (Nov)	57
X v Germany (1981), Application No 8741/79, 24 DR 137	96
Yeoman's Row Management Ltd and Anor v Cobbe [2008] UKHL 55, [2008] 1 WLR 1752, [2008] 4 All ER 713, [2008] WTLR 1461	141
Young, Re; Young v Young [1951] Ch 344, [1950] 2 All ER 1245, [1951] 1 TLR 262, ChD	29
Zielinski, Re; Korab-Karpinski v Lucas Gardiner [2007] WTLR 1655, ChD	130

Table of Statutes

References are to page numbers.

Administration of Estates Act 1925	
s 46	90
Administration of Justice Act 1982	2, 7, 19, 54, 107, 112, 121, 128, 130
s 17	22
s 20	11, 23, 24, 54, 105, 106, 110, 111, 112, 117, 120, 133, 191
s 20(1)	24, 106, 107, 108, 109, 118
s 20(1)(a)	112
s 20(1)(b)	108, 113, 114, 115
s 20(2)	106, 115
s 20(3)	106, 117
s 20(4)	107
s 21	8, 14, 106, 127
s 21(1)	9
s 21(1)(b)	13
s 21(2)	9
s 22	13
ss 27, 28	16
Sch 2 Uniform Law on the Form of an International Will	5, 16, 17
Art 2	17
Arts 3, 4	17
Art 5(1)–(3)	17
Arts 6, 7	17
Arts 9–14	18
Administration of Justice Act 1985	
s 49	188
Adoption and Children Act 2002	94
s 46(1)	94
s 51(2)	95
s 67(1), (2)	95
Births and Deaths Registration Act 1953	
s 15	87
s 22(1)	87
Children Act 1989	101
s 3(1)	92, 95
s 8	101
Civil Partnership Act 2004	165, 166, 168
Pt 5, Chap 1	125
Pt 5, Chap 3	126
s 210(2)(b)	125
s 211(2)(b)	125
Sch 4	124
Sch 4, Pt 1, para 2	126
Sch 5, Pts 1, 2	171
County Courts Act 1984	
s 32	183
s 40(2)	179
Data Protection Act 1998	49
Family Law Act 1986	
Pt II	126
s 46(1), (2)	166
Family Law Reform Act 1969	19
Family Law Reform Act 1987	167

Forfeiture Act 1982	94	s 3	171, 172
		s 3(4)	168, 173
Human Fertilisation and		s 3A	174
Embryology Act 1990	167	s 4	115, 169, 170
s 30	167	ss 5–7	173
Human Fertilisation and		s 8	150, 175
Embryology Act 2008	90, 167	s 9	155, 156, 175
s 4(1)	90	s 9(1)	154–155
s 39	90	s 9(2)	156
Sch 3	90	s 9(4)	155
Human Fertilisation and Embryology		s 10	175
(Deceased Father) Act 2003	90, 167	s 11	137, 140, 141, 150, 175
Human Rights Act 1998	98	s 11(2)	140
Human Tissue Act 2004	86, 88	ss 12, 13	140
Pt 1	86, 87	s 14	171
s 1(1)	86	s 14A	171
s 1(2), (3)	87	s 23	169
s 2	86, 88	s 25	174–175
s 2(4)	88	s 25(1)	165
s 2(6), (7)	88	s 25(4)	165
s 3	86, 88	Interpretation Act 1978	7, 20
s 3(5)	88		
s 4	89	Law of Property Act 1925	
s 7	90	s 36(2)	153
s 27(4)	89	s 40	138, 140
s 54	88	s 177	122
Sch 1	86, 87, 88	Law of Property (Miscellaneous	
Sch 1, Pts 1, 2	86, 87	Provisions) Act 1989	
		s 2	138, 149
Inheritance and Trustees' Powers		Law Reform (Succession) Act	
Act 2014	155, 168, 173, 174	1995	125, 166
s 4	168	Legitimacy Act 1976	167
s 6	154	Limitation Act 1980	
Sch 2	154	s 28	170
Sch 3	169		
Inheritance (Provision for Family		Marriage (Same Sex Couples) Act	
and Dependants) Act		2013	124, 125, 126, 164
1975	3, 4, 115, 116, 126, 140,	s 6	126
	145, 150, 154, 156, 162, 163,	s 9(1)–(3)	125
	164, 166, 167, 168, 170, 171,	s 11	122, 123, 124
	175, 179, 194	s 11(1)–(7)	123
s 1(1)	164	s 11(1), (2)	164
s 1(1)(d)	168	s 13	126
s 1(3)	168	s 15	165
s 2	4, 140, 172, 173	s 17(4)	126
s 2A	168	Sch 3	122, 123

Marriage (Same Sex Couples) Act 2013 *(continued)*		s 19(2)(b)	102
		s 116	91, 94, 95, 97, 98, 99, 100, 101, 102
Sch 3, Pt 1, para 1	123–124		
Sch 3, Pt 1, para 1(a), (b)	164	s 116(1)	102
Sch 3, Pt 1, para 2(1)–(3)	166	s 116(2)	103
Sch 3, Pt 2, para 5(2)	164–165	s 117	185
Sch 4	122, 123	s 122	27, 189
Sch 4, Pt 1, para 1	124	s 122(1), (2)	189
Sch 4, Pt 7	123	s 123	189, 190
Sch 7, para 21	126	Statutory Declarations Act 1835	
Matrimonial Causes Act 1973	168	s 16	27
ss 23, 24	171		
Mental Capacity Act 2005	32, 40, 41, 42, 43, 48, 50, 197, 198	Trustees Act 2000	
		s 28	30
s 1	40		
s 1(2)	197	Wills Act 1837	2, 7, 19, 26, 27, 30, 83, 110, 124, 126, 202
s 2	42, 61		
s 2(1)	41	s 9	19, 22, 24, 25, 30, 54, 55, 88, 89, 111
s 3	41, 42, 61		
s 3(1)	42	s 9(a)	21, 24
s 4	198	s 9(b)	24, 110, 111
s 16	43	s 14	29
s 16(2)(a)	197	s 15	21, 29
s 18	43	ss 18–22	121
s 18(1)(i)	197	s 18	121, 122
s 50	199	s 18(2)–(4)	122
Sch 2, para 4(3)–(5)	202	s 18A	125
Mental Capacity Act 2005 Code of Practice		s 18B	124
		s 18B(3)–(6)	124
para 4.12	41	s 18C	126
para 4.33	42	s 18C(1)(b)	126
		s 18C(3)	126
Public Health (Control of Disease) Act 1984		s 19	129, 132
		s 20	126–127, 131
s 46	92	s 24	8
		Wills Act 1963	16
Race Relations Act 1976	10	s 1	16
		s 2	17
Senior Courts Act 1981	102, 189	s 4	17

Table of Statutory Instruments

References are to page numbers.

Births and Deaths Registration (Northern Ireland) Order 1976, SI 1976/1041 (NI 14)	
art 21	87
art 25(2)	87
Civil Procedure Rules 1998, SI 1998/3132	181
Pt 1 Overriding Objective	177
r 1.1	177
r 1.1(2)	178
rr 1.2, 1.3	177
Pt 2 – Application and Interpretation of the Rules	
r 2.11	188
Pt 6 – Service of Documents	185, 186
rr 6.17–6.31	185
rr 6.32, 6.33	119
r 6.35	120, 186
PD6B – Service out of the Jurisdiction	120, 186
Pt 7 – How to Start Proceedings – the Claim Form	119, 183
Pt 8 – Alternative Procedure for Claims	103
Pt 15 – Defence and Reply	
rr 15.4, 15.5	120
Pt 16 – Statement of Case	
r 16.4	187
r 16.5(1), (2)	187
r 16.5(6)	187
r 16.9	186
Pt 18 – Further Information	190
Pt 19 – Parties and Group Litigation	182
r 19.4	183
Pt 20 – Counterclaims and other Additional Claims	186, 187
Pt 24 – Summary Judgment	170
Pt 31 – Disclosure and Inspection of Documents	190
r 31.12	190
r 31.16	188

Civil Procedure Rules 1998, SI 1998/3132 *(continued)*
    Pt 36 – Offers to Settle   194
    Pt 38 – Discontinuance   194
    Pt 44 – General Rules about Costs   194
        r 44.3   53
    Pt 57 – Probate and Inheritance   119, 175, 177
        r 57.1(2)   177
        r 57.2   177
        r 57.2(2)   179
        r 57.2(3)   183
        r 57.3   119
        r 57.4(2)   185
        r 57.4(3)   186
        r 57.5   186
        r 57.5(2)(a)   119
        r 57.5(3)   186
        r 57.6(1)   183, 184
        r 57.6(2)   184
        r 57.7   119, 184
        r 57.7(3), (4)   184
        r 57.7(4)(c)   75
        r 57.7(5)   186, 193
        r 57.8   187
        r 57.10(1)–(3)   187
        r 57.11   188, 194
        r 57.11(1)   193
    PD57 Probate   177, 186
        para 2.1   183, 184
        paras 2.3, 2.4   185
        para 3.2   184, 186
        para 3.3   185
        para 4.1   182
        para 6.1   188
        para 7.2   183
        paras 9–11   119, 191
        para 10.1   119, 192
        para 10.2   192
        para 11   120
        para 11.1   192
        Annex   184
    Pt 64 – Estates, Trust and Charities   101, 102
        r 64.2   102
    Pre-Action Protocol   175, 192, 195
    Pre-Action Protocols   177
    General Pre-Action Protocol   183, 190

Court of Protection Rules 2007, SI 2007/1744
    Pt 8 – Permission
        r 51(1)   199
        r 52(2)   199
    Pt 9 – How to Start Proceedings   199
        r 70   200
    PD9B – Notification of other persons that an application form has been issued   200
    PD9F – Applications Relating to Statutory Wills, Codicils, Settlements and Other Dealings with P's Property – effective from 1 July 2015   199
        para 9   200
    PD64F   200

Draft Non-Contentious Probate Rules 2013   6

Marriage (Same Sex Couples) Act 2013 (Commencement No 2 and Transitional Provision) Order 2014, SI 2014/93   126

Non-Contentious Probate Rules 1987, SI 1987/2024   26, 90, 99, 177, 181, 182
    r 12   26
    r 12(1)–(3)   26, 27
    r 13   20, 61
    r 16   27
    r 20   103
    r 22   98, 103
    r 30   99
    r 44   180
    r 44(3)   180
    r 44(10)   181
    r 44(12)   181
    r 45   185
    r 50   131
    r 54   131
    r 55   117, 191
    r 55(1), (2)   118, 191
    r 55(3)   191
    r 55(4)   118, 191

Rules of the Supreme Court 1965
    Ord 5   181
    Ord 85   101, 102

Wills and Administration Proceedings (Northern Ireland) Order 1994, SI 1994/1899 (NI 13)
    art 5   88, 89

Table of Conventions

References are to page numbers.

Convention on the Conflicts of Laws Relating to the Form of Testamentary Dispositions, which was concluded on 5 October 1961 at the Ninth Session of the Hague Conference on Private International Law and was signed by the UK on 13 February 1962	16
Convention providing a Uniform Law on the Form of an International Will was concluded at Washington on 26 October 1973	5, 16
Annex	5
Council Regulation (EC) No 1347/2000 of 29 May 2000 on jurisdiction and the recognition and enforcement of judgments in matrimonial matters and in matters of parental responsibility for children of both spouses (2000) OJ L160/19	166
European Convention for the Protection of Human Rights and Fundamental Freedoms 1950	85, 86, 96, 97, 98, 99, 170
Art 8	91, 96, 100, 101
Art 8(1)	86, 96, 97, 98, 100
Art 8(2)	96, 97, 100
Art 9	96, 97, 101

Chapter 1

Introduction

Disputes over wills and inheritance have been soaring since 2006. In 2011, they were 64% higher than in 2006. Trust property disputes increased from 10 in 2006 to 111 in 2010. The 2012 statistics showed a rise in probate and trust disputes of almost 14% between 2010 and 2011 (Ministry of Justice Judicial and Court Statistics 2010/11).

There are many reasons for this rise. In some cases, the disputes arise because of intestacy. In others, it is because the deceased's will has not been properly prepared. This is particularly the case in relation to DIY wills where the formalities of making a valid will have not been properly complied with. Nothing in life is certain or stagnant and so circumstances change, but it is not unusual to find that the deceased's will has not been updated to take account of changed circumstances, such as the dissolution of the deceased's marriage which has the effect of revoking a will, or to set out the deceased's intention at the time of, or shortly before, his/her death. Disputes can be avoided if a properly prepared will is made and the deceased's intentions are discussed and made clear with the family before death. Often, relatives are aggrieved at being left out of the will and resort to challenging the validity of the will. Where the deceased went through a number of marriages, and there are children from each marriage, things can become fractious between the children of each marriage. Further complications arise where, in addition to children and step-children from the deceased's marriage(s), the deceased also cohabited with a partner and had children as a result of that cohabitation. In such a scenario, the deceased's partner, his children from his marriage(s), any step-children whom he treated as his children, and the children from his cohabitation with his most recent partner will all be entitled to contest the will.

In many instances, disputes arise concerning the testator's/testatrix's alleged lack of mental capacity to make a will. Over the years, the elderly population has increased, and with it the number of adults who lack capacity to make decisions concerning their personal welfare, health and property affairs which includes the disposition of their assets on death. However, age itself is not a barrier to making a will. The issue in each case will be to determine whether at the relevant time the deceased had the mental capacity to make the appropriate decision and to give instructions. Issues relevant to testamentary capacity and where it is appropriate to apply for a statutory will are considered in Chapters 4 and 15.

Problems may also arise in the following situations: where the will was made by the testator/testatrix without legal advice, poor draftsmanship, using a 'cut and paste' procedure to draft a will, and using template precedents without ensuring that the content suits the particular case of the client, as occurred in *Austin v Woodward* [2011] EWHC 2458 (Ch).

1.1 WILLS AND CODICILS

The document which governs the disposition of property on death is a will or testament, in a prescribed form. It sets out the wishes and intentions of the person making it (the testator/testatrix) regarding how that person would like his/her assets disposed of on his/her death. The will comes into effect on the death of the testator/testatrix. During the lifetime of the testator/testatrix the document has no legal effect; it merely stands as a declaration of intention of the testator/testatrix. The testator/testatrix is free during his/her lifetime to transfer, dispose of or deal in any way with any of the property referred to in his/her will. The testator/testatrix may at any time revoke or vary the will, but to be effective, the revocation or variation must be made in accordance with the provisions relating to the making of a will. The revocable nature of a will may not be compromised by a declaration that it is irrevocable.

The will may be supplemented by a codicil, which is a document similar to a will but executed after a will has been made. The purpose of a codicil is to add to, vary or revoke any of the provisions set out in the will. However, to be valid and effective, a codicil must also comply with the formalities which apply to wills.

1.2 FORMALITIES RELATING TO WILLS

The form and manner in which a will should be made are set out in the Wills Act 1837 as amended by the Administration of Justice Act 1982. The formal requirements are as follows:

    (a)   the will must be in writing;
    (b)   the will must be signed by the testator/testatrix or by some other person in his/her presence and by his/her direction;

Introduction 3

- (c) it must be clear that the testator/testatrix intended by his/her signature to give effect to the will;
- (d) the signature must be made or acknowledged in the presence of two witnesses present at the same time;
- (e) each witness must attest and sign the will or acknowledge his/her signature in the presence of the testator/testatrix.

1.3 GROUNDS FOR CHALLENGE

The validity of a will may be challenged if any one of the above conditions is not met or there is uncertainty regarding any one of them. There are also other grounds on which the will may be challenged. These include the following:

- (a) at the date of the will the testator/testatrix did not have the mental capacity to make a will;
- (b) at the time when the document was made and the testator/testatrix signed it he/she did not have the intention to make a will and for the document to be given effect to on his/her death;
- (c) at the time when the will was made the testator's/testatrix's mind was affected by undue influence, want of knowledge and approval, fear, fraud or by other matters which vitiated his/her intentions;
- (d) the intention of the testator/testatrix is not ascertainable or capable of being ascertained from the words used in the will;
- (e) the beneficiary described in the will cannot be identified or is not capable in law of taking the gift;
- (f) the subject matter of the gift is not ascertainable;
- (g) the will was revoked.

The legal requirements for making a will are considered in more detail in Chapters 2 and 3, with examples provided of cases where the circumstances surrounding the making of the will led to the will being challenged and declared invalid.

Each of the above grounds for challenging a will is considered in the following chapters.

1.4 STATUTORY RIGHT TO CHALLENGE

The provisions of the Inheritance (Provision for Family and Dependants) Act 1975 (I(PFD)A 1975) give certain categories of claimants, who are considered as dependants of the deceased, the right to bring a claim for financial provision against the estate of the deceased if the deceased has failed to make such provision for the claimant. This statutory right, however, does not limit the testator's/testatrix's freedom to dispose of his/her estate, nor does it give the court the jurisdiction to rewrite the deceased's will. The Preamble to the Act makes it clear that the objective of the Act is not to interfere with these rights but 'to make fresh provision for empowering the court to make orders for the making out of the estate of the deceased person of provision' for certain categories of persons who fulfil the criteria set out in the Act. A claim for an order under section 2 may be made only on the ground that the disposition of the deceased's estate effected by his/her will or the law of intestacy, or the combination of the will and that law, is not such as to make reasonable financial provision for the claimant. When dealing with a claim under the Act it is not the function of the court to correct what may appear to be an injustice, or to make a fair or fairer division of the deceased's estate, but to give effect to the objective of the Act in cases which fall within its ambit. Where such a claim succeeds, the interests of those taking under the will may be adjusted, but only to the limited extent provided for in the Act. These provisions apply equally to dispositions of property made other than by will (see para 1.5) subject to the provisions of the relevant sections of the Act (see Chapter 13), as the court has power to reduce or nullify the effect of any contract or to direct the donee to provide such funds or other property as may be necessary to make financial provision for a claimant under the Act. The court may direct the personal representatives of the deceased not to make any payments or transfer property under the contract, settlement or other transaction, other than as specified by the court.

It is thus possible for a claimant, in appropriate cases, while not seeking to challenge the validity of a will, to seek relief by way of a declaration that the will should take effect subject to the deceased's equitable obligations, for example, where there is an agreement to make mutually binding wills, or pursuant to the terms of a contract entered into by the deceased in his/her lifetime, or where the deceased's conduct raises issues of proprietary estoppel under the doctrine of *donatio mortis causa*.

1.5 OTHER TESTAMENTARY DISPOSITIONS

In addition to making a disposition by will which takes effect on the death of the testator/testatrix, assets may be transferred by a person during his/her lifetime but to take effect on death. This can be achieved by:

    (a)   an *inter vivos* disposition;
    (b)   transferring property into joint names so that, on the death of one of the joint tenants the property automatically passes to the survivor;

(c) *donatio mortis causa*;
(d) nominating the person who is to receive the property under a trust deed or the rules of a pension scheme.

These dispositions do not constitute part of the will and, therefore, issues arising from any such disposition are not a direct challenge to the validity of the will. However, a person taking under such a transaction may make a claim against the estate to give effect to the transaction, which may in turn affect dispositions made in the will. Alternatively, beneficiaries taking under the will may challenge the validity of such dispositions made during the lifetime of the deceased. These are discussed in Chapter 13.

1.6 INTERNATIONAL WILLS

The Convention providing a Uniform Law on the Form of an International Will was concluded at Washington on 26 October 1973. An Annex to the Convention sets out the requirements for the form of an international will, which is embodied in Schedule 2 to the Administration of Justice Act 1982. The requirements are intended to come into force on a day to be appointed jointly by the Lord Chancellor and the Home Secretary. These requirements should be used as a guide when the testator/testatrix is not domiciled in England and Wales or where the testator/testatrix is domiciled in England and Wales and has property outside England and Wales. These requirements are dealt with in Chapter 2, paras 2.5 and 2.6.

1.7 PROSPECTIVE REFORMS

The Law Commission's *Twelfth Programme of Law Reform*, Law Com No 354, published on 23 July 2014 includes a project to undertake a general review of the law of wills with particular focus on:

> four key areas that have been identified as potentially needing reform: testamentary capacity, the formalities for a valid will, the rectification of wills, and mutual wills. It will consider whether the law could be reformed to encourage and facilitate will-making in the 21st century: for example, whether it should be updated to take account of developments in technology and medicine. It will also aim to reduce the likelihood of wills being challenged after death, and the incidence of litigation. Such litigation is expensive, can divide families and is a cause of great stress for the bereaved. (Part 2, para 2.32)

The need for reform in the particular areas identified is discussed in later chapters, and in particular in Chapters 3, 4, 9 and 11, which specifically deal with these issues.

Practitioners should also note that the Draft Non-Contentious Probate Rules 2013 are currently under revision following the end of the consultation period. It was anticipated that the final draft would be approved and published, or at least available, before this work went to press, but the rules in their final form are not available. It has not been possible to get any indication when the new rules will be issued.

The aim of this book is to provide a simple, easy to follow basic guide to challenging a will or other testamentary provision. It is not intended to provide an exhaustive and detailed study, nor would it be possible to do so within the framework of this work. Where it is intended to pursue a claim, reference should be made to the standard textbooks on the subject.

Chapter 2

Form, Content and Interpretation of a Will

2.1 INTRODUCTION

Every will must be in writing, but there is no legal requirement for it to use any formal language so long as it sets out clearly the wishes and intentions of the testator/testatrix. Disputes, however, may arise if the intention of the testator/testatrix is not clear or if the beneficiary under the will or property to which reference is made cannot be identified or traced. In such instances, issues of construction and interpretation inevitably arise. This chapter considers the issues which could result in a will being challenged and how the court may resolve the differences which may arise between the competing parties.

2.2 NATURE AND FORM OF A WILL

The form and manner in which a will is to be made are set out in the Wills Act 1837 as amended by the Administration of Justice Act 1982.

Every will, other than a privileged will, i.e. a will that extends to soldiers in actual military service and to mariners or seamen at sea, must be in writing. The Interpretation Act 1978 provides that in any Act, unless the contrary intention appears, 'writing' is to be construed to include 'typing, printing, lithography, photography and other modes of representing and reproducing words in a visible form and expressions referring to writing are to be construed accordingly'.

There is no requirement that the will should be made on any particular material or that it should be made using any specific words as long as the testator's/testatrix's intention and his/her wishes as to the disposition of his/her assets or part of the assets and the appointment of executors and trustees appear clear from the language used. There is also no requirement that the will should be dated (contrast with an international will; see para 2.6). Where a date is not included or a wrong date is inserted it does not invalidate the will, but evidence of the date on which the will was executed will need to be called for before the will is admitted to proof.

2.3 UNCERTAINTY RELATING TO INTENTION, SUBJECT MATTER OR DONEE

A will is a document which sets out the wishes of the person making it as to how he/she intends that his/her assets should be distributed on his/her death. Thus unless a contrary intention is expressed, the will takes effect on his/her death (section 24 of the Wills Act 1837) and it may be revoked or varied at any time during the person's lifetime. Until death occurs, the ownership and control of the assets of the testator/testatrix remain with him/her with the right to dispose of these assets or any part of them during his/her lifetime. Where no valuable consideration was given, in the absence of any proof, the disposition will be construed as a gift to the donee (see *Re Fleming's Will Trusts* [1974] 1 WLR 1552). When a will is prepared, care should be taken to set out the wishes and intentions of the testator/testatrix clearly, not only in relation to his/her current situation, but also where possible in relation to future foreseeable events. If a very specific description is made of a chattel or other possession which is subsequently replaced, the gift may fail.

In the case of a donee of a gift or a class of persons in whose favour a gift is made, the will applies to the donee or those in the class of persons at the time when the will was made unless a contrary intention is indicated. It is important, therefore, to ensure that the beneficiaries are clearly identified. Similarly, in relation to the property gifted. If the disposition is ambiguous or the words used are meaningless, the disposition may be challenged on the ground of uncertainty.

Where an ambiguity arises and the validity of the will is challenged, the court in general is reluctant to hold a gift void for uncertainty. It will attempt to look for evidence from which the testator's/testatrix's intention can be ascertained, and where possible it will try to adopt a construction which avoids finding the whole testamentary disposition invalid or void for uncertainty. The court, however, has no power to rewrite a will. The court's duty when dealing with a challenge on the ground of uncertainty is to give effect to the intentions of the testator/testatrix by resorting to circumstantial evidence, adopting a robust and common-sense approach and seeking, as far as possible, to interpret the words used so as to keep within what the testator/testatrix had in mind (*Aitken's Trustees v Aitken* 1927 SC 374). In so doing, the court starts from the principle that the testator's/testatrix's intention should be ascertained by considering the whole will, together with any other evidence. If the intention is able to be so ascertained, then the form or language used in setting out that intention is not important.

In so far as wills and codicils of a testator/testatrix dying after 1 January 1983 are concerned, section 21 of the Administration of Justice Act 1982 permits the use of extrinsic evidence to assist in the construction and interpretation of a will where the words in a testamentary document appear to be meaningless or ambiguous. Section 21(2) permits the admissibility of extrinsic evidence including evidence of the testator's/testatrix's intention to assist in the construction and interpretation of a will:

(a) in so far as any part of it is meaningless;
(b) in so far as the language used in any part of it is ambiguous on the face of it;
(c) in so far as evidence, other than evidence of the testator's/testatrix's intention shows that the language used in any part of it is ambiguous in the light of the surrounding circumstances (section 21(1)).

Where the words in the will are ambiguous, contradictory or obscure, appear to be meaningless in the context in which they are used, or have more than one meaning, the court will consider all the circumstances to ascertain what the testator/testatrix meant to convey by the words used, and will adopt a construction which it considers the most likely to indicate what the testator/testatrix intended. However, where the words used are clear and unambiguous, the court will not admit evidence to show that the testator's/testatrix's intention was different from that which is evident from the language used in the will. In construing a will, the court is concerned with:

(a) examining the words used by the testator/testatrix in the will to express his/her intention; and
(b) ascertaining how those words identify the donees and the subject matter of the disposition in question or clarify any other issues raised.

If the court is able to ascertain the intention of the testator/testatrix, it will go on to consider whether there is anything which prevents that intention being put into effect and, if not, how best it can be put into effect.

Extrinsic evidence may be adduced to identify persons or things referred to in the will. It may be adduced to clarify an ambiguity regarding the identity of a person, for example to show that there exists another person or subject matter to which the words in question refer or could refer. Where, even after admitting extrinsic evidence, the words used in a will lend themselves to more than one meaning, or may be taken to apply to more than one person or subject matter, further evidence may be admitted to clarify the matter further (*Re Ray, Cant v Johnstone* [1916] Ch 461) to enable the court to put itself in the position of the testator/testatrix at the time he/she made the will. If the testator/testatrix during his/her lifetime referred to a beneficiary by a nickname or referred to a person by a name other than his/her true name, evidence may be called to show that the name or description given applies to that person and not to any other person. Where a dispute arises or where it is not clear what the testator/testatrix intended, the court will wherever possible consider the will as a whole and give effect to the testamentary gift.

Gibbs v Harding [2007] EWHC 3 (Ch) is an example of one such case. In that case, the testatrix made a will as she was dying in hospital. The will was written for her in manuscript which she duly executed. It stated:

> I Sister Joseph Harding (Winsome Joy Harding) being of sound mind and aware of what I am doing, wish to revoke my last will and testimony made previous to today's date.
> I am not satisfied with certain aspects of the contents of that said will which are contrary to my express wishes.
> If I should die in the meantime before making another will it is my wish that everything I possess be taken over by the Diocese of Westminster to hold in trust for the Black community of Hackney, Haringey, Islington and Tower Hamlet. (*Gibbs v Harding* [2007] EWHC 3 (Ch) at [1])

The issue turned on whether the last paragraph of the will created a valid testamentary gift and, if so, on what terms. The various possibilities canvassed were whether she intended the estate to be held:

(a) on trust for the Roman Catholic Diocese of Westminster absolutely;
(b) by the Roman Catholic Diocese of Westminster on charitable trusts;
(c) by the Roman Catholic Diocese of Westminster on trust for the Caribbean Community Centre.

Having considered case law and the provisions of the Race Relations Act 1976, Lewison J (as he then was) held that the clause should take effect as a gift to the Roman Catholic Diocese of Westminster for charitable purposes.

2.4 EXAMPLES OF CASES OF CONSTRUCTION OF WILLS

Rawstron and Pearce v Freud [2014] EWHC 2577 (Ch) is a recent example where the court took the natural and ordinary words used in the context of the will to construe the disposition in the will of Lucian Freud. The will had been professionally drawn and left the residue of the estate as follows:

> I GIVE all the residue of my estate (out of which shall be paid my funeral and testamentary expenses and debts) and any property over which I have a general power of appointment to the said Diana Mary Rawstron and the said Rose Pearce jointly. (*Rawstron and Pearce v Freud* [2014] EWHC 2577 (Ch) at [4])

The defendant, who was Freud's illegitimate son, argued that the residuary estate was given to the two named persons to hold on trusts which were not set out in the will and imposed a half secret trust. He wished to explore this issue and to argue, if the trust was deemed half secret, whether it had been validly created. Richard Spearman QC took into account the fact that the clause referred to the claimants by name; that although one of the beneficiaries was the testator's solicitor, the gift of the residue was subject to a secret trust under which Rawstron did not stand to benefit; that an earlier will which had been revoked was in terms different to the will in dispute. He concluded that:

> ... in the light of (a) the natural and ordinary meaning of the words used in clause 6 of the Will; (b) the overall purpose of the Will, (c) the other provisions of the Will, (d) the material factual matrix when the Will was made and (e) common sense, I consider that the Claimants' interpretation of clause 6 of the Will is to be preferred to that suggested by the Defendant. (*Rawstron and Pearce v Freud* [2014] EWHC 2577 (Ch) at [64])

(See also Lord Neuberger's approach to the interpretation of wills, set out in *Marley v Rawlings & Anor* [2014] UKSC 2.)

In *Parkinson v Fawdon* [2009] EWHC 1953 (Ch), Mr Fawdon (F) and Mr Hindle (H) made mirror wills and appointed each other as executors, and both wills provided for the same alternative executors. H predeceased F and therefore under H's will, F was his executor. On the death of F, only one of the substitute executors could be identified. There was no one who matched the description of the other executor, 'Mark Parkinson of 215 Ditching Road Brighton', who was also a residuary beneficiary with a 50% share. The claimant, Justin Parkinson, contended that the intended reference was to him. He commenced proceedings for the rectification of the deceased's will by replacing 'Mark Parkinson' with 'Justin Parkinson'. Before it could be decided (in accordance with section 20 of the Administration of Justice Act 1982) that the will did not, by reason of a clerical error or a failure to understand the testator's instructions, carry out the testator's intentions, the court had first to decide what the testator meant. The defendant, Edith Fawden, counterclaimed for a determination upon the proper construction of the will and the events which happened, in order to determine whether or not the claimant, Justin Parkinson, was the person referred to as 'Mark Parkinson' in the will, and for a grant to issue accordingly.

In H's will, Mark Parkinson was described as the testator's nephew. When the wills were executed, however, the occupants of 215 Ditching Road were H's niece, her husband, Alan, and their children, Justin and Kirby. The claimant Justin was thus H's great-nephew. There were no other members of H's family who were connected with Ditching Road or had the surname Parkinson, nor was there any person who was H's nephew other than Justin. There was thus no clerical error or other ambiguity.

The court applied the principle in *Resch's Will Trusts* [1969] 1 AC 514 that the court could take into account as an aid to construction: (a) all the persons and facts known to the deceased at the time when he made his will; and (b) any document which is substantially contemporaneous with the will and is of an important character and which shows who the testator had in mind and intended by the misdescription.

The court held that the intended reference was clearly to a male member of H's family and that it would be unusual save within a very close family relationship to refer to the husband of a niece as a 'nephew', but that it would not be unusual to refer to a great-nephew as a 'nephew'. In the absence of any other person fitting the description given, the court held that the reference to Mark Parkinson was a misdescription of Justin Parkinson, the claimant whom the deceased intended to appoint as executor and to receive the share in his residuary estate.

In *Esson v Esson* [2009] EWHC 3045 (Ch), the dispute between the children and step-children of the deceased concerned the construction of the codicil of the deceased. The deceased (D) died in November 2006 survived by her three children from her first marriage and three step-children from her second marriage. D and her second husband (H) made mirror wills with each of them leaving their share of the matrimonial home to their own children and the residue to all the children from both marriages.

Subsequently, D's mother died leaving one half of her estate to D. D invested this in a separate bank account. She then executed an undated home-made codicil which identified this account as the 'residue of the monies left to me by my mother' with the statement that H 'is in full agreement that should I predecease him, all monies in this account should be divided equally between my grandchildren'. H predeceased D and on D's death the issue between the prospective beneficiaries related to the effect of the codicil. Read literally, it meant that the money in the account fell into the residue to be divided between D's children and step-children as residuary legatees. D's son, however, contended that the words 'should I predecease him' should be read as 'even if I should predecease him' or, alternatively, for rectification or for the codicil to be admitted to probate without the offending words.

The judge was not convinced that the words should be given their literal meaning as he took the view that D was concerned enough about her share of her mother's estate to execute a codicil, that the money was from her mother, that she kept it in a separate account and that she wanted it to remain in her family. However, since there was an ambiguity the judge considered it appropriate to resolve the issue by admitting extrinsic evidence from D's sister's sons under section 21(1)(b) of the Administration of Justice Act 1982 which supported the conclusion that the money was intended for the grandchildren.

In *Harrison v Gibson* [2005] EWHC 2957 (Ch), the court considered the implications of section 22 of the Administration of Justice Act 1982 and, on the facts, found that there was doubt as regards what the testator intended. Section 22 provides:

> Except where a contrary intention is shown it shall be presumed that if a testator devises or bequeaths property to his spouse in terms which in themselves would give an absolute interest to the spouse, but by the same instrument purports to give his issue an interest in the same property, the gift to the spouse is absolute notwithstanding the purported gift to the issue.

By Clause 2 of his will, the testator made an absolute gift to his widow of his financial assets. Clause 3 read, 'the bungalow I leave in trust to my wife ... On her death the bungalow is to be sold and cash raised is to be equally divided between my children'. After his signature at the end of the will he added, 'no doubt if mum runs into money problems you can sort something out ... Like selling [the] bungalow'.

The widow died in 2004, having been predeceased by her husband. The widow left the bungalow on trust for sale with a direction to divide the proceeds between the four children in unequal shares. This led to the issue of her entitlement under her husband's will and whether Clause 2 of his will gave the widow an absolute interest so that the proceeds of the bungalow would pass to the children in unequal shares or whether she received a life interest, in which case the children would take in equal shares.

The court decided that despite the words 'terms which in themselves would give an absolute interest' used in section 22 of the Administration of Justice Act 1982, where there was doubt as to the effect of the words used, the words used by the husband in his will should be interpreted having regard to the terms of the will as a whole. Similarly, the question of whether there was a contrary intention should be determined upon a fair reading of the will as a whole in the light of any admissible extrinsic evidence. Following this approach, the judge held that the conditions for the application of the statutory presumption of an absolute gift did not apply, but, even if he was wrong, the will showed a sufficient contrary intention to displace the statutory presumption. The widow had, therefore, a life interest only and the proceeds of the bungalow passed to the children in equal shares.

In *Pinnell v Anison* [2005] EWHC 1421 (Ch), by his will dated 8 May 2001, the deceased left his residuary estate to his brother, Philip Moran, and his sister 'Doreen Hall of 48 Nelson Street, Fenton, Stoke on Trent, Staffordshire'. The deceased died in April 2003. At the date of his will, he had one sister Doreen who was known as Doreen Anison but she did not live at 48 Nelson Street. A person named Doreen Hall lived at 48 Nelson Street but she died in February 2002. There was no evidence to suggest that she was in any way related to the deceased or that she was or had been in a relationship with the deceased. In those circumstances, looking at the will as a whole, the judge came to the conclusion that the deceased wished to benefit his sister Doreen Anison as the bequest in the will could not otherwise be explained.

In *Ross v Perrin-Hughes* [2004] EWHC 2559 (Ch), the issue was whether the bequest in a home-made will referring to 'my apartment' was intended to pass the property free of mortgage and to include the freehold. The deceased had purchased a lease of a first floor flat and the freehold of two maisonettes which formed the premises. The purchases of these properties were made separately but contemporaneously. The flat was purchased subject to a mortgage of £30,000 with an endowment policy which was assigned to the mortgagees. In the deceased's will made after his engagement to the defendant, he bequeathed 'my apartment and contents thereof to my friend Irene Perrin-Hughes'. In addition, he bequeathed 50% of the residue of his estate to his friend Irene and the remaining 50% to his two brothers. The court held that taking the steps of obtaining an endowment policy, assigning it to the mortgagees and later increasing the premiums on the policy were all indications that the deceased intended that the mortgage should be redeemed from the proceeds of the endowment policy. However, although the deceased was made aware of the distinction between leasehold and freehold property, his use of the words 'my apartment' in his will was ambiguous. The court could, in those circumstances, admit extrinsic evidence under section 21 of the Administration of Justice Act 1982 to establish that, despite being advised, the deceased did not in fact make any distinction between leasehold and freehold, i.e. the flat and the maisonettes. Had he intended to do so, he would have specifically done so.

Other older cases which illustrate how the court construes and interprets an ambiguity include *Re Doland's Will Trust, Westminster Bank Ltd v Phillips* [1970] Ch 267, *Re James's Will Trusts, Peard v James* [1962] Ch 226 and *Re Harper's Will Trusts, Haller v Attorney General* [1962] Ch 78.

In *Re Doland's Will Trust, Westminster Bank Ltd v Phillips* [1970] Ch 267, the testator provided for his residuary estate to be disposed of in percentages, in some cases to named persons absolutely, and in other cases to named persons, but if they predeceased him, to their children. He gave 2% to William Frederick

Lewis absolutely but he also got Lewis's wife to be one of the attesting witnesses. The testator then added a proviso:

> Provided that if the trusts or any of the shares aforesaid of my residuary estate shall fail my trustees shall stand possessed of my residuary estate upon trust for [two named persons] in equal shares absolutely but should either of them predecease me then for the survivor of them absolutely or should they [the named persons] ... both predecease me then for such of their children living at my death absolutely and if more than one in equal shares absolutely.

It was held that there was such a contradiction between what was set out in the proviso and the residuary disposition in the will that the conclusion could be drawn that the will was defective. The court, however, sought to ascertain the intention of the testator from the will as a whole, and found that there was a clear indication of a conflict between the intention which appeared to be expressed in the proviso and the intention which was clearly expressed in other parts of the same clause. In those circumstances, the court held that the intention of the testator was that, if a gift of a particular share of residue failed then that share only was to be held in trust for the persons named in the proviso. The gift to Lewis failed because his wife was an attesting witness and the court treated the will as though it did not contain that disposition.

In *Re James's Will Trusts, Peard v James* [1962] Ch 226, the issue was whether the testator used the word 'surviving' in the sense of being alive at and after the time of the event to be survived or in some other secondary sense. It was held that the words should be given their natural meaning, although the testator, or the draftsman of his will, showed himself to be somewhat careless, and that the testator clearly used the words in the proper sense, without wholly appreciating the effect on the scheme of his disposition.

In *Re Harper's Will Trusts, Haller v Attorney General* [1962] Ch 78, the testatrix provided that the residue of her estate should be accumulated for a period of 10 years, and thereafter certain legacies should be paid to named charities. The gift was followed by a clause directing that the residue of her estate should be divided between:

> such institutions and associations having for their main object the assistance and care of soldiers, sailors, airmen and other members of HM Forces, who have been wounded or incapacitated during the recent world wars in such manner and in such proportions as my said executors and trustees may in their uncontrolled discretion select and deem appropriate.

The issue before the court concerned the effect, if any, to be given to this clause. The gift failed for uncertainty of the object.

Thus when seeking to challenge the validity of a will on the basis of uncertainty, ambiguity or obscurity, careful consideration should be given to all the available evidence to prove or disprove the issue(s) raised, and to assess and weigh the nature, quality and strength of that evidence and all the surrounding circumstances. It is only when there is overwhelming and convincing evidence of the interpretation sought that a challenge would be justified. The decision in *Parkinson v Fawden* [2009] EWHC 1953 (Ch) indicates that a wider approach will be taken when determining identity than in construing what is alleged to be a meaningless provision.

2.5   WILLS WHERE THERE IS A FOREIGN ELEMENT

A will with a foreign element usually arises where the testator/testatrix is domiciled outside England and Wales or if domiciled in England and Wales has property situated outside England and Wales. The law which governs the will in such cases depends on whether the property is classed as movable or immovable property. In general, all interests in land are considered to be immovable including land held in trust. The rules which apply to the validity of a will with a foreign element in relation to both movable and immovable property are governed by the Wills Act 1963. This Act resulted following the Convention on the Conflicts of Laws Relating to the Form of Testamentary Dispositions, which was concluded on 5 October 1961 at the Ninth Session of the Hague Conference on Private International Law and was signed by the UK on 13 February 1962. This eventually resulted in the Convention providing a Uniform Law on the Form of an International Will, concluded at Washington on 26 October 1973. The aim of the Convention is to provide uniformity in private international law on the formalities of a will. The relevant provisions of the Convention are now set out in sections 27 and 28 of, and Schedule 2 to, the Administration of Justice Act 1982. These provisions are intended to govern the validity of a will in relation to both movable and immovable property. It would be advisable, therefore, to follow these provisions where appropriate.

Section 1 of the Wills Act 1963 provides that a will is properly executed if it complies with the internal law of the place where it was executed, any place where the testator/testatrix was domiciled or habitually resident, or of which he/she was a national when the will was made, or the place where he/she was domiciled or habitually resident, or of which he/she was a national at the time of his/her death. Validity of a will in relation to movables is governed by the law of the place of the testator's/testatrix's domicile at death, and validity as to immovables by the law of the place where the property is situated, i.e. the *lex situs*. The testator/testatrix may, however, determine the law he/she wishes to apply to its construction expressly or by implication in the will. Where it is intended that the will should be construed in accordance with English law then, as is the case in commercial agreements, the will should include an express declaration to that effect. In the absence of any express provision, any issue which arises in relation to construction of a will is governed by the law of the testator's/testatrix's domicile when he/she made the will (see section 4).

Section 2 of the Wills Act 1963 sets out the provisions which apply to a will executed on board a ship or aircraft, and a will of immovables.

2.6 REQUIREMENTS OF INTERNATIONAL WILLS

The requirements of international wills are set out in Schedule 2 to the Administration of Justice Act 1982 and provide as follows:

- The will must be of a single testator/testatrix (Article 2).
- The will must be made in writing but it need not be written by the testator/testatrix himself/herself. It may be written in any language and by hand or any other means (Article 3).
- The testator/testatrix must declare in the presence of two witnesses and of a person authorised to act in connection with international wills that the document is his/her will and that he/she knows its contents but it is not necessary for him/her to divulge its contents to them (Article 4).
- The testator/testatrix must sign the will in the presence of two witnesses and the authorised person. If he/she has previously signed the will, he/she must acknowledge his/her signature in their presence (Article 5(1)). The witnesses and the authorised person must there and then attest the will by signing the will in the testator's/testatrix's presence (Article 5(3)). If the testator/testatrix is unable to sign, he/she must indicate the reason to the authorised person who must make a note of this on the will. The testator/testatrix may be authorised by the law under which the authorised person was designated to direct another person to sign on his/her behalf (Article 5(2)).
- The signatures must be placed at the end of the will. If the will consists of several sheets, each sheet must be signed by the testator/testatrix or a person on his/her behalf if he/she is unable to sign or by the authorised person. Each sheet must be numbered (Article 6).
- The date of the will is the date on which the authorised person signed the will and the authorised person is under a mandatory duty to note the date at the end of the will (Article 7).
- In the absence of any mandatory rule relating to the safekeeping of a will, the authorised person must ask the testator/testatrix whether he/she wishes to make a declaration about its safekeeping. If the testator/testatrix makes such a declaration and if he/she so requests, the place

where he/she intends the will to be kept must be mentioned in the prescribed certificate referred to in Article 10.
- The authorised person must attach the prescribed certificate to the will (Article 9). He/she must keep a copy of the certificate and deliver a copy to the testator/testatrix (Article 11).
- In the absence of evidence to the contrary, the certificate of the authorised person must be treated as conclusive proof of the formal validity of the will, but the absence or irregularity of a certificate will not affect the formal validity of the will (Articles 12 and 13).
- An international will is subject to the ordinary rule of revocation of wills (Article 14).

It is usual, therefore, where the testator/testatrix is domiciled outside England and Wales for his/her will to deal with his/her immovable property situated in England and Wales, and to advise the testator/testatrix to make a separate will in relation to all his/her other assets in accordance with the law of his/her domicile. In the case of a testator/testatrix who is domiciled in England and Wales but has property both in and outside England and Wales, the testator/testatrix should be advised to make a foreign will particularly in relation to immovables in the foreign country.

There are all sorts of permutations on which an international will may be challenged in relation to its form and content where there is a foreign element; for example, if a foreign will exists and the English will contains the usual revocation clause, it will have the effect of revoking all wills unless it contains a clause that the revocation is to apply only to the property referred to in the will and not the foreign will. The above summary is intended to provide a brief overview only in relation to issues which may arise where there is a foreign element. The ambit of this publication is limited to property in England and Wales and the challenges which may be made where the formalities in relation to the making of a will are not complied with or there are other grounds on which its validity may be challenged under English law.

Chapter 3

Execution of a Will

3.1 FORMAL REQUIREMENTS

The formal requirements for the making of a will are set out in section 9 of the Wills Act 1837, as substituted by the Administration of Justice Act 1982. Section 9 as amended provides that:

> No will shall be valid unless—
>
> (a) it is in writing and signed by the testator, or by some person in his presence and by his direction; and
> (b) it appears that the testator intended by his signature to give effect to the will; and
> (c) the signature is made or acknowledged by the testator in the presence of two or more witnesses present at the same time; and
> (d) each witness either—
>
>   (i) attests and signs the will; or
>   (ii) acknowledges his signature, in the presence of the testator (but not necessarily in the presence of any other witness),
>
> but no form of attestation shall be necessary.

Additionally, save in the case of a privileged will (see Chapter 2, para 2.2), a person must be 18 years of age before he/she can make a valid will (Wills Act 1837, as amended by the Family Law Reform Act 1969).

These requirements seem quite clear and simple to follow but it is easy to be careless and to overlook the most basic points. It is, therefore, not surprising that in many instances errors have arisen in the execution of a will. Thus the first and obvious ground for challenging the validity of a will is that it was not duly executed in accordance with the provisions of section 9 of the Wills Act 1837 as amended. It is, therefore, essential to have some knowledge of what the requirements mean and how the courts have interpreted the statutory provisions.

3.2 WILL MUST BE IN WRITING

With the exception of a privileged will (see Chapter 2, para 2.2), no will is valid unless it is in writing. No particular form of words is required but the writing, in whatever form, must express the wishes of the testator/testatrix as to the disposition of his/her estate or part of it and appoint an executor. The Interpretation Act 1978 provides that in any Act unless the contrary intention appears, the word 'writing' is to be construed as including 'typing, printing, lithography, photography and other modes of representing and reproducing words in a visible form and expressions referring to writing are construed accordingly'. A will in shorthand is acceptable, as is a will produced in Braille, but in such a case when the will is lodged for probate it should be accompanied by a transcription by a competent person and verified by a sworn statement.

3.3 WILL MUST BE SIGNED BY THE TESTATOR/ TESTATRIX OR BY SOME OTHER PERSON AT HIS/HER DIRECTION

To be valid, the will must be signed by the testator/testatrix or by some other person in the testator's/testatrix's presence and at his/her direction. It matters not in what form the signature appears in the will as long as it was intended to represent the testator's/testatrix's signature and to give effect to the testamentary disposition, particularly where the testator/testatrix is disabled, for example if he/she is illiterate or blind. In the case of a testator/testatrix who is blind or illiterate, rule 13 of the Non-Contentious Probate Rules 1987 (SI 1987/2024) provides that:

> Before admitting to proof a will which appears to have been signed by a blind or illiterate testator or by any other person by direction of the testator, or which for any reason raises doubt as to the testator having had knowledge of the contents of the will at the time of its execution, the district judge shall satisfy himself that the testator had such knowledge

The will may be signed with the testator's/testatrix's name. Initials may suffice (see *Re Savory's Goods* (1851) 15 Jur 1042), as may a partial signature or mark (*Re Blewitt's Goods* (1880) 5 PD 116) or a thumb print (*Re Finn's Estate* (1935) 105 LJP 36). The words 'your loving mother' have been held to represent the name of the testatrix and to suffice as a signature (*Re Cook's Estate, Murison v Cook* [1960] 1 WLR 353). A rubber stamp has been held to be sufficient (*Perrins v Holland & Ors* [2010] EWCA Civ 840). A mark made by a seal would be sufficient, provided there is proof that the sealing was intended to be the testator's/testatrix's signature and not merely used as a sealing process. A signature which was incomplete due to the testator's/testatrix's weakness has been accepted (*Chalcraft, Chalcraft v Giles* [1948] P 222). Where a testator's hand was guided in order for him to make his mark, it was held to be sufficient (*Wilson v Beddard* (1841) 12 Sim 28, see also *Barrett v Bem & Ors* [2011] EWHC 1247 (Ch), discussed below). Where a wrong name was placed against the mark of the testator but the real name appeared at the beginning of the will, it was held not to invalidate the will (*Re Clarke's Goods* (1858) 1 SW & Tr 22). The signature in whatever form, however, must be in its original form. A photocopied signature will not be acceptable even if it is subsequently acknowledged in the presence of two witnesses who then attest the photocopy. This is because a photocopy of the will with a photocopied signature would not be regarded as a document which is signed by the testator/testatrix (see *Lim v Thompson* [2009] EWHC 3341 (Ch)).

Section 9(a) of the Wills Act 1837 as amended provides for situations where, due to physical frailty, weakness or disability, a testator/testatrix is unable to sign his/her will by providing that some other person may sign on his/her behalf provided he/she is present when the signature is made and it is done at his/her direction. Much will depend on the condition of the testator/testatrix and the specific facts of the case whether, in the circumstances, the will is considered to be signed by the testator/testatrix or at his/her direction. In *Barrett v Bem & Ors* [2011] EWHC 1247 (Ch), handwriting experts concluded it was unlikely that the deceased signed the will which was the subject matter of the dispute, and on that evidence the grant of probate was revoked. Three weeks after that decision was made, nurses who were at the bedside of the deceased when he signed the will stated that the deceased had the pen in his hand when he signed the will, but that his daughter A and A's daughter were present and held his hand to stop it shaking. It was held that in the 'peculiar, some might say extraordinary circumstances' in this case, the deceased knew and approved the will and validly directed A to sign it on his behalf. Although A was the main beneficiary under the will, it was also held that in the circumstances of the case it did not offend the provisions of section 15 which makes a gift to an attesting witness 'utterly null and void', as this provision did not apply to a beneficiary who merely signed a will on the testator's/testatrix's behalf at his/her direction. However, in such circumstances the court would have to be satisfied that the will represented the true wishes and intentions of the deceased (*Barry v Butlin* (1838) 2 Moo PCC 480). In a case where the will is signed by a person other than the testator/testatrix but at his/her direction, that person must sign either the testator's/testatrix's name or his/her name for the purpose of giving effect to such direction, and the attestation clause must indicate that the will was signed by the other person in his/her own name or that of the testator/testatrix by his/her direction and in the presence of the testator/testatrix. It should also confirm that the will was read by or read over to the testator/testatrix and was understood by him/her and approved by him/her. The validity of the will may, therefore, be challenged where there are grounds for believing that these requirements were not followed.

3.4 POSITION OF THE SIGNATURE

Although it is usual for the testator/testatrix to place his/her signature at the foot of a will, it does not invalidate a will if the signature appears elsewhere than at the end or foot of the document because section 9 of the Wills Act 1837, as amended by section 17 of the Administration of Justice Act 1982, does not stipulate where the signature should be placed. In *Wood v Smith* [1993] Ch 90, the testator made a handwritten will with his signature at the start of the will and then wrote out his will disposing of his assets. He did not otherwise sign the will at the foot of the document or elsewhere. When the witnesses attested the will, he told them that he signed the will at the top and that it could be signed anywhere. It was contended that the will was invalid and that the purported signature, when made, was made on a document which was not a will containing any disposition. The Court of Appeal held that the writing of his name by the testator amounted to his signature as the testator indicated in clear terms to the attesting witnesses that he regarded his name written by him as being his signature. The fact that the will was signed before the terms of the will were written did not invalidate the will, as the writing of the signature and the dispositive terms were all done in one operation. The signature did not necessarily have to be appended to the document after the substantive testamentary contents were written out. A signature in the margin has, in special circumstances, been held to be valid (*Re Roberts' Estate* [1934] P 102).

The testator's/testatrix's signature if not on the paper on which the will is written must be physically connected with the will when it is signed and attested (*Re Little, Foster v Cooper* [1960] 1 All ER 387). Wherever the signature is made it must, however, be shown that the testator/testatrix intended by his/her signature to give effect to his/her will. In *Re Bean's Estate* [1944] P 83, probate was refused because the testator did not sign the will but placed the will in an envelope, marked it with the words 'the last will and testament of' and then printed his name and address on the envelope containing the will and named the executors and the date. If the will is signed by the testator/testatrix but is not attested and then placed in a sealed envelope and, subsequently, the envelope is signed by the testator/testatrix and attested by two witnesses with a statement that the envelope contained the testator's/testatrix's will, it will be held to be validly executed (see *Re Nicholls, Hunter v Nicholls* [1921] 2 Ch 11). On the other hand, in *Re Mann's Goods* [1942] P 146, the testatrix wrote her will in the presence of witnesses, marked it with the words 'this is my last will and testament' and signed it intending that the signature should be the signature of her will. It was attested by the witnesses and then placed in the envelope and sealed. It was held that the signed envelope and the attested document together formed the will.

3.5 EXECUTION OF THE WRONG WILL

It was established in *Meyer's Estate* [1908] P 353 that if the testator/testatrix executed a will of another person by mistake as his/her own, it would not be valid and probate will be refused. This principle has now been overruled by the Supreme Court in *Marley v Rawlings & Anor* [2014] UKSC 2. The case involved Mr and Mrs Rawlings who, in 1999, made mirror wills leaving their estate to one another and eventually the estate was to pass to M, whom they treated as their son and who was the couple's sole carer. Solicitors acting for both parties dealt with the execution of the wills but in error handed the wrong wills to the couple. Neither the parties nor the solicitor and his secretary who witnessed the signatures noticed the error. It also went unnoticed on the death of Mrs Rawlings. The discrepancy did not come to light until Mr Rawlings' death in 2006 when his two sons, on discovering that on the face of their father's will everything was to pass to M, noticed the mistake and argued that the will was not valid. M applied for rectification on the basis that the mistake arose as a result of an administrative oversight and error, and that the court had the power to rectify the error under section 20 of the Administration of Justice Act 1982 (see Chapter 9). In affirming the High Court's earlier decision, Black LJ said, 'This is a conclusion I have reached with great regret, but Parliament made very limited changes to the law in 1982 and it would not be right for a court to go beyond what Parliament then decided'. On 5 July 2012, the Supreme Court granted permission to appeal. The appellant contended, first, that Mr Rawlings' will properly interpreted should be read as if it was the document signed by his wife; secondly, that the extent of Mr Rawlings' knowledge and approval of the contents of the will was such that it could be validated; and, thirdly, that the will should be rectified to give effect to Mr Rawlings' intentions. The court declined to decide on the first issue of interpretation because interpretation was not the basis upon which the courts below had decided the case and it was not the ground primarily relied on by the appellant, therefore very limited argument had been advanced before the court. The court, therefore, proceeded on the basis that it failed on interpretation (*Marley v Rawlings & Anor* [2014] UKSC 2 at [41]). The court rejected the second contention, because to do so would involve 'converting what is a simple and beneficial principle of severance into what is almost a word game with haphazard outcomes' (for full reasons, see [41]–[49]). Allowing the appeal on the ground of rectification, the court held that as a general proposition, the greater the extent of the correction sought, the steeper the task for a claimant who is seeking rectification. However, there was no reason in principle why a wholesale correction should be ruled out as a permissible exercise of the court's power to rectify. The court stated that the circumstances of the case gave rise to a classic case of rectification subject to two other points. There could be no doubt as to what both Mr Rawlings wanted and how he would have expressed himself if he had appreciated the mistake (see [54]). On the first of the two points raised as to whether the document was a 'will', although the will purports to be the will of Mrs Rawlings, there is no doubt that it cannot be hers as she did not sign it. As it was Mr Rawlings who signed it, it can only have been his will and it is he who is claimed in these proceedings to be the testator for the purposes of section 9 of the Wills Act 1837. The court, therefore, held that section 9(a) appears to be satisfied. On the second point, the court held that although the will does not make sense at least if taken at face value, that is a matter for 'a court construction'. There is no doubt from the face of the will as well as from the evidence that it was Mr Rawlings' intention at the time he signed the will that it should have effect and, therefore, section 9(b) was also satisfied (see [59]).

The court also held that it would still be open for the appellant to invoke section 20 of the Administration of Justice Act 1982. A document does not have to satisfy the formal requirement of section 9 of the Wills Act 1837 or of having the testator's full knowledge and approval before it can be treated as a will which is capable of being rectified. If section 20 could not be invoked to rectify a document which was currently formally invalid into a formally valid will, that would cut down on its operation for no apparently sensible reason (see [60] and [62]). The court, having accepted that there is an argument for saying that it does nothing to discourage carelessness, nevertheless held that section 20(1) should be given a wide rather than a narrow meaning. In this case, there was clearly an error which could be characterised as 'clerical' because it arose in connection with office work of a routine nature and, therefore, it follows that it was susceptible to rectification. The court, therefore, allowed the appeal and held that the will should be rectified.

Despite the decision of the Supreme Court, practitioners should take care to supervise the execution of a will to avoid having to make an application for rectification, challenges that could be made to such an application and of course the possibility of a claim for negligence.

3.6 ACKNOWLEDGEMENT OF SIGNATURE IN THE PRESENCE OF WITNESSES

Section 9 of the Wills Act 1837 as amended provides for a signature that has previously been made to an unattested will to be acknowledged by the testator/testatrix in the presence of two or more witnesses present at the same time. The acknowledgement may be made expressly by words or by gestures such as nodding (*Hadler's Estate, Goodall v Hadler* (1960) *The Times*, 20 October). The will may be acknowledged by implication, such as by producing the will with the signature visibly apparent to the witnesses who must both be present together at the same time and requesting them to subscribe to it (*Re Davies' Estate, Russell v Delaney* [1951] 1 All ER 920). If the witnesses affirmatively state that they looked and there was no signature present on the document presented to them or that the document was folded or in some way covered so that the signature was not visible to them, probate will be refused. Where a testator/testatrix makes a will and later decides to alter it and dictates the alteration to another person, who copies the alteration by hand into the will, which is then checked by the testator/testatrix and confirmed by adding that the will was altered, and dates it in the presence of two witnesses who attest the will, the will cannot be admitted to probate in its altered form.

3.7 ATTESTATION IN THE PRESENCE OF WITNESSES

Under section 9 of the Wills Act 1837 the testator/testatrix must sign or acknowledge his/her signature in the presence of two or more witnesses present at the same time and each witness must either attest and sign the will or acknowledge his/her signature in the presence of the testator/testatrix. If the testator/testatrix signs in the presence of only one witness, the defect may be remedied by the testator/testatrix acknowledging his/her signature in the presence of both witnesses. The first witness must then also acknowledge his or her prior signature followed by the second witness signing the will in the presence of both the testator/testatrix and the first witness.

This means that the testator/testatrix must sign or acknowledge his/her signature in the presence of both witnesses and before either of the witnesses has signed or acknowledged their signatures, but see *Mulhall v Mulhall* [1936] IR 712 where one of the witnesses was in another room but the door between them was open, which was held to be sufficient. As long as the witnesses saw or had the opportunity to see the testator/testatrix signature, it matters not that they were unaware of the nature of the document that they were being asked to sign and signed. This provision can lead to confusion, as illustrated in *Couser v Couser* [1996] 1 WLR 1301, where the testator drafted his will and signed it. He then took it to his friends (a couple) for attestation. When he arrived at their house, only the wife was present. She signed the will as a witness. A few minutes later her husband joined them. The wife told him what she did but expressed doubts about the validity of her attestation. The testator nevertheless asked the husband to sign the will bearing the signatures of himself and the wife, and informed the husband that he signed the will. The husband signed the will in the presence of his wife (who continued to protest that what was done was invalid), and the testator. On the testator's death, his son contended that the will was not duly executed on the grounds that the testator did not acknowledge his signature in the presence of the two witnesses at the same time, and the female witness did not subscribe the will after the testator had acknowledged his signature. It was held that the testator not only acknowledged his signature to the female witness but also subsequently did so in her presence and with her knowledge when her husband had attested the will. The testator had, therefore, acknowledged his signature in the presence of the two witnesses, and the female witness, by protesting about the invalidity of her signature, also acknowledged her signature at the time. The will was, therefore, validly executed.

The witnesses' signatures do not have to be in any particular part of the will or codicil provided that the signatures were clearly intended to attest the testator's/testatrix's signature. Where the signatures appear on a separate sheet of paper, it must be shown by a sworn statement that the sheet was attached to the will with the testator's/testatrix's signature by, for example, a pin or that it was stapled together. Where the names of the witnesses appear on the reverse of the will, it will be presumed that the will was duly executed even if the witnesses or either of them cannot be traced to confirm what actually occurred (*Harnett v Elliott* [1958] 2 All ER 1).

3.8 EVIDENCE OF ATTESTATION

Although no form of attestation clause is necessary, for evidential purposes, every will and codicil should contain such a clause stating that the will was signed by the testator/testatrix in the presence of the two witnesses present at the same time. The standard clause usually states that the testator signs in the presence of the witnesses and they sign in his presence. If an attestation clause is not included and it is not evident from the will itself whether the will was executed as required by the Wills Act 1837 or if there appears to be any doubt about whether the requirements were complied with, the doubt may be overcome by providing evidence to that effect. The evidence of the two witnesses who attested the signature of the testator/testatrix is usually relied upon to prove due execution and, in the absence of any other evidence to the contrary, the court is bound by that evidence. If both witnesses are not available, at least one of the witnesses' sworn statement confirming that execution occurred as required by statute will suffice. The district judge also has a discretion, under the Non-Contentious Probate Rules 1987, to dispense with evidence. Rule 12 provides:

> Evidence as to due execution of will
> 12.—(1) Subject to paragraphs (2) and (3) below, where a will contains no attestation clause or the attestation clause is insufficient, or where it appears to the registrar (*now district judge*) that there is doubt about the due execution of the will, he shall before admitting it to proof require an affidavit as to due execution from one or more of the attesting witnesses or, if no attesting witness is conveniently

available, from any other person who was present when the will was executed; and if the registrar, after considering the evidence, is satisfied that the will was not duly executed, he shall refuse probate and mark the will accordingly.

(2) If no affidavit can be obtained in accordance with paragraph (1) above, the registrar (*now district judge*) may accept evidence on affidavit from any person he may think fit to show that the signature on the will is in the handwriting of the deceased, or of any other matter which may raise a presumption in favour of due execution of the will, and may if he thinks fit require that notice of the application be given to any person who may be prejudiced by the will.

(3) A registrar (*now district judge*) may accept a will for proof without evidence as aforesaid if he is satisfied that the distribution of the estate is not thereby affected.

(See also rule 16 of the Non-Contentious Probate Rules 1987.)

Evidence may be given by affirmation or statutory declaration under section 16 of the Statutory Declarations Act 1835.

Situations where an affidavit/statement of execution is likely to be required include where the will or codicil has been signed in two places, where the signature of the testator/testatrix appears below that of the witnesses or where the will is signed by a mark or by the direction of the testator/testatrix. Where evidence of due execution is not available because, for instance, the witness has died, cannot be traced or lacks capacity, a sworn statement from any other person who was present at the execution of the will may be acceptable. If the witness is available but is not co-operating, pursuant to section 122 of the Senior Courts Act 1981, the High Court may order any person it reasonably believes has knowledge of any document which is or purports to be testamentary to attend court for examination in open court. Failure to attend or to answer any questions will render the person guilty of contempt of court.

Where the will on the face of it is regular and there is an attestation clause, the court will apply the presumption *omnia praesumuntur rite esse acta* – all things are presumed to have been done rightly and regularly – and presume that the will was executed in compliance with the provisions of the Wills Act 1837. In such a case, it will require the strongest evidence to rebut the presumption of due execution, as for example in *Sherrington v Sherrington* [2005] EWCA Civ 326, where the court inferred the intention of a witness to attest from the fact of the presence of the testator's signature, the attestation clause and underneath that clause the signature of the witness. This principle was applied in *Re Wright, Kentfield v Wright* [2010] EWHC 1607 (Ch), where the claimant and one attesting witness claimed that both witnesses were not present at the same time but the defendant and the other witness gave evidence that that they were.

Where the attestation clause is irregular and unusual in form the presumption will have less force and it would be possible to rebut it (*Lim v Thompson* [2009] EWHC 3341 (Ch)). In *Murrins v Matthews* [2006] EWHC 3419 (Ch), the presumption was rebutted because although the will was signed by two witnesses, there was no address given for them nor could they be found. Since the sole beneficiary of the will was 'overwhelmingly likely' to have been involved in the preparation of the will, and there was no evidence by the attesting witnesses as to its execution, the will was held to be invalid on the ground that it was not validly executed.

The presumption and the need for the strongest evidence to rebut it was considered in *Re Rawlinson, Kayll v Rawlinson* [2010] WTLR 1443, where there was 'common ground that the attestation clause was wrong'. David Richards J said:

> ... the presumption of due execution ... is an important presumption which requires the strongest evidence before the court will rule that a will apparently executed in proper form was not in fact validly executed ... I have not relied on the presumption for two reasons. First, where I have direct and conflicting evidence of a recent event, I considered it right, if possible, to resolve the conflict by findings of fact ... Secondly, it is not at all clear to me how far the presumption of due execution can apply as regards the presence of witnesses when the testator signs the will or acknowledges his signature, when it is common ground that the attestation clause is wrong. Contrary to the terms of the attestation clause, the will was not signed by the deceased in the presence of both witnesses. Where that is established fact, the presumption cannot derive from the terms of the attestation clause and, as it appears to me, some evidence of due execution by later acknowledgment, in the presence of both witnesses, is required. But I reach no firm conclusion on this and, in the light of my findings [that there was such an acknowledgment] it is unnecessary to analyse the extent to which the presumption applies in this case. (*Re Rawlinson, Kayll v Rawlinson* [2010] WTLR 1433)

The inability of a witness to recall or to have a vague recollection of what occurred when the will was executed is insufficient in itself to rebut the presumption (*Channon v Perkins* [2005] EWCA Civ 1808).

3.9 COMPETENCE OF WITNESSES

There is no statutory provision which disqualifies a person from witnessing a will. Witnesses should be of sound mind and capacity and of fixed abode. They should not be under a disability which prevents them from seeing or being aware of the act done. It is considered that a blind person is not capable of witnessing a will as he/she is not able to see what he/she is witnessing (see

Re Gibson (Deceased) [1949] P 434, where the question was left open as to whether a blind man could witness a will).

Section 14 of the Wills Act 1837 provides that a will is not to be considered invalid by reason of the fact that the person who attested its execution, either at the time of execution of the will or subsequently, is found to be 'incompetent to be admitted as a witness to prove execution'. There is no rule which disqualifies a child from witnessing a will, but a will attested by a child may be challenged on the basis of lack of mental capacity to understand the nature of the act done.

Section 15 of the Wills Act 1837 applies where a person attests the execution of a will and, under that will, any beneficial device, legacy, estate, interest, gift or appointment, of or affecting any real or personal estate, is given or made to that person or to his/her wife/husband/civil partner. Such a device, etc in so far as concerns the person attesting the execution of such a will, or that person's wife/husband/civil partner or any person claiming under that person or that person's wife/husband/civil partner, will be null and void, but the person who attested the will may be admitted as a witness to prove the execution of the will or to prove its validity or invalidity. If a witness is a person to whom or to whose spouse/civil partner the will makes a gift, the attestation is valid but the gift fails (section 15). This provision does not apply to a beneficiary of a will who has signed the will on behalf of a testator/testatrix and by his/her direction (*Barrett v Bem & Ors* [2011] EWHC 1247 (Ch)).

There are exceptions to this rule, which include gifts made in the following circumstances:

(a) a beneficial interest will not be lost if it is conferred on a witness under a secret trust and the witness is unaware of it at the time of attestation (*Re Young, Young v Young* [1951] Ch 344);

(b) where the witness or his/her spouse/civil partner does not witness an earlier will containing the gift but witnesses a codicil to that will, even if the codicil confirms the will or it is clear from the circumstances that the testator/testatrix does not intend to revoke the will;

(c) where a gift is made to an attesting witness or his/her spouse/civil partner in a fiduciary capacity;

(d) where a donee under the will attests a codicil which increases the donee's share in the residue under the will; or where a codicil confirms a will containing a gift to an attesting witness to the will;

(e) if three or more persons attest the will and at least two of them were persons who (and whose spouse/civil partner) took no gifts under it, no gift to any other witness or his/her spouse/civil partner is lost;

(f) a donee who or whose spouse/civil partner has witnessed the will may have his/her gifts restored if the will is confirmed by a codicil which is not witnessed by him/her or his/her spouse/civil partner;

(g) where the donee marries or enters into a civil partnership with the witness after the attestation took place;

(h) after 1 February 2001, if the will makes provision for a trustee or a personal representative acting in a professional capacity to receive payment from the deceased's estate (i.e. a 'charging clause'), such a payment is not treated as a gift (section 28 of the Trustees Act 2000).

In summary, therefore, where on the face of it a will appears to be duly executed, the presumption that it has been executed in accordance with the requirements of the Wills Act 1837 applies. This does not mean that the will cannot be challenged. It is obvious from the commentary given above that a challenge can be made, but that strong, clear and reliable evidence will be required to rebut the presumption.

It should also be noted that the formalities for the execution of a valid will as set out in section 9 of the Wills Act 1837 are currently the subject of a review by the Law Commission. In particular, the review will consider whether the formalities could be applied more flexibly, and whether there is any 'scope for taking more advantage of technology'.

Chapter 4

Testamentary Capacity

4.1 INTRODUCTION

For a will to be valid, the testator/testatrix must be a person who is aged 18 or over and have the mental capacity to make the will. Claims contesting the validity of wills, particularly of those who are elderly or are mentally disabled, have been and are likely to remain an increasing source of litigation. They are the most difficult mainly because it is not always clear whether the person had capacity when instructions were first taken and, if he/she had capacity at that time, whether it persisted. The issue of testamentary capacity is also intertwined with the principle that it is essential to the validity of a will that the testator/testatrix should have knowledge of and approve the contents of his/her will. In challenging the validity of a will on the basis of lack of testamentary capacity, it is essential to draw a distinction between the ability to understand, which is the test of capacity, and actual understanding, which is not. (The subject of knowledge and approval is considered in Chapter 5.) It is, therefore, not surprising that when a will is challenged on the basis of lack of testamentary capacity, it is also claimed that the testator/testatrix did not know, understand and approve the contents of the will, and also that due to his/her vulnerability undue influence was exerted on him/her (see Chapter 6). Failure to ascertain whether the testator/testatrix has the appropriate capacity to give instructions and to understand the nature of the act of making a will is an invitation for litigation and a claim for professional negligence and costs. In the majority of cases where the validity of the will is challenged on the ground of lack of testamentary capacity, the observation made by Briggs J (as he then was) in *Re Key (Deceased), Key v Key & Others* [2010] EWHC 408 (Ch) at [6] applies, that the significant element or responsibility for the situation which arose in that tragic case was due to the failure of the solicitors to comply with the *Golden Rule* and the guidance given by the Law Society (see para 4.3) which led to the increased difficulties and aggravated the 'depths of mistrust'. Although the *Golden Rule* is not a rule of law, it is good practice to follow the guidance. The difficulties which may arise are avoidable by ensuring that the basic rules are followed and consideration is given to the impact of provisions set out in the

Mental Capacity Act 2005 (MCA 2005). The factors which need to be established to challenge lack of testamentary capacity are considered below.

4.2 TEST OF TESTAMENTARY CAPACITY UNDER COMMON LAW

The test for testamentary capacity under common law was set out in *Banks v Goodfellow* (1870) LR 5 QB 549, in which Cockburn CJ referred to it as follows:

> It is essential that a testator shall understand the nature of his act and its effects; the extent of the property of which he is disposing; shall be able to comprehend and appreciate the claims to which he ought to give effect, and, with a view to the latter object, that no disorder of mind shall poison his affections, pervert his sense of right, or prevent the exercise of his natural faculties, that no insane delusion shall influence his will in disposing of his property and bring about a disposal of it which, if his mind had been sound, would not have been made. (*Banks v Goodfellow* (1870) LR 5 QB 549 at 565)

However, a will cannot be invalidated simply because the testator/testatrix was moved 'by capricious, frivolous, mean or even bad motives'.

There are thus four key factors which must be met to establish testamentary capacity. They are that the testator/testatrix must understand:

(a) the nature of the act of making a will;
(b) the effect of making a will;
(c) the nature and extent of the property of which he/she is disposing;
(d) the claims on his/her estate of those whom he/she is benefiting and also of those whom he/she is excluding and in relation to the latter:

> no disorder of mind shall poison his affections, pervert his sense of right, or prevent the exercise of his natural faculties, that no insane delusion shall influence his will in disposing of his property and bring about a disposal of it which, if his mind had been sound, would not have been made. (*Banks v Goodfellow* (1870) LR 5 QB 549 at 565)

4.2.1 Nature of the act of making a will

Those taking instructions must ensure that the person giving instructions for the making of his/her will has a broad understanding of the process of making a will, such as that the will comes into effect only on death; that until death occurs, ownership of the property remains with him/her; and that he/she has the right at any time before his/her death to revoke or vary his/her wishes and thus the will.

4.2.2   Effect of making a will

Care must be taken to establish that the person giving the instructions for the making of his/her will understands the ambulatory nature of a will and that although he/she might wish to bequeath a certain property to a named beneficiary, circumstances may change between the making of the will and date of death, in that the property may not be in existence at the date of death, its value may have increased or decreased or the beneficiary may predecease him/her, in which case the gift will fail. He/she should be able to consider alternative options.

4.2.3   Nature and extent of the property being disposed of

This means that the client should be able to understand and have knowledge or recollection of the property he/she owns, for example his/her legal title to the property and whether he/she is the sole owner of the property or whether it is jointly owned with another, and if the latter the legal implications of ownership by survivorship. He/she should be able to identify other interests that he/she may have such as pension rights, rights under insurance policies, shares, etc. The recent case of *Pearce v Beverley* [2013] EW Misc 10 (CC) is an example where the facts raised doubts as to whether the testator understood the extent of his property and whether he had an understanding of the claims of his daughter and his grandchildren on his estate. The testator in that case was suffering from mental and physical problems, he was unable to speak when the will was drawn and executed, and the instructions were given by the defendant. The evidence also indicated that he denied he had a daughter, which was inexplicable given his good relationship with her. This raised doubts about whether the testator had the mental capacity to make a will and whether, when the will was executed, he had knowledge of what he was doing and was able to approve this (see Chapter 5). It was also found on the facts that he was the subject of undue influence by the defendant.

4.2.4   Claims on the estate

This involves the testator/testatrix understanding and appreciating his/her moral responsibilities and obligations which he/she has towards others; the ability of distinguishing between the needs of those for whom he/she is responsible and assessing their needs and being able to balance the competing interests of others.

If he/she chooses to ignore, exclude or differentiate between such potential beneficiaries, he/she should have the capacity to give his/her reasons for so doing. This has been referred to as being able to consider the moral claims of persons 'who are fitting objects of the testator's bounty' (*Broughton v Knight* (1873) LR 3 P & D 64), but as long as he/she is capable of considering these moral claims, there is no legal obligation for him/her to leave any property to these persons. There is no need for any testator/testatrix to act 'in such a manner as to deserve approbation from the prudent the wise and the good' (*Bird v Luckie* (1850) 8 Hare 301). A testator/testatrix has the freedom to leave his/her assets to whomsoever he/she pleases. However, the fact that he/she disregarded such moral obligations may raise doubts on whether he/she indeed had capacity (see *Battan Singh v Amirchand* [1948] AC 161 where, although the testator had three nephews to whom he was close, he claimed he had no living relatives and left his assets to creditors). The case of *Pearce v Beverley* [2013] EW Misc 10 (CC) is a recent example where the testator denied he had a daughter and excluded her from his will without any explanation. His action on the facts was found to be irrational.

4.2.5 Capricious, frivolous, mean or even bad motives

A will cannot be invalidated simply because the testator/testatrix makes an unwise decision. For a will to be valid, the law does not require that the testator/testatrix should have a perfectly balanced mind or that he/she should be motivated to please or do good. Where the will is rational on its face and duly executed, it will be presumed that the testator/testatrix had testamentary capacity. The burden of proving otherwise and rebutting the presumption will fall on those who seek to allege lack of capacity to adduce evidence of the testator's/testatrix's mental incapacity. Once there is credible evidence before the court which casts doubts on the testamentary capacity of the testator/testatrix, the burden of proof shifts onto those who seek to propound the will to prove that he/she did have the appropriate mental capacity (*Cowenbergh v Valkova* [2008] EWHC 2451 (Ch) at [247]; *Sherrington v Sherrington* [2005] EWCA Civ 326 applied. See also *Pearce v Beverley* [2013] EW Misc 10 (CC)). If the opposing party proves a real doubt as to capacity, the burden will revert to the propounder of the will (*The Vegetarian Society & Anor v Scott* [2013] EWHC 4097 (Ch)).

4.3 ASCERTAINING TESTAMENTARY CAPACITY – THE GOLDEN RULE

Ascertaining whether a would-be testator/testatrix has testamentary capacity is essential when that person is elderly or has suffered, or is suffering, from serious illness. This should be achieved by instructing a medical practitioner to assess the testator's/testatrix's capacity to make a will where he/she is elderly, has suffered or is suffering from serious illness, as set out in *Kennard v Adams* (1975) *The Times*, 29 November, and in *Re Simpson, Schaniel v Simpson* [1977] NLJ 487 by Templeman J (as he then was):

> In the case of an aged testator or a testator who has suffered a serious illness, there is one golden rule which should always be observed, however straightforward matters may appear, and however difficult or tactless it may be to suggest that precautions be taken; the making of a will by such a testator ought to be witnessed or approved by a medical practitioner who satisfied himself of the capacity and understanding of the testator, and records and preserves his examination and finding.
>
> There are other precautions which should be taken. If a testator has made an earlier will this should be considered by the legal and medical advisers of the testator and, if appropriate, discussed with the testator. The instructions of the testator should be taken in the absence of anyone who may stand to benefit, or who may have influence over the testator. These are not counsels of perfection. If proper precautions are not taken injustice may result or be imagined, and great expense and misery may be unnecessarily caused. (*Re Simpson, Schaniel v Simpson* [1977] NLJ 487)

This has now come to be known as the *Golden Rule*. In order to reconcile the operation of this rule with a solicitor's and his/her staff's duty of confidentiality in relation to the affairs of the client, the Law Society suggests that when a doctor witnesses a patient's signature on a document, there is a strong inference that the patient had the requisite capacity (see *Assessment of Mental Capacity: A Practical Guide for Doctors and Lawyers* (British Medical Association and the Law Society, 4th edn, 2015). The Law Society also recommends that, where there is any doubt about the patient's capacity, the doctor should not witness the patient's signature on a document unless: (a) the doctor has formally assessed his/her capacity; and (b) the doctor is satisfied, on the balance of probabilities, that the patient has the requisite capacity to enter into the transaction effected by the document and makes a formal record of his/her examination and findings. Where the testator/testatrix lacks capacity, application should be made to the Court of Protection for a statutory will to be made (see Chapter 15).

Although it is recommended that the *Golden Rule* should be followed, it is not a rule of law and thus not absolute. If it is not strictly observed, it does not necessarily lead to criticism, nor does it follow that if it is observed, capacity cannot or will not be challenged, and if challenged the court will find that the testator had capacity. Recent authorities have shown that much will depend on the strength of the evidence adduced before the court. The issue is one for the decision of the court:

> It is not to be delegated to experts, however eminent, albeit that their knowledge and experience may be an invaluable tool in the analysis, affording insight to the

workings of the mind, otherwise beyond the grasp of laymen, including for that purposes, lawyers and in particular judges. (*Re Key (Deceased), Key v Key & Others* [2010] EWHC 408 (Ch) at [98])

The rule was considered in *Buckenham v Dickinson* [1997] CLY 4733. In that case, the testator was 93 years of age, partially blind and deaf. It was reported by a neighbour, who had experience in dealing with the elderly, that he virtually cut himself off from everybody. A medical assessment of his capacity was not undertaken. His wife was the informant of what his wishes were, which were at variance with those set out in an existing will. The solicitor, however, took steps to read out aloud the contents of the will to the testator in short spells and on each interruption asked the testator if he understood and approved what was read out. The will was challenged by the testator's son on the ground that the deceased did not have testamentary capacity or that the requirement of knowledge and approval was lacking. The court held that although the testator had capacity, he did not have actual understanding to know and approve the contents. In considering the failure by the solicitor to observe the *Golden Rule*, Judge Cooke said:

> Now of course what *Simpson* does not say, although counsel tries to submit that it does is that a failure to observe the golden rule will invalidate the will; it says nothing of the kind, but it points very starkly to the problems that professionals face when they are drawing wills and they do not take these precautions or precautions as near to them as the practicalities require. (*Buckenham v Dickinson* [1997] CLY 4733)

When taking instructions for a will, and where the instructions were in fact given by someone other than the testator/testatrix and the testator/testatrix was merely being asked to agree to someone else's proposition, the use of open rather than closed questions was an essential minimum of good practice.

The effect of the *Golden Rule* was considered in *Cowderoy v Cranfield* [2011] EWHC 1616 (Ch), where capacity was upheld. The case concerned an elderly woman who left the property in which she lived to her neighbour, the defendant, who befriended her, cared for her and visited her regularly. The will was challenged by her grand-daughter on the grounds of lack of capacity, knowledge and approval, and that the defendant procured the will by exercising undue influence. The solicitor failed to carry out an assessment in accordance with the guidelines of the *Golden Rule*. Although the evidence indicated that the testatrix had good days and bad days, the court found she had capacity and rejected the claim of undue influence. When dealing with the failure to observe the *Golden Rule*, Morgan J said:

> The so-called Golden Rule as to the role of a solicitor involved in the preparation and execution of a will is that in the case of an aged testator, or one who has been seriously ill, the solicitor should arrange for a medical practitioner first to satisfy

himself as to the capacity and understanding of the testator, and to make a contemporaneous record of his examination and findings: see *Key v Key* at [6]. A friend or a non-medical professional adviser may fail to detect defects in mental capacity which would become apparent to a trained and experienced medical examiner who understood the legal test for testamentary capacity. The application of the Golden Rule assists in the avoidance of subsequent disputes as to capacity. However, in the present case, where the Golden Rule was not followed, and a dispute as to capacity has arisen and has to be resolved by the court, non-compliance with the Golden Rule does not demonstrate a lack of capacity. The issue must be decided by the court by applying the correct legal principles to the court's findings of fact. (*Cowderoy v Cranfield* [2011] EWHC 1616 (Ch) at [137])

In *Re Key (Deceased), Key v Key & Others* [2010] EWHC 408 (Ch), the will was made by an elderly testator who was bereaved from the death of his wife when he gave instructions for the preparation of his will, and the solicitor did not obtain a medical assessment. Briggs J (as he then was) held that the will was invalid, and stated that:

> Without in any way detracting from the continuing authority of *Banks v. Goodfellow*, it must be recognised that psychiatric medicine has come a long way since 1870 in recognising an ever widening range of circumstances now regarded as sufficient at least to give rise to a risk of mental disorder, sufficient to deprive a patient of the power of rational decision making, quite distinctly from old age and infirmity. The mental shock of witnessing an injury to a loved one is an example recognised by the law, and the affective disorder which may be caused by bereavement is an example recognised by psychiatrists, and that, although there did not appear to be any reported case dealing with the effect of bereavement on testamentary capacity, the *Banks v. Goodfellow* test must be applied so as to accommodate this, among other factors capable of impairing testamentary capacity. (*Re Key (Deceased), Key v Key & Others* [2010] EWHC 408 (Ch) at [95])

Many of the cases which have followed *Banks v Goodfellow* (1870) LR 5 QB 549 relate to cognitive behaviour and dementia, and although affective disorder such as depression, including that caused by bereavement, is more likely to affect powers of decision-making than comprehension, the effect of bereavement on a person is a relevant factor to be taken into account. This is because although the person in that condition may have the capacity to understand what his/her property is, and even who his/her relatives and dependants are, he/she may not have the mental energy to make any decision of his/her own and there is thus an increased risk of the person being led by suggestions made by third parties. It may also cause severe reactions such as impaired concentration and attention, the ability to take in things and to remember them and impaired cognitive impairment (see *Re Key (Deceased), Key v Key & Others* [2010] EWHC 408 (Ch)). However, grief following a bereavement cannot be relied on to support a case on the ground of lack of testamentary capacity, where there is no evidence or unconvincing evidence that following the bereavement the testator suffered from depression or such severe grief that it prevented him from making a rational decision or was unduly influenced before or at the time or immediately after the will was executed, and there is no recorded medical evidence to support the finding of lack of testamentary capacity. In *Dharamshi & Others v Velji & Others* [2013] EWHC 3917 (Ch), on the facts, the claim based on lack of testamentary capacity due to bereavement failed, but the court gave useful guidance on when a testator's grief may give rise to lack of testamentary capacity. The case differed from *Re Key* (above) in that in *Re Key* there was also clear evidence that the testator's daughter had pressurised him to make the will, whereas in *Dharamshi* the evidence established that the testator had acted on his own and carefully selected those he wished to benefit, and had sought legal advice.

Medical evidence which establishes that the testator had capacity may not always be conclusive. Other factors may result in the court concluding that the testator lacked capacity when he made the will. In *Sharp v Adam* [2006] EWCA Civ 449, the Court of Appeal allowed an appeal notwithstanding that medical assessment confirmed that the testator had capacity. In that case, the testator suffered from multiple sclerosis which was known to lead to some impairment of the mind. He made a will in 1997, under which his two daughters were the principal beneficiaries. In 2001, he revoked the will and executed another will disinheriting his two daughters and leaving his estate to two employees. The solicitors followed the *Golden Rule* and obtained an assessment of his capacity which concluded that the testator had capacity. The validity of the 2001 will was challenged. At the trial, two experts were divided in their opinion on capacity. The trial judge concluded that the testator lacked capacity on the basis that although the first three elements of the test in *Banks v Goodfellow* (1870) LR 5 QB 549 were met, the fourth element of the test was not. The reason for that conclusion was that the total exclusion of his daughters raised the question whether his mind was impaired so as to deprive him of the ability to think clearly and enable him to make a rational decision. The claimant appealed, relying in the main on the fact that the *Golden Rule* was implicitly followed. The Court of Appeal came to the conclusion that it was a finely balanced decision and, because it could not find any rational explanation for the testator completely excluding his daughters from whom he was not estranged, it could not be shown that the will as a whole was rationally made, and on the evidence the testator's decision to exclude his daughters was an indication of cognitive decline which the experts confirmed was a feature of multiple sclerosis.

Given the fact that the solicitors went to great lengths to ensure that the *Golden Rule* was complied with, the conclusion reached in this case may be explained on the basis that it turned on its specific facts. However, a more plausible explanation may be that as the sticking point in the case was the fourth element of the test in *Banks v Goodfellow* (1870) LR 5 QB 549, this element is an important factor which should be given weight when determining the issue of testamentary capacity. Where a rational reason is given for excluding someone to whom the testator/testatrix has a moral obligation, it may establish or confirm capacity. But where the decision cannot be explained by considering the will as a whole, it may lend support to challenging capacity. The Court of Appeal, however, emphasised that where the *Golden Rule* has been followed 'it will require very persuasive evidence to enable the court to dislodge that conclusion'.

In contrast, in *Re Perrins (Deceased), Perrins v Holland & Anor* [2009] EWHC 1945 (Ch), although the testator suffered from an aggressive form of multiple sclerosis and left everything to his cohabitant, A, and his only son was to receive one half of the estate only if A predeceased him, the court held that he had capacity. An experienced legal executive took instructions and formed the view that the testator had capacity. A draft will was sent to him but no response was received for a year. The next communication was from A after a bill was sent for the preparation of the draft. She requested a copy of the will and an enduring power of attorney. Subsequently, the will was executed after the contents were briefly gone through with the testator. The son's challenge on capacity was based on irrationality in his father excluding him. The court heard conflicting evidence on the testator's capacity but held that what mattered was that the testator had capacity when he gave instructions (see further para 4.4).

Similarly, in *Re Ritchie* [2009] EWHC 709 (Ch), the testatrix whose estate was valued at £2.5 million executed a will when she was aged 88 disinheriting her children and leaving her assets to the National Osteoporosis Society. She was known to suffer from obsessive compulsive disorder. Her solicitors took care to seek out an explanation for her decision which included allegations of theft, violence towards her and neglect. These were denied by the children and found to be untrue, although they accepted that the testatrix believed these allegations. It was held that her testamentary capacity was affected and the will was invalid. The observations made by Mummery and Scott Baker LJJ in *Hawes v Burgess* [2013] EWCA Civ 74 (see [60] and [69]), that the court should not readily invalidate a will that has been drafted by an experienced solicitor who oversees the execution of the will and records in a note that he was satisfied that the testator had testamentary capacity, appear to contradict the need to adhere to a clinical assessment required under the test in the *Golden Rule*. In so doing, it fails to take account of the fact that not all experienced solicitors are qualified to make the very discrete assessment or adopt a procedure from which such an assessment can be achieved, and the obvious risks of relying on such a non-clinical assessment are overlooked.

4.4 AT WHAT STAGE IS ASSESSMENT OF CAPACITY RELEVANT?

The time which elapses between when the first intention and move is made to make a will and when it is finally and formally executed can vary from a few days to years. There are innumerable reasons why delay occurs, but once the first step is taken the most common reason for the delay is the need to establish the person's testamentary capacity to make a will. Difficulties may be encountered where the would-be testator/testatrix is under temporary disability which may lift or where the person has fluctuating capacity, in which case capacity is very much time-specific. In such cases, problems may arise if the testator/testatrix had capacity when instructions were given but subsequently loses capacity and does not regain it. In such cases, the rule in *Parker v Felgate* (1883) 8 PD 171 applies: the will is valid if the testator/testatrix had capacity when instructions were taken from him/her but his/her condition deteriorates between giving instructions and when the will is executed, provided it can be established that: (a) he/she had capacity when he/she gave instructions for the will to be prepared; (b) the will as drafted was in accordance with those instructions; (c) at the time he/she executed the will, he/she was capable of understanding that he/she was executing a will for which he/she gave instructions.

The rule in *Parker v Felgate* (1883) 8 PD 171 was applied in *Clancy v Clancy* [2003] EWHC 1885 (Ch). In that case, the court upheld the testatrix's will although her testamentary capacity was doubtful at the time of execution. The evidence established that she had capacity when she gave instructions for the will to be drawn up. When she received the draft 6 days prior to her death, she confirmed the contents of the will to her solicitor. Two days before her death the will was executed and at that point her capacity was doubtful. Applying the rule in *Parker v Felgate*, it was held that it was sufficient that when she signed the will she understood that she was signing a document which contained the instructions she gave 4 months earlier. Similarly, in *Re Perrins (Deceased), Perrins v Holland & Anor* [2009] EWHC 1945 (Ch) (see para 4.3), the testator who suffered from multiple sclerosis was found to have capacity when he gave instructions but not when the will was executed some 5 months later. The will was held to be valid on the basis of the rule in *Parker v Felgate*. This principle was also applied to an *inter vivos* transaction in *Singellos v Singellos* [2010] EWHC 2353 (Ch).

4.5 MENTAL CAPACITY ACT 2005 AND THE TEST FOR CAPACITY UNDER COMMON LAW

The MCA 2005 came into force on 1 October 2007. Section 1 sets out the fundamental principles which must be considered in every decision made under the Act. These include:

(a) a person must be assumed to have capacity unless it is established that he/she lacks capacity;
(b) a person is not to be treated as unable to make a decision unless all practicable steps to help him/her to do so have been taken without success;
(c) a person is not to be treated as unable to make a decision merely because he/she makes an unwise decision.

The Act thus reinforces the common law presumption that an adult has full capacity to make decisions for himself/herself unless it is proved otherwise. The onus of proving incapacity rests on the person who alleges it. Under the common law test, it is for the person propounding the will to prove its validity even though there is a presumption that a will, which is duly executed, was made by a person who has capacity, where its contents are rational and there is nothing that casts doubt on the testator's/testatrix's capacity.

The MCA 2005 also sets out a definitive test for assessing whether a person has capacity to make a specific decision at the material time. It is thus issue- and time-specific. It provides for a two-stage process. The first stage is the diagnostic stage which is set out in section 2(1), and the second stage is the functional stage which is set out in section 3.

4.5.1 Diagnostic stage

Section 2(1) of the MCA 2005 provides that 'a person lacks capacity in relation to a matter if at the material time he is unable to make a decision for himself in relation to the matter because of an impairment of, or disturbance in the functioning of, the mind or brain'. Hence before a decision is made on behalf of a person who appears to lack capacity, the first question which needs to be answered is whether that person has been diagnosed as having an impairment of, or disturbance in, the functioning of the mind or brain. If he/she does not, it is assumed that he/she has capacity. The MCA 2005 Code of Practice at paragraph 4.12 sets out some conditions which could lead to such impairment or disturbance. These include conditions of dementia, significant learning difficulties, long-term effects of brain damage, mental or physical conditions which cause confusion, concussion following a head injury, and symptoms of alcohol and drug abuse. If the person is diagnosed as having an impairment or disturbance in the functioning of the mind, one still needs to question whether or not it affects the person's ability to make particular decisions at the 'material time', because the impairment may be temporary, in which case if there is no urgency, all practical steps must be taken to assist the person to make the decision and, where appropriate, to wait until the person is able to make the decision for himself/herself.

4.5.2 Functional stage

Section 3(1) of the MCA 2005 confirms the common law position in providing that a person is unable to make a decision for himself/herself if he/she is unable:

(a) to understand the information relevant to the decision. The information relevant to the decision includes information about reasonably foreseeable consequences of deciding one way or another or failing to make the decision. However, in order to enable the person to understand the decision he/she has to make, he/she must be given the information in a way that is appropriate to his/her circumstances. Furthermore, in order to enable the person to understand the consequences of his/her decision, the person must be given information about the nature of the decision to be made, the reasons for the need to take the decision and the likely effect of making it and refusing to make it;

(b) to retain that information. But the fact that he/she is able to retain the information for a short time only does not prevent him/her from being regarded as able to make the decision;

(c) to use or weigh that information as part of the process of making the decision; or

(d) to communicate his/her decision (whether by talking, using sign language or any other means). The person must be supported and assisted to overcome any disability he/she may have, where appropriate by a person with the necessary skills.

It should be noted that in *Sharp v Adam* [2006] EWCA Civ 449, the Court of Appeal did not consider that the test in *Banks v Goodfellow* (1870) LR 5 QB needed to be reformulated in the light of the MCA 2005. In *Re Devillebichot (Deceased)* [2013] EWHC 2867 (Ch), the issue of whether the testator had the requisite testamentary capacity was considered by reference to the test in *Banks v Goodfellow*. There does not appear to be any reference to the provisions of sections 2 and 3. In *Turner v Phythian* [2013] EWHC 499 (Ch), the judge referred in passing to the test applied under the Act as being relevant but did not determine the issue on that test because he 'did not hear any submissions as to whether this test differed from the common law test' (see [39]). It is submitted that future cases where capacity is in issue should consider the application of the statutory definition if not as replacing the test in *Banks v Goodfellow*, then alongside that test so as to incorporate it as it reflects the common law but with account being taken of the advancement in modern medicine and adopting plain language (e.g. see *Re Key (Deceased), Key v Key & Others* [2010] EWHC 408 (Ch) (discussed at para 4.3). The MCA 2005 Code of Practice at paragraph 4.33 expressly refers to the common law test and states that the statutory definition does not replace the common law test, but the new definition may be adopted if the judge considers it appropriate. The fact that the statutory provision that the person's capacity is issue- and time-specific is akin to the common law principle is best illustrated by the cases referred to in para 4.4, which established that testamentary capacity is determined when the decision is taken to make the will and instructions are given to give effect to that decision. It is, however, important to make the distinction that *Banks v Goodfellow* limits the application of the test to any person who is 'aged or who has been seriously ill', whereas the MCA 2005 test has wider application. Under the MCA 2005, the assessment of capacity is not limited to the medical practitioner. The fourth element of the *Banks v Goodfellow* test, which until very recently was regarded as significant, is very much part of the conditions recognised as resulting in impairment or disturbance in the functioning of the mind or brain. In *Scammell v Farmer* [2008] EWHC 1100 (Ch), although the court held that the question of whether or not a particular testator had capacity when the will was made does not fall within the scope of the MCA 2005 but under the common law, the differences between the statutory test and the common law test were referred to. For further discussion on the need for an approach to testamentary capacity that takes into account the test of capacity under the MCA 2005, see Annabel Lee and Alex Ruck Keene, 'Testamentary Capacity' [2013] 3 Eld LJ 272.

Where there is doubt on the would-be testator's/testatrix's capacity, guidance may be sought from the Court of Protection and, if lack of capacity is found, the court has the power to make or authorise the making of a statutory will on behalf of the person who lacks capacity (sections 16 and 18 of the MCA 2005).

4.6 DELUSIONS

The fact that a person suffers from delusions concerning a particular belief or matter does not necessarily lead to the conclusion that he/she is incompetent to make a will if, in all other respects, he/she appears to be rational. Capacity may be said to be lacking if it influences or is capable of influencing the decision he/she takes in the provisions he/she makes in the will. The test to be applied in such cases is whether, viewed objectively, the particular delusion is of such a nature and extent that no person in full control of his/her senses could believe it.

The starting point is that a testator/testatrix has the freedom to make his/her will as he/she pleases, and he/she is entitled to dispose of his/her property as he/she wills no matter how capricious he/she may be in so doing. In *Broughton v Knight* (1873) LR 3 P &D 64, Sir John Hannen said:

> Everyone is left free to choose the person on whom he will bestow his property after death entirely unfettered in the selection he make think proper to make. He may disinherit, either wholly or partially, his children, and leave his property to

strangers to gratify his spite, or to charities to gratify his pride, and we must give effect to his will, however much we may condemn the course he has pursued. (*Broughton v Knight* (1873) LR 3 P & D 64 at para 137)

However, where the testator/testatrix has antipathy towards a person, for example his/her children, and it can be shown that he/she was deluded, the party setting up the will must prove that the delusion did not influence his/her decision. As Sir John Hannen went on to say in *Broughton v Knight* (1873) LR 3 P & D 64:

> But there is a limit beyond which one feels that it ceases to be a question of harsh unreasonable judgment of character, and that the repulsion which a parent exhibits towards one or more of his children must proceed from some mental defect in himself ... there is a point at which such repulsion and aversion are themselves evidence of unsoundness of mind. (*Broughton v Knight* (1873) LR 3 P & D 64 at para 137)

The fourth element in the test in *Banks v Goodfellow* (1870) LR 5 QB 549 best deals with the circumstances where delusions can be said to affect capacity:

> If the human instincts and affections, or the moral sense, becomes perverted by mental disease; if insane suspicion or aversion take the place of natural affection; if the reason and judgment are lost, and the mind becomes a prey for insane delusions calculated to interfere with and disturb its functions – in such a case it is obvious that the condition of the testamentary power fails, and that a will made under such circumstances ought not to stand. (*Banks v Goodfellow* (1870) LR 5 QB 549 at 565)

It follows, therefore, that if the first three elements of the test are met but the fourth is not and there is no rational explanation for the decision taken by the testator/testatrix, the court may find that capacity was lacking. The following are examples of cases where the court so found. In *Re Ritchie* [2009] EWHC 709 (Ch), the deceased left her estate worth £2.5 million to charity and disinherited her children in the deluded but false belief that her children stole from her, physically abused her and neglected her. Similarly, in *Sharp v Adam* [2006] EWCA Civ 449, the court could find no rational explanation for the testator disinheriting his daughters and found that the deceased lacked capacity, although the solicitor went to great lengths to establish that the testator had capacity when he executed his will. In *Kostic v Chaplin* [2007] EWHC 2298 (Ch), the deceased left his entire estate valued at over £8 million to the Conservative Party. Evidence was adduced to show that the deceased was extremely deluded and paranoid about a number of things. The court found that the deceased's insane delusions affected his testamentary capacity and held the will invalid. But in *Carr & Others v Beaven & Others* [2008] EWHC 2582 (Ch), two of the three wills of the testator were challenged by his children.

Before making the first will in 1998 the testator suffered a stroke. Under that will the children were to receive modest legacies. In February 2000, he gave instructions to his solicitor for a new will disinheriting his children but granting a lease of a cottage which formed part of the estate to his employee. Before the will was executed he changed his instructions. The will was executed in March but, at the time, the solicitor was concerned about the testator's capacity and advised the testator's wife to have him assessed by his doctor who, in turn, made a referral to a consultant psychiatrist. In November 2000, the testator made his last will drawn by a friend, an experienced solicitor, who was satisfied that the testator had capacity and that he knew and approved what he wished and gave reasons for why he changed his mind. Medical evidence confirmed that patients who suffer from dementia have lucid periods when they have capacity to make decisions. On the combined evidence of the solicitor and the doctor, the judge was satisfied that the testator had capacity.

The difficulties which arise in cases where delusion is raised lie in the fact that the issue of capacity becomes apparent after death. The issue of whether the deceased had capacity can only be discerned from past medical records and secondary evidence. Medical records are often brief and deal with the immediate medical condition of the deceased at the time and are often insufficient. Even where the solicitor took steps beyond the call of duty, as in *Re Ritchie* [2009] EWHC 709 (Ch), the court has found that the deceased lacked capacity. Often, the medical evidence obtained at the time proves to be inadequate and uninformative. In determining the issue of capacity, the court will consider the contents of the will and all the surrounding circumstances. Where reasons are given by the deceased for his/her decision, information about the truth or otherwise of the facts and allegations and the general demeanour of the deceased will be relevant factors. It is only when the court is satisfied that the delusion could not, in the circumstances, be taken to have had any influence on the decision taken by the deceased that it will hold that the deceased had capacity.

4.7 SENILITY, CONFUSION AND LUCID INTERVALS

The mere fact that the testator/testatrix was of advancing years when the will was made does not suffice to invalidate the will for lack of testamentary capacity. Although, in the cases which have highlighted the problem, the testator/testatrix has been in the main over 70 years of age and in ill health (see *Re Simpson, Schaniel v Simpson* [1977] NLJ 487; *Buckenham v Dickinson* [1997] CLY 4733 – testator was 93, deaf and partially blind; and *Re Key (Deceased), Key v Key & Others* [2010] EWHC 408 (Ch) – testator was 89), it is nevertheless prudent to obtain medical evidence of capacity. The evidence must show that the testator's/testatrix's mental ability and understanding was reduced to such an extent that he/she did not understand and appreciate the act of making a will and its effect on those who may have a possible claim on the estate, as required under the *Banks v Goodfellow* (1870) LR 5 QB 549 test. Where the evidence shows that the testator's/testatrix's mental condition varied, as in the case of someone suffering from senile dementia, for a will to be valid it must be shown that the will was made during a lucid period. Evidence that the *Golden Rule* was followed, although not always determinative, will go some way to establishing capacity.

In *Re Loxton (Deceased), Abbot v Richardson* [2006] EWHC 1291 (Ch), evidence showed that the elderly testatrix was unable to recall or focus on the persons she wished to benefit, although she was able to understand what was in her will and approve it. It was held that she lacked capacity. This is an example which demonstrates the link between capacity and the ability to know and approve a will. Conversely, in *Re Perrins (Deceased), Perrins v Holland & Anor* [2009] EWHC 1945 (Ch) where, despite the fact that the testator was physically and mentally disabled by multiple sclerosis, there was a close relationship between him and his son, whom he disinherited, and over a year had elapsed before the will was finally executed, the court nevertheless held that he had capacity when he gave instructions for his will in April 2000. Evidence showed that he was able to recall and process information, to identify his assets, and to answer hypothetical questions. He was able to make the decision of how he wished his estate to be disposed of. He thus had capacity when he gave instructions, although not when the will was executed. Applying the rule in *Parker v Felgate* (1883) 8 PD 171, the will was held to be valid. See also *Re Parsons* [2002] WTLR 237, where the testator was held to have capacity. The testator was elderly, in poor health and suffered a stroke on the same day that he signed his will (which he did by making a thumb print) after having been examined by a doctor, who confirmed that he had testamentary capacity. In *Richards v Allan* [2001] WTLR 1031, the testatrix was 84 years of age and prone to confusion. She had lucid periods interspersed with periods of confusion. Evidence from her doctor confirmed that she was confused on the day she signed her will. She was held to lack capacity.

4.8 DRUNKENNESS

The fact that the testator/testatrix was drinking when he/she signed his/her will is not in itself sufficient to invalidate the will for lack of testamentary capacity. Where the evidence discloses that the testator/testatrix was drunk, for it to have any effect on the issue of capacity it must be shown that the testator/testatrix was incapable of knowing the nature of the act which he/she was carrying out. The relevant issue in such a case is whether, at the time he/she gave instructions and executed the will, he/she was clear in his/her mind how he/she wished to dispose of his/her property, that he/she was aware of the nature and effect of what he/she was doing, how he/she wished to dispose of his/her property and why. *Chana (Gavinder) v Chana (Harjit Kaur)* [2001] WTLR 205 illustrates how the court applied the test set out in *Banks v Goodfellow* (1870) LR 5 QB 549. In that case, the testator and one of the attesting witnesses were drinking when the will was executed. The will was drafted by a friend who was a business man and a local councillor with some experience of drafting wills. The testator indicated to him that he did not wish to leave anything to his sons as they had physically and verbally abused him. One of his sons was severely disabled and the testator was aware of the disability. Ten months after executing his will, the testator died of alcoholism. Applying the test in *Banks v Goodfellow* (see above), the court held that the testator had a clear understanding of his wishes, what he intended to do and its effect.

4.9 LANGUAGE AND LITERACY

It is essential for those who prepare a will to ensure that language is not presenting a barrier in obtaining instructions and advising the client. If in doubt, it would be prudent to instruct an independent and qualified interpreter or, where appropriate, a skilled sign language interpreter, and to keep a full record and have it endorsed as an accurate record by the interpreter. The attestation clause should also confirm that the will was translated/interpreted or read to the testator/testatrix before its execution. A will may be challenged on the ground that the testator/testatrix lacked understanding of the language in which the will was drawn, that he/he was illiterate or that the interpreter instructed was not suitably qualified in the language or dialect familiar to the testator/testatrix (see *Chana (Gavinder) v Chana (Harjit Kaur)* [2001] WTLR 205, where this issue was raised but rejected on the facts).

4.10 MEDICAL EVIDENCE AND ITS LIMITATIONS

When seeking to observe the *Golden Rule*, the obvious and first choice tends to be the testator's/testatrix's doctor, but not all doctors are aware of the requirement of the rule nor do they have the necessary specialist expertise to undertake the assessment. To instruct a professional expert with the right expertise will involve delay and expense and the testator's consent. The testator/testatrix may not be willing or may be hesitant about obtaining the assessment and this, too, has the potential of causing delay. Where a solicitor is dealing with an elderly or seriously ill client, time is likely to be of the essence. All these factors make the obvious choice of the doctor being an appropriate first call understandable. However, the chances are that the doctor's report will not deal with a psychiatric assessment, but an opinion based on his dealing with the patient concerning his/her health and not the discrete issues which are pertinent to the *Golden Rule*.

A good example of such a case is *Re Ritchie* [2009] EWHC 709 (Ch), where the report was provided on the basis of the testatrix's visit to her doctor for a number of symptoms 5 weeks earlier. There was no formal psychiatric assessment. In cross-examination, the doctor agreed that he based his opinion on the fact that she was able to answer questions which related to her symptoms, and that he was not told of the contents of the will. This case was the first case where he was asked for an assessment on testamentary capacity. As the judge observed, the doctor based his opinion:

> on a medical examination five weeks earlier on an unrelated medical matter. He based his assessment on Mary's ability to answer his questions appropriately and his ability to make an assessment for her circumstances and orientation. He was not aware that the will cut out her children. He did not carry out any formal assessment. (*Re Ritchie* [2009] EWHC 709 (Ch) at [187])

Since under the MCA 2005 capacity is decision-specific, it follows that to establish lack of capacity it must be shown that the testator/testatrix was given all the information necessary to make a will and asked questions which are directed to ascertaining that he/she knows and understands all the relevant factors necessary to establish testamentary capacity.

In *Scammell v Farmer* [2008] EWHC 1100 (Ch), the doctor referred the testatrix to a consultant psychiatrist for an assessment because she was forgetful. The psychiatrist's initial conclusion was that she was in the early stages of 'Alzheimer's disease of late onset'. He prescribed medication to slow down deterioration of memory loss and functional abilities. The Community Mental Health Nurse also recorded that the testatrix had short-term memory loss, but in all other respects she was self-sufficient and had no psychiatric history. Subsequently, the testatrix was given the standard mini mental state examination (MMSE) in which she scored well. On the basis of the examination and the tests undertaken, the consultant psychiatrist concluded:

> I wish to make the following observations regarding the assessment of the mental capacity in people with memory disorder. Alzheimer's disease is the commonest type of dementia. People in the early stages of or with a mild degree of dementia of Alzheimer's disease of late onset type, are able to make choices and decisions. This would depend on the complexity of the information to be grasped and retained in memory, in arriving at an informed decision. Mrs. Scammell was able to make an informed decision regarding receiving treatment with Reminyl, accepting professional help such as community nursing input, and attending

psychiatric outpatient's clinic. (*Scammell v Farmer* [2008] EWHC 1100 (Ch) at [50])

The consultant psychiatrist went on also to state that his study of the documentation did not yield sufficient information to enable him to form an opinion with regard to her mental capacity to make a will, but he confirmed that she displayed a degree of strength of mind and decision-making ability in demanding a reduction in the dosage of her prescription.

In assessing the evidence, the judge commentated that:

> the tests administered were directed at assessing a different capability than the capacity to make a Will. They were largely directed at memory and Irene's powers of recall. As was pointed out in *Banks v. Goodfellow*, the possession of an imperfect memory is not to be equated with an absence of testamentary capacity. The professionals never tested Irene Scammell's ability to recollect the names of her immediate family, in other words those she had a 'moral responsibility' at least to consider as objects of her bounty; nor – as one would expect – did they examine her ability to comprehend the extent of her estate. (*Scammell v Farmer* [2008] EWHC 1100 (Ch) at [94])

However, on assessing all the evidence in this case, the judge was able to find that the testatrix had testamentary capacity when she made the will which was the subject of the proceedings, and that she had the knowledge of and approved the contents of the will.

Thus when a doctor is instructed, unless the assessment given directly relates to the issue of testamentary capacity, the evidence is open to challenge. Even when the MMSE is undertaken, it is not in itself necessarily determinative of capacity or lack of it, but the results are useful evidence to be considered with all the other evidence. There is of course an added advantage when the medical assessment is given by someone who has known the testator/testatrix and also has been provided with information of the test to be applied to assess testamentary capacity and information about the nature and extent of the estate, the nature of the testator's/testatrix's relationship with his/her family and friends and details if any of previous wills. It may also involve the sharing of other information relating to the personal circumstances of the individual. Those instructed will inevitably require the consent of the testator/testatrix before disclosure of this information can be given, as they are bound by the duty of confidentiality under the codes of their profession and the Data Protection Act 1998.

In such situations, in the first instance every effort should be made by the solicitor or legal adviser to explain to the person wishing to make a will the reason why it is necessary to disclose the information to the medical expert and of the consequences if a thorough assessment and report is not obtained, including if appropriate to inform the person that in the absence of agreement he/she would have to decline to act. Helpful guidance on creating the right environment for assessing capacity is set out in *Assessment of Mental Capacity: A Practical Guide for Doctors and Lawyers*, 4th edn, 2015), which solicitors would be well advised to follow where appropriate. Failing this, courts have confirmed that in appropriate circumstances, disclosure in confidence may be made without consent to those with a proper interest in having the information in question. In such cases, it may be necessary to strike a balance between confidentiality and the need to act in the best interests of the client (see *W v Egdell* [1990] Ch 359 at 419(E), and *R (Stevens) v Plymouth City Council & Anor* [2002] EWCA Civ 388 at [49]). The Law Society recommends that where a solicitor cannot obtain the client's consent to the disclosure of confidential information or has not obtained consent in advance in anticipation of the need for disclosure, advice should be sought of the Solicitors Regulation Authority (see *Assessment of Mental Capacity: A Practical Guide for Doctors and Lawyers*, 4th edn, 2015).

Those who wish to challenge the will obviously are not content to rely on the available evidence. They will usually rely on the deceased's medical records to instruct medical experts in the field to give an opinion, which is of course retrospective and without a physical assessment of the deceased. The only other additional evidence the expert will be provided with are the witness statements which are bound to be conflicting and biased and from those who have a vested interest in the estate. At best, the expert may give a preliminary report, but subject to hearing the witness's evidence at the trial. The danger is that this process runs the risk of the expert witness straying across the boundary into domain which is solely that of the court.

The issue of whether the testator/testatrix has testamentary capacity is problematic and there is no easy solution. The matter is made more difficult because if the will is challenged on the basis of lack of capacity, the burden of proof rests on the person who propounds the will to prove that the testator/testatrix had capacity. It is thus important to ensure that the *Golden Rule* and the test of capacity set out in the MCA 2005 are followed, and when seeking an assessment on capacity the letter of instructions should bear in mind the guidance given in *Assessment of Mental Capacity: A Practical Guide for Doctors and Lawyers*, 4th edn, 2015.

4.11 EVIDENCE AND STANDARD OF PROOF

There is a presumption that the testator/testatrix had testamentary capacity and where a will appears to be regular and its contents rational, unless the validity of the will is challenged, it will be presumed to be valid. If capacity is challenged, it is for the person propounding the will to prove that the testator/testatrix had testamentary capacity and understanding in accordance with the test in *Banks v Goodfellow* (1870) LR 5 QB 549. Where the will is validly executed and appears rational on its face, the burden shifts to the person who challenges the will to raise doubts about capacity. Once real doubt is established on capacity, the burden will shift back again on the propounder (see e.g. *Pearce v Beverley* [2013] EW Misc 10 (CC) and *The Vegetarian Society & Anor v Scott* [2013] EWHC 4097 (Ch)).

The standard of proof is the civil standard, that is, on the balance of probabilities.

All relevant and documentary evidence will be admitted to prove or disprove the issues raised. Evidence from witnesses regarding the testator's/testatrix's demeanour before, at the time and after instructions to draw up the will, and when the will was executed is relevant, but not necessarily conclusive if there is other evidence, such as medical evidence or from those who were closely involved with the testator/testatrix and his/her care. Evidence of the solicitor to whom instructions were given would be admissible and it is usually relevant to confirm the test in *Banks v Goodfellow* (1870) LR 5 QB 549 and whether, and to what extent, the *Golden Rule* was followed and, if not, the reasons.

4.12 CONCLUSION

The golden rule for solicitors is, if in doubt, observe the *Golden Rule*. It is always prudent to keep meticulous records and attendance notes at every step (see *Ross v Caunters* [1980] Ch 297). Where a medical practitioner is instructed, the practical suggestions for solicitors instructing a medical practitioner should be followed. The medical practitioner who is involved should not be asked to attest the will unless he/she has assessed the testator's/testatrix's capacity, and is satisfied on the balance of probabilities that the testator/testatrix has the requisite capacity to make a will; and should be asked to make a formal record of his/her findings. When a will is challenged, this evidence will go some way to assist the person propounding the will to discharge the burden of proof. In the absence of such evidence, the risk is that the will may be declared invalid. Where there is a real concern about the testator's/testatrix's mental capacity and his/her decision-making abilities, guidance from the Court of Protection should be requested to consider the testator's/testatrix's status and, if appropriate, to authorise the making of a statutory will.

Those who wish to challenge the will on the ground of testamentary capacity will need to consider all the factors raised above. They will also need to scrutinise what evidence is available on the testator's/testatrix's physical and mental condition and all the surrounding circumstances to see whether there is any weakness or failure in the procedure which should have been followed, and then to consider whether or not there is sufficient evidence to raise doubts. The Law Commission in its project on the law of wills will be undertaking a review of testamentary capacity with particular reference to the criteria in *Banks v Goodfellow* (1870) LR 5 QB 549 and their inconsistency with legal and clinical development, and the problems resulting from the increase in the population of those who are affected by medical conditions that affect capacity (see Law Commission, *Twelfth Programme of Law Reform*, Law Com No 354, 23 July 2014).

Chapter 5

Knowledge and Approval

5.1 INTRODUCTION

A person propounding a will must show that, at the time the will was executed, the testator/testatrix knew, understood and approved the contents of the will. Due execution of a will, which on the face of it appears to be rational and fair, raises the presumption that the testator/testatrix had knowledge and approval.

Problems in this context usually arise where:

(a) there was a mistake in the preparation of the will;
(b) the testator/testatrix suffered from some disability, such as blindness, deafness or illiteracy;
(c) there is doubt about the testator/testatrix's testamentary capacity (see Chapter 4);
(d) the circumstances surrounding the preparation and execution of the will are suspicious.

Since those who seek to challenge a will on the basis of lack of knowledge and approval are not always aware of the precise circumstances in which the will was made, it is not unusual for challenges made on this ground also to include allegations of undue influence, assertions that the testator/testatrix lacked testamentary capacity and claims that there was want of execution (see *Pearce v Beverley* [2013] EW Misc 10 (CC), referred to in Chapter 4). In cases where such allegations are not raised in the pleading as grounds for challenge, these grounds are often raised by implication, but in so doing the objectors expose themselves to costs being awarded against them if they fail to make out their case (*Re Stott* [1980] 1 WLR 246, and rule 44.3 of the Civil Procedure Rules 1998 (SI 1998/3132) (CPR)).

5.2 MISTAKE

A mistake in the drafting of the will may give rise to the belief that the testator/testatrix did not know of the error and, therefore, did not approve of the provisions. Drafting errors may arise as a result of the testator's/testatrix's own inadvertence, an error by the draftsman or the deliberate act of another. Drafting errors are likely to occur with the use of information technology and especially where template precedents are cut and pasted. In some instances, the errors may be rectified by the court under powers developed at common law and section 20 of the Administration of Justice Act 1982. This subject is covered more fully in Chapter 9.

Where the mistake relates to the whole of the will, probate is generally refused, as it would be difficult to satisfy the court that the testator/testatrix knew and approved the contents of the will. An error in the execution of the will is an example where the court may rule that the testator did not know, understand and approve the contents of the will. In *The Goods of Hunt* (1875) 3 P&D 250, the testatrix, who lived with her sister, prepared two wills. By mistake, the testatrix executed the will prepared for her sister. The wills were drawn in similar terms but the court refused probate on the ground that the testatrix did not know and approve 'any part of the contents of the will she executed as she did not know and approve of any part of the contents of the paper as her will, for it is quite clear that if she had known of the contents she would not have signed it'. *Re Meyer* [1908] P 353, was a similar case where sisters signed each other's will by mistake. The will was challenged on two grounds. The first that it 'must appear that the testator intended by his signature to give effect to the will'. The court agreed and held that the testatrix had not intended to sign the document she signed but a different one. Secondly, as in *The Goods of Hunt*, it was argued that knowledge and approval of the contents of the will were lacking.

More recently, in *Marley v Rawlings & Anor* [2011] EWHC 161 (Ch), a couple wished to make mirror wills each leaving everything to the other, and the survivor leaving everything to Mr Marley, who was their carer and whom they both treated as their son. However, in error they executed the wrong will. Neither of the two witnesses, who attested the will, noticed the error. The error was also not picked up when the wife died and the property passed to the husband by survivorship. On the husband's death, the couple's two sons on wishing to challenge the will noticed the error. They challenged the will on the ground that the will was not signed by the testator and, therefore, did not comply with section 9 of the Wills Act 1837. Mr Marley sought rectification of the will under the Administration of Justice Act 1982. At first instance, Proudman J rejected this argument and held the will invalid. On appeal ([2012] EWCA Civ 61), the Court of Appeal unanimously dismissed the appeal. Reliance was placed on foreign authorities to support Mr Marley's case, but neither Proudman J nor the Court of Appeal was convinced by them. Apart from the fact that the will did not comply with the requirements of section 9, it did not provide confirmation of the testator's approval of the contents. The contents of the will showed that he did not give effect to the will. However, on further appeal, the Supreme Court ruled (*Marley v Rawlings & Anor* [2014] UKSC 2) that, having regard to the circumstances in which the will was executed, there was clear evidence of the testator's intentions and from which knowledge and approval could be identified. The error could be considered as a 'clerical error' and open to rectification (see Chapter 3, para 3.5 and Chapter 9).

5.3 DISABILITY

Where the testator/testatrix suffered from a disability which may have made it difficult for him/her to understand and approve the contents of his/her will, the court will require convincing evidence that the will sets out the testator's/testatrix's intentions. The evidence includes cases where instructions were taken from a testator/testatrix who was hard of hearing, or deaf and dumb, where the person was blind or illiterate, where the testator/testatrix suffered from a speech defect and was unable to read, write or speak, or suffered from some other disability which adversely affected his/her ability to comprehend and understand the contents of the will or that the document was his/her will which will operate on his/her death. Where a will has been read over to a testator/testatrix or the contents have been brought to his/her knowledge in some other way, it will be sufficient evidence to support knowledge and approval unless the circumstances and the manner in which this was done brings the matter into question and rebuts the presumption (*Garnett-Botfield v Garnett-Botfield* [1901] P 335). In *D'Eye v Avery* [2001] WTLR 227, the testator suffered a severe stroke in 1986 and subsequently he was placed in the care of the Court of Protection because he was unable to make himself understood and to manage his affairs. In 1988, D took him to a bank, where instructions to draw up a will were given entirely by D for the testator's estate to be left to D. On a second visit to the bank, the will was executed in the presence of D. The will was not read over to the testator. On his death, the will was challenged by the testator's next of kin. The court refused to grant probate on the ground that the testator did not understand the disposition he was making and lacked the knowledge and approval required.

5.4 LACK OF TESTAMENTARY CAPACITY

It is essential to the validity of a will not only that the testator/testatrix had testamentary capacity when the will was executed but also that he/she had the ability to know, understand and approve the contents of the will. These two requirements are often misunderstood and taken to mean that at the time the will was executed the testator/testatrix must have the opportunity and the ability to reconsider his/her wishes, and that therefore he/she should also have testamentary capacity at this stage. Recent authorities have confirmed that this is not how these two requirements should be applied and that a clear distinction should be made between them. The interplay between these requirements has been highlighted in recent decisions where the testator/testatrix had capacity when giving instructions for the preparation of the will but did not have capacity when the will was signed. As explained in Chapter 4, para 4.4, in the majority of cases it is inevitable for time to elapse between the giving of instructions for the making of a will and when the will is executed. Where this occurs, recent authorities have confirmed that the issue should be approached by applying the rule in *Parker v Felgate* (1883) 8 PD 171, which remains good law. In *Re Perrins (Deceased), Perrins v Holland & Anor* [2009] EWHC 1945 (Ch) at first instance, Lewison J applied the rule. On appeal, the Court of Appeal (*Perrins v Holland & Ors* [2010] EWCA Civ 840) referred to the distinction between testamentary capacity and knowledge and approval, and stated that the purpose of the enquiry into knowledge and approval is to ascertain whether the will represents the testator's/testatrix's true intention and that the rule in *Parker v Felgate* was consistent with that principle. The Court of Appeal expanded on this in *Gill v Woodall* [2010] EWCA Civ 1430. It held that to determine whether the testator/testatrix knew and approved the contents of his/her will, the correct approach was to consider the factual and medical evidence, and to ask whether the testator/testatrix appreciated what was in the will when it was signed. Other earlier cases where this principle was applied include *Minns v Foster* [2002] All ER (D) 225 (Dec), where the last will of the deceased, which was executed in 1999, one year before his death aged 96 in 2000, was challenged on the grounds of testamentary capacity and want of knowledge and approval. The deceased suffered from short-term memory loss but it was held that he understood 'the business in which he was engaged' at the time he executed the 1999 will. Evidence disclosed that he discussed tax issues and the needs of the two beneficiaries under the will, and understood the nature and extent of his property, which clearly indicated that he had testamentary capacity. Although the claimant, who was the deceased's niece, helped to set up the meetings with the solicitor and there was no evidence whether the deceased read the will or whether its contents were read over to him, he obviously read the first draft and corrected it. The claimant was not present when he gave instructions and executed the will. There was thus no basis for the challenge on the ground of want of knowledge and approval.

5.5 SUSPICIOUS CIRCUMSTANCES

If a will is prepared and executed under suspicious circumstances which suggest that the will, or any provision in it, did not express the intentions of the testator/testatrix, it will not be admitted to probate unless the suspicion is removed by satisfactory evidence of the testator's/testatrix's knowledge and approval. A classic example is where a person prepares or causes the preparation of a will for the testator, and under that will the person himself is a substantial beneficiary. In such a case, the suspicions will cause the court:

> to be vigilant and jealous in examining the evidence in support of the instrument, in favour of which it ought not to pronounce unless the suspicion is removed and it is judicially satisfied that the paper propounded does express the true wish of the deceased. (*Barry v Butlin* (1838) 2 Moo PCC 480)

In *Wyniczenko v Plucinska-Surowka* [2005] EWHC 2794 (Ch), the testatrix, who was Polish, moved to England with her husband in the 1960s. She remained in contact with her family in Poland and in particular with her niece, P. Her husband died in 1986. In August 1993, she made a will appointing P and a Polish lawyer her executors. The will contained bequests of legacies including £40,000 each to her sister and P. On 19 February 2002, several weeks before her death, when she was visually impaired and with deteriorating grasp of English, she made a DIY will naming W, a tradesman she met in 1996, her sole beneficiary. W drafted the will. He maintained that he did so at her instructions. He then showed the will to the testatrix while he was taking her to hospital for an appointment. He did not explain the terms of the will to her nor did he suggest that she should consider including other members of her family in the will. W subsequently obtained a letter from one of the doctors at the surgery (not the testatrix's doctor) confirming her capacity. When she died in April 2002, W did not inform the testatrix's relatives of the death or the cremation. P learned of the death 2 months later when she was unable to get in touch with her. When contacted, W was evasive and unco-operative. P challenged the will. The judge held that the circumstances in which the will was prepared and executed and its contents raised suspicion. These included the fact that, unlike her first will, the second will did not include any charitable bequests, the will was written in English and the terms of the will were not explained to her. W's conduct after the will was executed also raised suspicion. The 1993 will was declared valid and the 2002 will was pronounced invalid.

In *Franks v Sinclair* [2006] EWHC 3365 (Ch), the circumstances and the manner in which the will was prepared and executed raised a 'significant degree of suspicion'. The contest related to two wills prepared by the testatrix, one in 1992 which was prepared by a solicitor neighbour, leaving everything to her grandson. The second will made in 1994 was prepared by her son, who was a solicitor, leaving her estate to her two children. It was this second will which was disputed on the grounds that the testatrix did not know or approve the terms of the will. The matters which raised suspicion were that the terms were so different from the first will, particularly as it disinherited the grandson with whom she had a close relationship, and there were concerns regarding the preparation of the will. The son did not advise his mother to seek independent advice, in breach of the guidance on the professional conduct of solicitors. The will contained complex clauses which the judge considered would be 'gobbledegook' to a layperson, and although the son said that he read out the will to his mother, the judge found that she would not have understood any of it unless explained in plain language. The son also failed to keep any attendance records of the instructions, preparation and execution of the will. His evidence was inconsistent and unreliable. It was held that the testatrix did not know or approve the 1994 will.

Similarly, in *Westendrop v Warwick* [2006] EWHC 915 (Ch), the testatrix made a will in 2003 in which she made provision for a half share of the property she owned to go to her sister's children and the residue she left to be divided in equal third shares to her daughter J from whom she had been estranged, J's first husband, K, and M who was the son of the testatrix's late husband from his first marriage. In March 2004, J re-established her relationship with her mother. To the astonishment of all those who had had close contact with her, the testatrix went to live with her daughter, J, on 5 August 2004. On 31 August, when the testatrix was unwell, she made a new will leaving everything to J. She died on 10 September. In evidence, J's second husband, Mark, conceded that he conceived the idea of a new will and drafted it. The issues raised were whether the testatrix had capacity and whether she knew and approved the disposition. On the evidence, the judge found that there were doubts about the testatrix's capacity when she executed the will and that he was not satisfied that she knew or approved the contents.

It will be observed that the degree of suspicion is likely to vary according to the circumstances of the case. It may be slight and easily dispelled or may be so 'grave that it can hardly be removed', such as in *Franks v Sinclair* [2006] EWHC 3365 (Ch) and *Wintle v Nye* [1959] 1 WLR 284 (where the facts were similar). In *Ticehurst, Midland Bank Executor and Trustee Co v Hankinson* (1973) *The Times*, 6 March, where the will was prepared by correspondence with a solicitor through an amanuensis, who was the wife of one of the beneficiaries, the court refused to admit the will to probate. More recently, in *Hawes v Burgess* [2013] EWCA Civ 74, the testatrix altered her previous will, in which she had split the estate between her three children, to disinherit her son. The new will was drawn by a solicitor with the involvement of one of the daughters. The daughter could not give a satisfactory account of what had occurred when instructions were taken for the second will. The court held that the will had been executed in suspicious circumstances and the suspicions had not been dispelled. The propounders of the will had not been able to prove that the testatrix had known and approved of the contents of the will. In contrast, in *Sharp v Hutchins* [2015] EWHC 1240 (Ch), the beneficiary under the will was able to dispel the allegation of lack of knowledge and approval and suspicious circumstances. Mr Butcher was a pensioner. He made a new will about 2 months before his death, leaving his entire estate valued at about £500,000 to Mr Sharp, a builder who had befriended him. The will excluded all the beneficiaries named in the previous will. Beneficiaries of the earlier will contended that the testator did not know and approve the contents of the will. They were, however, unable to provide any evidence to support this claim. Their evidence relating to the circumstances surrounding the execution of the will also did not establish any suspicion. The court found that Mr Sharp had discharged the burden of proving that the testator had understood what was in his last will when he signed it and what its effect would be, because the will was consistent with the testator's earlier will. It was short and had been prepared using a widely available template. One of the witnesses to the will was his financial adviser, and the testator had shown the will to Mr Sharp and read it to him.

5.6 STANDARD AND BURDEN OF PROOF

The burden of proof lies on the party propounding the will, as laid down in *Barry v Butlin* (1838) 2 Moo PCC 480 and now known as the rule in *Barry v Butlin*:

> The rules of law according to which cases of this nature are to be decided do not admit to any dispute, so far as they are necessary to the determination of the present appeal ... These rules are two: the first that the *onus probandi* lies in every case upon the party propounding the Will; and he must satisfy the conscience of the Court that the instrument so propounded is the last Will of a free and capable Testator. The second is, that if a party writes or prepares a Will, under which he takes a benefit, that is a circumstance that ought generally to excite the suspicion of the Court, and calls upon it to be vigilant and jealous in examining the evidence in support of the instrument, in favour of which it ought not to pronounce unless the suspicion is removed, and it is judicially satisfied that the paper propounded does express the true Will of the deceased.
>
> The strict meaning of the term *onus probandi* is this, that if no evidence is given by the party on whom the burden is cast, the issue must be found against him. In all cases the *onus* is imposed on the party propounding a Will, it is in general discharged by proof of capacity, and the fact of execution, from which the knowledge of and assent to the contents of the instrument are assumed, and it cannot be that the simple fact of the party who prepared the Will being himself the Legatee, is in every case, and under all circumstances, to create a contrary presumption, and to call upon the Court to pronounce against the Will, unless additional evidence is produced to prove knowledge of its contents by the deceased. A single instance, of no infrequent occurrence, will test the truth of this proposition. A man of acknowledged competence and habit of business worth £100,000 leaves the bulk of his property to his family. And a legacy of £50 to his confidential attorney, who prepared the will: would this throw the burden of proof of actual cognizance by the Testator, of the content of the will, on the party propounding it, so that if such proof were not supplied, the will would be pronounced against it? The answer is obvious, it would not. All that can truly be said is, that if a person whether attorney or not, prepares a will with a legacy to himself, it is most suspicious circumstance, of more or less weight, according to the facts of the particular case: in some of no weight at all, as in the case

suggested, varying according to the circumstances; for instance the *quantum* of the legacy, and the proportion it bears to the property disposed of, and numerous contingencies; but in no case amounting to more than a circumstance of suspicion, demanding the vigilant care and circumspection of the court in investigating the case and calling upon it not to grant probate without a full and entire satisfaction that the instrument did express the real intentions of the deceased. Nor can it be necessary, that *in all such cases*, even if the testator's capacity is doubtful, the precise species of evidence of the deceased's knowledge of the will is to be in the shape of instruction for, or reading over the instrument. They form, no doubt, the *most* satisfactory, but they are not the *only* satisfactory description of proof, by which the cognizance of the contents of the will may be brought home to the deceased. The court will naturally look for such evidence; in some cases it might be impossible to establish a will without it, but it has no right in every case to require it. (*Barry v Butlin* (1838) 2 Moo PCC 480 at 482–483)

This test was approved by the Court of Appeal in *Fuller v Strum* [2001] EWCA Civ 1879. The nature of the evidence required will depend on the degree of doubt and suspicion, and the circumstances surrounding the preparation of the will and its execution.

The test of whether the testator/testatrix knew and approved his/her will is an objective one. The standard of proof is the civil standard (the court must be satisfied on the balance of probabilities that the contents of the will truly represent the intentions of the testator/testatrix). This standard nevertheless permits a degree of flexibility, so that where the allegations are serious, the burden is heavier than in cases where they are less serious or trivial. The case of *Atter v Atkinson* (1869) LR 1 P&D 665 may give the impression that the standard of proof is that which applies in criminal cases because it stated that:

> if you have to deal with a will in which the person who made himself take a large benefit, you ought to be well satisfied, from evidence calculated to exclude all doubt, that the testator not only signed it but he knew and approved of its contents. (*Atter v Atkinson* (1869) LR 1 P&D 665)

However, *Fuller v Strum* [2001] EWCA Civ 1879 clearly indicates that this is not the case. Longmore LJ reviewed the earlier authorities and said:

> I am satisfied that there is no basis for an approach that requires, in all cases, that a person propounding a will which he has prepared and under which he takes a benefit, must satisfy the court by evidence which excludes all doubt – or by evidence which excludes all reasonable doubt (the standard required in criminal proceedings) – that the testator knew and approved the contents of the will. The standard of proof required in probate proceedings (as in other non-criminal proceedings) is satisfaction on the preponderance (or balance) of probability. But the circumstances of the particular case may raise in the mind of the court a suspicion that the testator did not know and approve the contents of the document which he has executed which is so

grave that, as Viscount Simmonds observed in *Wintle v Nye*, it can hardly be removed. (*Fuller v Strum* [2001] EWCA Civ 1879 at [72])

Where there are no unusual or suspicious circumstances, evidence which establishes that the will was read by, or read over to the testator/testatrix, who was at the time capable of understanding what he/she was reading or hearing and its effect, having regard to any moral or other obligations he/she may have had at the time to persons close to him/her is generally sufficient to discharge the burden and standard of proof (see *Hart v Dabbs, sub nom Re Dabbs (Lawrence Stanley) (Deceased)* [2001] WTLR 527). If the testator/testatrix merely casts his/her eye over the will, it may not be sufficient to establish knowledge and approval of the contents (*Re Morris* [1971] P 62).

If the testator/testatrix suffered from a physical disability, for example if he/she was mute and instructions were taken through a sign language interpreter, evidence of the sign language used and how and by whom it was interpreted together with evidence of the testator's understanding and approval of the will, should be produced to discharge the burden of proof. Where the testator/testatrix was blind or illiterate, evidence that the will was read over to him/her before the will was executed should be provided. Rule 13 of the Non-Contentious Probate Rules 1987 provides that in such cases:

> Before admitting to proof a will which appears to have been signed by a blind or illiterate testator or by another person by direction of the testator, or which for any other reason raises doubt as to the testator having had knowledge of the contents of the will at the time of its execution, the district judge or registrar shall satisfy himself that the testator had such knowledge.

In *Buckenham v Dickinson* [1997] CLY 4733, where the testator was deaf and partially blind, it was held that further affirmative evidence of knowledge and approval is required when the testator is deaf and blind, and it must be shown to the satisfaction of the court that the will was read over to the testator in the presence of witnesses or that the testator otherwise knew of its content. It is thus essential that the attestation clause in the will should include a statement that the testator/testatrix signed the will after the will was read over to him/her in the presence of the witnesses and that he/she appeared to approve and understand the contents in the presence of the witnesses. There may, however, be circumstances where this clause within the attestation clause may not suffice, and, depending on the degree of doubt and suspicion raised, other evidence may be required. (See also *Re Key (Deceased), Key v Key & Others* [2010] EWHC 408 (Ch), and the concept under the rule in *Parker v Felgate* (1883) 8 PD 171 and the decision-making capacity which forms the basis of the test of 'capacity' under sections 2 and 3 of the MCA 2005.)

5.7 CONCLUSION

The issue of whether the testator/testatrix knew and approved the contents of the will is often linked with capacity and undue influence. Clear evidence of the circumstances in which the will was prepared and executed will be required. Evidence of the relationship between the testator/testatrix and the person who was present or assisted him/her when instructions were given and the will was made and executed, and the extent and nature of the disability or vulnerability of the testator/testatrix will be crucial.

Chapter 6

Undue Influence

6.1 INTRODUCTION

A will made as a result of undue influence will not be admitted to probate. There are, however, two points which need to be recognised before a will is challenged on this ground. First, that there is no presumption of undue influence in the case of a will. Secondly, and one which follows from the first, is that the burden of proving undue influence is on the party who alleges it. In relation to the first, as Scarman J said in *Re Fuld* [1968] P 675:

> Lord Penzance once said of the issues of testamentary capacity, knowledge and approval, undue influence and fraud, that they very often merge into one another. That position has now been made abundantly clear by the decision of the House of Lords in *Wintle v Nye* ... it may well be that positive charges of fraud and undue influence will not feature as largely in the pleadings of probate case, now that *Wintle v Nye* has been decided ... (*Re Fuld* [1968] P 675 at 722)

Yet it has frequently been relied on as an additional ground with lack of knowledge and approval, and lack of capacity. Although in many cases it is rejected (but see *Pearce v Beverley* [2013] EW Misc 10 (CC), and *Schrader v Schrader* [2013] EWHC 466 (Ch), where undue influence was successfully established), undue influence continues to be raised to challenge both testamentary and lifetime gifts.

This may be due to misconception and confusion of what it means and when it may be appropriately raised, and failure to appreciate that because there is no presumption the burden of proving it lies on the person who alleges it. Some cases suggest that in order to succeed, strong evidence is required, whereas others suggest a shift towards a less strict evidential proof. The reason for the differences may be because much depends on the circumstances and the factual situation. It may also depend on whether the disposition is made in a will or is a lifetime transaction. The person who alleges undue influence must prove it and the evidential burden of proving it is difficult. It should only be relied on as a last resort and only if there is substantial evidence to prove it. Be aware though that if the claim fails, it is likely that the claimant will have to bear the costs of the litigation.

In the case of a lifetime gift, a presumption of undue influence may arise in relation to certain relationships.

6.2 WHAT CONSTITUTES UNDUE INFLUENCE

Where a will is challenged on the ground of undue influence, the person making the claim must show that the testator/testatrix was coerced into making the will or disposition in the will, which he/she did not wish to make, and that the will or disposition was made not of his/her own volition but as a result of the influence of the third party who dominated the testator's mind. It has been stated that, 'It is only when the will of the testator is coerced into doing that which he does not desire to do that it can be regarded that the third party's actions amount to undue influence' (*Wingrove v Wingrove* (1885) 11 PD 81).

Although there is no presumption of undue influence, the challenge is more commonly raised in cases where the testator/testatrix was weak, frail, in ill health, dependent on another for his/her care or suffering from impaired mental capacity. That, of course, does not exclude a challenge being made where the testator/testatrix was of sound mind and understanding and in good health. Undue influence may take many forms. The coercion may be brought about by physical force, such as occurred in *Chana (Gavinder) v Chana (Harjit Kaur)* [2001] 2 WTLR 205. It may result from mental pressure being put on an individual, for example where extreme pressure is exerted on the testator/testatrix to the extent that it breaks his/her will and he/she gives in to the pressure. Pressure which does not result in the testator/testatrix succumbing his/her will so that it becomes that of the person exerting the pressure does not amount to undue influence. Often, coercion is confused with influence, and where the line is drawn before influence becomes unacceptable is blurred. The principle which applies was stated in *Hall v Hall* (1868) LR 1 P&D 481 as follows:

> Persuasion appeals to the affections or ties of kindred, to a sentiment of gratitude for past services, or pity for future destitution, or the like – these are all legitimate, and may be fairly pressed on a testator. On the other hand, pressure of whatever character, whether acting on fear or the hopes, if so exerted as to overpower the volition without which no valid will can be made ... In a word the testator may be led but not driven; and his will must be the offspring of his own volition and not the record of someone else's.
>
> ...
>
> Persuasion is not unlawful, but pressure of whatever character if so exercised as to overpower the volition without convincing the judgment of the testator will

constitute undue influence, though no force is either used or threatened. (*Hall v Hall* (1868) LR 1 P&D 481).

Mere influence exercised over the testator/testatrix by another person does not constitute undue influence unless there is sufficient proof of coercion. Proof of motive and opportunity for the exercise of influence over the testator/testatrix is relevant, but even if this has led him/her to make a disposition for the benefit of that person to the exclusion of another, that alone is not sufficient to establish undue influence; there must also be proof of coercion which overpowered the volition of the testator/testatrix (*Craig v Lamoureux* [1920] AC 349). It must be shown that the influence which one had over the other was abused.

Lewison J in *Edwards v Edwards* [2007] EWHC 1119 (Ch) summarised the law as follows:

i) In a case of a testamentary disposition of assets, unlike a lifetime disposition, there is no presumption of undue influence;

ii) Whether undue influence has procured the execution of a will is therefore a question of fact;

iii) The burden of proving it lies on the person who asserts it. It is not enough to prove that the facts are consistent with the hypothesis of undue influence. What must be shown is that the facts are inconsistent with any other hypothesis. In the modern law this is, perhaps no more than a reminder of the high burden, even on the civil standard, that a claimant bears in proving undue influence as vitiating a testamentary disposition;

iv) In this context undue influence means influence exercised either by coercion, in the sense that the testator's will must be overborne, or by fraud;

v) Coercion is pressure that overpowers the volition without convincing the testator's judgment. It is to be distinguished from mere persuasion, appeals to ties of affection or pity for future destitution, all of which are legitimate. Pressure which causes a testator to succumb for the sake of a quiet life, if carried to an extent that overbears the testator's free judgment discretion or wishes, is enough to amount to coercion in this sense;

vi) The physical and mental strength of the testator are relevant factors in determining how much pressure is necessary in order to overbear the will. The will of a weak and ill person may be more easily overborne than that of a hale and hearty one. As was said in one case simply to talk to a weak and feeble testator may so fatigue the brain that a sick person may be induced for quietness' sake to do anything. A 'drip drip' approach may be highly effective in sapping the will;

...

ix) The question is not whether the court considers that the testator's testamentary disposition is fair because, subject to statutory powers of intervention, a testator may dispose of his estate as he wishes. The question, in the end, is whether in making his dispositions, the testator has acted as a free agent. (*Edwards v Edwards* [2007] EWHC 1119 (Ch) at [95])

Schrader v Schrader [2013] EWHC 466 (Ch) and *Pearce v Beverley* [2013] EW Misc 10 (CC) are two recent examples of the extent of the background history of the family and its dynamics that will need to be investigated in order for undue influence to be established. Undue influence was also proved in *Schomberg v Taylor* [2013] EWHC 2269 (Ch). In that case, the testatrix had made a second will disinheriting her step-children in favour of her nephews and nieces. The beneficiaries under the first will challenged the application to prove the second will on the ground of undue influence. Undue influence was found proved. The court took into account the testatrix's frail mental and physical state proved by medical and other evidence; evidence of pressure being exerted on the testatrix; the fact the she had had no relationship with her nephews and nieces; and the motives and financial circumstances of their father in exerting pressure on the testatrix.

6.3 CONFIDENTIAL/FIDUCIARY RELATIONSHIP

In contractual and other transactions if the parties are, at the time of the transaction, in a confidential relationship with each other, undue influence is presumed. In *Powell v Powell* [1900] 1 Ch 242, Farwell J said, 'the mere existence of the fiduciary relation raises the presumption and must be rebutted by the donee'.

Fiduciary relationships include, for example, those of a parent and child, doctor and patient, guardian and ward, solicitor and client, priest and parishioner. Such a relationship does not, however, raise a presumption to invalidate a will because, in most cases, such a relationship is the very reason for the testator/testatrix to provide a benefit; to show undue influence, the circumstances would have to be such as to demonstrate that the mind of the testator/testatrix was dominated.

In *Pearce v Beverley* [2013] EW Misc 10 (CC), the evidence established that the defendant exerted undue influence on the testator who was physically and mentally disabled and where the instructions for the drafting of the will were given by the defendant. In *Schrader v Schrader* [2013] EWHC 466 (Ch), while the claimant failed in establishing lack of testamentary capacity and absence of knowledge and approval, the court found that the testatrix was vulnerable and dependent on her son (the defendant) who lived with her and he, therefore, exerted undue influence on her to revoke her earlier will, in which she bequeathed her estate equally between her children, and make a new will in which she left her major asset to the defendant. *Re Howell* [1955] OWN 85 is an example of a case where a will was successfully challenged. In that case, the will was drafted by a parish priest, and left nearly all the testator's estate to the parish church. In *Gill v RSPCA* [2009] EWHC 2990 (Ch), a couple, Mr and Mrs G, made mirror wills leaving everything to each other and disinheriting their daughter, C, in favour of the Royal Society for the Protection of Cruelty to Animals (RSPCA). Each will contained a declaration that no provision was made for C because she was well provided for over a long period of time. Mr G predeceased Mrs G who inherited under his will and C had no reason to look at or challenge his will as she assumed that the estate passed to her mother. She was under the belief that when her mother died she would inherit the estate as she had always been close to her mother. On her mother's death, on discovering the true position, she challenged the will on the ground that her mother was under the undue influence of her husband. Evidence adduced disclosed that Mrs G suffered from severe agoraphobia and severe anxiety and was reclusive. She was also very dependent on her husband and unable to stand up to him. The RSPCA's argument was that when Mr G died, Mrs G was free from such pressure and was free to discuss matters with C and to change her will. The judge rejected this argument and found for C, stating that although there was force in that argument, the evidence adduced had to be considered as a whole and given the appropriate weight. On the facts, it was sufficient to discharge the high burden of proof placed on C. The RSPCA, having failed, was ordered to pay the costs of £1.3 million.

A gift made in the lifetime of the deceased, on the other hand, may be challenged on the basis of the presumption of undue influence where a fiduciary relationship exists; or where, in the absence of such a relationship, there has been coercion, domination or pressure, to set aside a gift made by the deceased during the lifetime of the deceased. The purpose of such a challenge would be to benefit the deceased's estate or for compensation to be paid to the estate.

6.4 NATURE OF THE UNDUE INFLUENCE

In *Royal Bank of Scotland v Etridge (No 2)* [2001] UKHL 44, the House of Lords identified circumstances in which undue influence could arise, whether the presumption is rebuttable and the factors which should be considered. The distinction between actual and presumptive undue influence was disapproved of. Lord Clyde said:

> the wisdom of the practice which has grown up ... of attempting to make classification of undue influence ... the attempt to build up classes or categories may lead to confusion. The confusion is aggravated if the names used to identify the classes do not bear their actual meaning. Thus on the face of it a division into

cases of 'actual' and 'presumed' undue influence appears illogical. It appears to confuse definition and proof. (*Royal Bank of Scotland v Etridge (No 2)* [2001] UKHL 44 at [92])

The categorisation of undue influence into 'actual' and 'presumed' has also been disapproved of by Lord Neuberger (*Aspects of Undue Influence*, 2005 STEP lecture). Undue influence may occur where the specific overt act of persuasion or overt acts of persuasive conduct results in the person on whom the pressure is exerted making a decision which was not of his/her own volition or for his/her benefit. This may occur, for example, by threats or the use of force, as in *Bradshaw v Hardcastle* [2002] All ER (D) 219 (Nov). The testator who was terminally ill transferred his home into the joint names of himself and his second wife of 3 years. Three days before his death, he executed a will leaving his estate to his daughter and at the same time signed a statement that he had made the transfer to his wife under duress. On his death, his daughter applied to have the transfer set aside. Evidence adduced proved that the wife conducted a campaign of harassment which was described by the court as 'nothing short of physical violence to break her husband's resistance'. The transfer was set aside on the ground of undue influence.

The case of *Daniel v Drew* [2005] EWCA Civ 507 is another example. In that case, MD was an aged aunt of D. Under a family trust, she inherited one half share of a farm on the death of her parents. D's mother, who inherited the other half, transferred her share to her two sons, one of whom was D. D was subsequently granted an agricultural tenancy of MD's one half share at an annual fixed rate of £1 for 5 years. Subsequently, MD assigned her beneficial interest to her son, S. At the end of the tenancy, when S asked for rent, disagreement broke out between S and D which resulted in D demanding that MD should attend the trustee meetings and when she refused he told her that if she did not retire as trustee he would issue proceedings against her. MD did not like any form of confrontation and became fearful of possible proceedings and resigned. Both the trial judge and the Court of Appeal ruled that MD was driven to resign by D's actions towards her and that this was a case of actual undue influence. The trial judge also took into account the forceful, ruthless and dominating character and actions of D against the fact that MD was elderly and a vulnerable individual. The Court of Appeal also stated that as a 'court of conscience' it had a duty to intervene to 'protect people from being forced, tricked or misled in any way by others into parting with their property'. D's argument that she was a free agent and made the decision of her own volition failed to rebut the presumption of undue influence.

Those who persist in differentiating between actual and presumptive undue influence would class the above two examples as actual undue influence.

The most common situation when influence exerted on another is considered undue influence (and thus considered by some to be 'presumed') is where there is a specific relationship between the persons concerned such as described above of, for example, the parent/child relationship and where the dependent party places trust and confidence in the other and it results in a transaction which cannot be explained. This test has been considered and applied in many cases. The criteria for this type of undue influence (referred to by some as presumptive undue influence) was referred to in *Turkey v Awadh* [2005] EWCA Civ 382. The Court of Appeal said that in cases where there was a relationship between the donor and donee of trust and confidence, the court had to consider whether:

(a) the relationship of trust and confidence was one which indicated that a potential influence may exist; and
(b) the transaction, which followed, was readily explicable.

If such a situation was established, the court had to consider whether the presumption was rebuttable.

In *Turkey v Awadh* [2005] EWCA Civ 382, the transaction which occurred was between a father, his daughter and her husband. The father agreed to rent a property owned by his daughter and her husband on mortgage. Subsequently, it was agreed that the father should have a long lease of the property in consideration of him discharging the outstanding mortgage and certain debts which they had. When the father sought to enforce the deed, they applied to set it aside on the grounds of 'presumed undue influence'. The court accepted that there was a relationship of trust and confidence between them but the transaction could be explained and, therefore, the presumption did not arise as the two conditions were not met.

In order to clarify and assist practitioners on how the courts have adopted this approach and to identify some of the factors, such as the nature of the pressure exerted, the personalities involved and their relationships and circumstances which have raised suspicion and vigilance of the court, further summaries of some of the cases where undue influence has been proved are set out below.

In *Pesticcio v Huet & Others* [2003] All ER (D) 237 (Apr) (Ch), Neuberger J (as he then was) set aside a deed of gift in favour of the donor's sister, in whom the donor placed trust and confidence, despite the evidence of the donor's solicitor. The court found that the solicitor failed to distinguish between the interests of the donor and those of the donee.

In *Williams v Williams* [2003] EWHC 742 (Ch), the donor was illiterate and unable to cope on his own. His brother and his sister-in-law persuaded him to relinquish one half share in his home to them. They gave up the tenancy of their council home and moved into the house to look after him. The solicitor who was involved in the transaction had discussions with the donor in the presence of the brother. The solicitor did not read his predecessor's file which contained information about the donor's disability and the disability was not brought to his attention at the time by the brother. All the correspondence that passed between the solicitor and the donor was read out to the donor by a third party. In the circumstances, the court held that the third party could only have been the brother and his wife, and found that the donee did not rebut the presumption of undue influence because the transaction was manifestly to the donor's disadvantage.

In *Watson v Huber* [2005] All ER (D) 156 (Mar), following the death of her husband, Mrs Watson went to live with her half sister, Ms Huber, and agreed to Ms Huber looking after her financial affairs. Ms Huber applied about 48% of Mrs Watson's estate for herself and her own family, and when challenged she argued that the transfers were gifts made to her by Mrs Watson. On the facts, there was clearly a relationship of trust and confidence, and the size of the gifts required an explanation, i.e. the two requirements of undue influence set out above were established. Ms Huber was unable to discharge the burden of proof to rebut the presumption. The gifts were set aside.

In *Hughes v Hughes* [2005] EWHC 469 (Ch), the dispute was between a mother and son. On the facts, the court held that the relationship between them was one of loving relationship and that the son was unlikely to have suggested the transactions. Thus neither of two conditions was satisfied.

In *Goodchild v Bradbury* [2006] EWCA Civ 1868, Goodchild was an elderly and needy man. He transferred land to his great nephew, Bradbury. The court found that on the facts their relationship raised the presumption of trust and confidence, and the size of the transfer could not be explained simply on the basis of their relationship. Moreover, Goodchild did not receive any advice from his solicitor. On the evidence given by Goodchild that he was not put under any pressure by Bradbury, the trial judge found for Bradbury. The Court of Appeal, however, disagreed and overturned the decision. It found that the absence of pressure was not decisive particularly as here the donor did not appreciate the magnitude of his actions and did not receive any legal advice.

In *Schrader v Schrader* [2013] EWHC 466 (Ch), Mann J referred to 10 factual points of evidence which led him to the conclusion that undue influence was proved. These were:

> (i) The vulnerability of Jessica. Although not sufficient to deprive her of capacity, it is an important point in relation to undue influence. She

was apparently an admirable lady in her mid-90s, but more uncertain after her 2005 fall.

(ii) Her dependency on Nick. This is an obvious factual point. It was not total – she still had will and strength of her own, but she was more dependent on him since her fall. She would have been very worried about his moving out and ceasing to look after her.

(iii) The non-engagement of Cullens in the making of the will. At one stage in his evidence Nick suggested that she was angry with the firm because they had lost some deeds, but then he said that she told him she had rung them and had been told that they did not do home visits. The latter reason is wrong. This is an unsatisfactory part of the evidence. The engagement of the will writer brought in a firm with no prior contact with the family. It was not clear whether instructions for the will would have been dealt with by anyone at Cullens with familiarity with the family, but Nick would not necessarily have known that.

(iv) The reason given to Miss Marks for giving the house to Nick was inaccurate, and its source is likely to have been Nick. The sale of his house was not a voluntary act by Nick. It was sold by the trustee in bankruptcy, and would have been sold by the mortgagee if the trustee had not sold it. Nick was maintaining the farm house after a fashion, but that is hardly a reason for giving him the whole house. Wanting him to have a roof over his head after she had died is an understandable sentiment, but it is not apparent that a half share would have been insufficient for this purpose. Nick suggested that she might have wanted to even things up between him and his brother, on the footing that the brother's activities had devalued the property anyway. I find this implausible. I do not think that Jessica would have thought like that. Nick, however, would, and it would provide a motivation for suggestions by him that he should have the house.

(v) There is no other identified reason why Jessica would, entirely of her own volition, wish to change her will in respect of the house.

(vi) Nick's personality is an important factor. I have made findings about that above. He was a forceful man with a forceful physical presence. I repeat that I find there was no question of physical abuse, or even of real emotional abuse. I am sure that he will have experienced frustrations in looking after his elderly mother which many less volatile personalities will experience. However, the fact is he was a powerful personality and his mother was much more vulnerable.

(vii) Nick's keenly felt view that he had not been treated equally with his brother is an important point. He would be more inclined to try to even things up. I think that he did so, by way of suggestion to his mother. He had clear views about his entitlement to his 'inheritance' – see above.

(viii) Nick's attempts in evidence to distance himself from a consideration of the will, and from acquiring knowledge of its contents, are an important point. The thrust of his evidence, until the marked up draft was produced, was that he did not really know much about the will.

He arranged for the will writer to attend, and took his mother to the execution meeting, but did not know about the gift in his favour until a little time afterwards. His evidence distanced him from the content of the will. However, it then became apparent that he participated in a consideration of the draft. I think it unlikely that he had simply forgotten that. Furthermore, it gave him an opportunity to see the gift to him. With his hatred for his brother, and his feelings of unequal treatment, it is unlikely that he would not have looked to see what it said, particularly when the gift to him was on the same page as some of his manuscript amendments (on my findings). I do not accept his evidence that he had a thing about wills and did not like contemplating them (even his own). In any event, I am sure that his interest in seeing how he and his brother were treated would have overcome any such emotional difficulties. His direct involvement in the terms of the will, coupled with his omitting it from his evidence, are very important factors in considering whether he applied some degree of improper influence towards the gift in his favour. On my findings he will have known that he was going to get the house, and with his views on entitlement and inheritance he would not have forgotten that either. His failing to give evidence about it is likely to be rooted in a perception that it would not be helpful to the picture that he wished to present to be volunteering it.

(ix) His not disclosing the will until steps were taken to prove the 1990 will some 6 months after the death is also significant in this context. I think it is more consistent with his being aware of the circumstances in which it was drawn (of which he was less than proud) and wanting to put off the evil day of having to propound it because he had misgivings about those circumstances.

(x) I do not think that Miss Marks' attempt to ascertain whether there was pressure on her, the fruits of which are recorded on her instruction form, are a particularly strong contra-indication in this case. If the usual more subtle form of undue influence is being applied, its victim would hardly be likely to answer 'Yes' to the question.

In all those circumstances I find that undue influence has been proved. I think that they require the inference that Nick was instrumental in sowing in his mother's mind the desirability of his having the house, and in doing so he took advantage of her vulnerability. It is not possible to determine any more than that the precise form of the pressure, or its occasion or occasions, but it is not necessary to do so. I am satisfied that this will results from some form of undue influence. (*Schrader v Schrader* [2013] EWHC 466 (Ch) at [97] and [98])

(For another example where lack of capacity and want of knowledge and approval was proved, see *Turner v Phythian* [2013] EWHC 499 (Ch).)

Where the testator/testatrix may have been influenced by an extra-marital relationship consideration, this does not amount to undue influence, for example where a mistress uses her influence to induce a man to make a will in her favour, provided that the will expresses the man's wishes (*Wingrove v Wingrove* (1885) 11 PD 81).

In cases where only part of the will has been affected by undue influence, that part will fail but the rest of the provisions may be admitted to probate unless the omission has the effect of frustrating the entire disposition.

6.5 FRAUD

As in the case of undue influence, a will or a gift in a will made as a result of fraud will not be admitted to probate. However, in the event that undue influence or fraud is established, it may be possible to refuse probate in respect only of that part of the will to which the fraud was directed, unless that would be untenable having regard to the tenor of the will taken as a whole.

Where fraud is alleged, it must be shown that the testator/testatrix was misled into doing what he/she did. In probate proceedings, fraud usually takes the form of false representation concerning a person's character or conduct, with a view to inducing the testator/testatrix to revoke a gift to that person or securing the exclusion of that person from benefit under the will (*Boyse v Rossborough* (1857) 6 HLC 2). When the issue of fraud is raised, it is usually in connection with testamentary capacity and undue influence.

6.6 BURDEN OF PROOF

The legal burden of proof of undue influence is on the person who makes the challenge (*Boyse v Rossborough* (1857) 6 HLC 2; *Tyrell v Painton* [1894] P 151; *Craig v Lamoureux* [1920] AC 349). This was confirmed by Lord Nicholls in *Royal Bank of Scotland v Etridge (No 2)* [2001] UKHL 44:

> whether a transaction was brought about by the exercise of undue influence is a question of fact. Here, as elsewhere, the general principle is that who asserts that a wrong has been committed must prove it. The burden of proving an allegation of undue influence rests upon the person who claims to have been wronged. This is the general rule. (*Royal Bank of Scotland v Etridge (No 2)* [2001] UKHL 44 at [13])

The person who makes the allegation must prove that the will, or such part of it is in issue, was made as a result of undue influence and/or fraud. In *Re Good*

(Deceased), Carapeto v Good [2002] EWHC 640 (Ch), the testatrix left the bulk of her estate to her housekeeper and the latter's husband. The court held that where the circumstances of the making of a will raise suspicion, it is not enough to show that the testator/testatrix had knowledge of the contents of the will and approved it, and that in all other respects the testator/testatrix had testamentary capacity. In that case, on the facts the court found that the testatrix was an intelligent and strong-minded person who sought advice before executing her will. She was aware of the contents of the will and its financial effect on her family as this was fully explained to her.

Discharging the burden in lifetime transactions will depend on the nature of the alleged undue influence, the personalities of the parties, the relationship between them and whether there is an explanation for the transaction. Where a relationship of trust and confidence is presumed, as in the case of a parent/child relationship and the transfer is questionable, an explanation for the disposition will be called for. In the absence of an explanation or plausible explanation, the inference will be that the transaction was prompted by undue influence.

Where a testator/testatrix is ill, weak or frail, proof of a relatively small amount of pressure may be sufficient to discharge the burden of proving undue influence.

6.7 STANDARD OF PROOF

The standard of proof is the civil standard, i.e. on the balance of probabilities, but where the allegations are serious, for example coercion, it would seem that the court will look for cogent evidence to disprove that undue influence did not occur (see *Killick v Pountney* [2000] WTLR 410).

6.8 EVIDENCE

Before making a challenge on the ground of undue influence, an assessment of all the surrounding circumstances should be undertaken to ascertain what evidence is available to support the allegation and the nature and strength of the evidence. Evidence of the physical and mental condition of the deceased/donor is relevant, as are his/her relationship with the beneficiary/donee, the beneficiary's/donee's conduct and whether the deceased/donor had the opportunity and benefit of legal advice.

6.9 PROCEDURE

Any party who wishes to contest the will on the ground that execution of the will was obtained by undue influence of the claimant and others acting with him must set out the contention specifically and give particulars of the facts and matters relied on (rule 57.7(4)(c) of the CPR). A word of warning, however: this contention should not be made unless there are reasonable grounds to support it (*Spiers v English* [1907] P 122 at 124), nor should it be relied on as an indirect way of contending that the gift was obtained as a result of fraud. However, where the will is challenged on the ground of want of knowledge and approval, it is permissible to cross-examine a witness to establish in the alternative that the party was fraudulent (*Wintle v Nye* [1959] 1 WLR 284).

Chapter 7

Forgery

7.1 INTRODUCTION

Forgery of a will is assumed to be rare because there are few reported cases. However, this may be due to the fact that the allegation is included within the grounds of lack of testamentary capacity, lack of knowledge and approval and undue influence, and where it is raised courts may reach their conclusions on grounds other than forgery. Recent prosecutions which have received some publicity are an indication that forgery of wills is not a rare incident. Michael Tringham, writing in the *New Law Journal* on 11 December 2009, gave three examples of cases in which police investigations resulted in criminal convictions.

The Scottish Law Reporter website has referred to the increase of incidents of forgeries in probate disputes in Scotland involving large to small estates, where wills have been altered or forged by the survivor of spouses or partners and other relatives of the deceased or others. One such reported recent case is *Sharon McGeever (AP) as legal representative of her daughter Sophie v Maureen Nicol* [2012] CSOH 115, where a mother faked the will of her dead son in order to get possession of her son's house so that it would not pass to his child and his former partner.

7.2 EVIDENCE

Many cases involve people going through convoluted and sometimes complex procedures and actions to weave a web of deceit in order to create a legitimate front and to conceal their tracks. These may involve falsifying documents, producing multiple wills or codicils, misappropriation of assets before and after the death of the testator/testatrix, providing false information to banks and other financial institutions and forming corporate bodies. The case of *The Solicitor for the Affairs of Her Majesty's Treasury v Doveton & Anor* [2008] EWHC 2812

(Ch) best illustrates the lengths to which a fraudster will go to legitimise his case. In that case, the Treasury Solicitor brought an action for the revocation of a grant of probate to and several dispositions made by Mr Doveton, who obtained a grant of probate of an alleged will dated 19 May 1977 claiming that he was a distant cousin of the deceased, Mrs Janovtchik. The ground of the claim was that the will was a forgery.

The deceased died on 8 November 2005. The Treasury Solicitor established that the estate was *bona vacantia* in about January 2006 and lodged a caveat. Mr Doveton applied for probate in May 2006 and discovered the caveat, whereupon he approached the Treasury Solicitor to remove the caveat. In support of his account, he sent a copy of the will and an account of his connection with the deceased and the circumstance in which he came to be in possession of the will. Despite the caveat being in place, Mr Doveton managed to obtain probate by manipulating the procedural process. He immediately set about to take possession of the deceased's property and to transfer funds into his accounts, and he then took steps to enter into a number of transactions in relation to his own assets and those of the deceased's estate transferring them to a company which he formed and which was incorporated in the British Virgin Islands. The Treasury Solicitor remained suspicious and commenced proceedings. The evidence adduced was contained in 10 files and took 6.5 court days.

The disputed will was a one-page A4 typed document. It contained a number of typographical discrepancies and spaces between letters, and the deceased's name was spelt as Janovtechnik. It made Mr Doveton, who would then have been 14 months old, one of the executors and the beneficiary under the will. Mr Doveton gave a convoluted account of how he came to be in possession of not only the deceased's will but also her husband's wills. The court found that Mr Doveton had a staggering disregard for the authority of the court, a propensity to lie or tell half truths and persistence in giving an untrue account of events. In relation to the credibility of Mr Doveton in finding that the disputed will was a forgery, the judge said:

> 129. In the end I go further, because in considering the totality of the evidence before the court in this action, there are several factors which I cannot avoid taking into account, and I list them here in brief, in no particular order of significance: —
>
> (a) The obvious falseness of the witnesses' signatures, coupled with Mr Doveton's access to those signatures.
> (b) The use of the surname Janovtechnik in the disputed will and the non-use of it in Mr Janovtchik's 1977 will.
> (c) The appointment of Mr Doveton as a 14-month-old child as an executor.

(d) The omission of Mr Janovtchik as a beneficiary of the disputed will.
(e) Mrs Jones's evidence that the name Janovtechnik on the death certificate, and therefore the bona vacantia website, was a mistake.
(f) Her evidence that Mr Doveton had told her that he found the death on that website.
(g) The lack of any independent evidence of any relationship at all between the Futchers or Dovetons and the Janovtchiks.
(h) The disputed will being apparently typed by a person unfamiliar with old-style typewriters.
(i) The pictorial signature on the disputed will having no equivalent in any document traced to Mrs Janovtchik, other than those in Mr Doveton's possession and produced by him.
(j) Mr Doveton's failure to serve the warning on the Treasury Solicitor.
(k) The use of the sum £274,000 in the form PA1.
(l) The rapid extraction of cash from the estate accounts, followed by the only marginally less rapid transfer of funds to Switzerland and then Liechtenstein.
(m) The similarities and differences in Mr Janovtchik's 1977 will, in particular the appearance of a new typewriter ribbon, coupled with Mr Doveton's purchase of such a ribbon (or such ribbons) and his implausible evidence in relation to that purchase.
(n) His implausible evidence about the custody of the disputed will between 1977 and 2000, coupled with his failure to contact Mrs Janovtchik when, if his version of events is true, he found the wills.

130. Taking account of all these points, I return to the essential choice identified by Dr Barr, namely that the signature on the disputed will was either a pictorial signature (and a rare one unless Mr Doveton's second set of pictorial signatures was genuine), or a forgery by someone making no attempt to copy a genuine one. The totality of the evidence, including also the evidence of Mrs Janovtchik's signature on the probate copy of her husband's 1994 will, leads me to the firm conclusion that the disputed will is a forgery. Despite the seriousness of that finding, and the seriousness of the possible consequences to Mr Doveton, I am satisfied of that conclusion not only on the balance of probabilities, and in the end I have no real doubt at all. Mr Peto described the case against Mr Doveton as overwhelming, and having considered it with the thoroughness which it deserves I have reached the conclusion that he was right.

131. I shall therefore make an order revoking the grant of probate made in favour of Mr Doveton on 28 July 2006, and I shall pronounce formally against the validity of the disputed will. I shall also order that a grant of letters of administration be granted to the Treasury Solicitor if so entitled. These last three words are added because, to date, there is no evidence of which I am aware to show that there are no relatives of Mrs Janovtchik capable of sharing her estate on intestacy. It was assumed throughout the hearing that there are no such relatives, but as far as I can see that is no more than an assumption at this point. (*The Solicitor for the Affairs of Her Majesty's Treasury v Doveton & Anor* [2008] EWHC 2812 (Ch) at [129]–[131])

7.3 INTERFACE BETWEEN CIVIL ACTION AND FORGERY AS A CRIMINAL OFFENCE

Forgery is also a criminal offence. Charges may, therefore, be brought against the perpetrators, in which case the prosecution must be dealt with before the probate action can be heard. Where a probate action has been commenced, an application for that action to be stayed until the end of the criminal trial may be made. If the charges result in a conviction, that can be relied on as sufficient proof for probate to be refused and the will to be held invalid but it may not be conclusive. A conviction may be proved to be unsafe where, for example, subsequently, further evidence is discovered to show that the conviction cannot stand or is unsafe. This is best demonstrated by the widely reported case of estate agent, Chris John, who died in September 2008. Mr John was separated from his wife. Although divorce proceedings were issued, a decree absolute had not been granted. Following his separation from his wife, Mr John lived with Gillian Clemo. A few days after his death, Ms Clemo found a will which was executed in 1999 and witnessed by her and another. By his will, Mr John appointed his sister as an executor and guardian of his teenage daughter who was the main beneficiary. Mrs John produced a codicil making her the sole beneficiary of the estate and she alleged that Ms Clemo forged the 1999 will. Ms Clemo was charged with forgery.

In the meantime, Mrs John admitted that she forged the codicil. She received a caution but the prosecution against Ms Clemo continued. At her trial in May 2011, a handwriting expert testified that the disputed will was in fact genuine but the jury nevertheless convicted her and she was fined.

Following the conviction, Mrs John sought a declaration from the High Court that the 1999 will produced by Ms Clemo was invalid and that Mr John died intestate. However, a further will was discovered by Mr John's sister, which was in identical terms in all respects to the one previously found by Ms Clemo. Mr John's sister opposed the probate action commenced by Mrs John. At the hearing, a second handwriting expert testified that both wills were genuine. It seemed that the deceased executed two copies of the same will and it was the top copy which produced the suspicious looking indentations found by Ms Clemo. That will was upheld and Mrs John's application for a declaration of intestacy was rejected.

Other cases involving close family members and relatives reported in the *New Law Journal* include a case of a daughter who used a DIY will writing kit of the kind sold in high street retailers in an attempt to inherit her father's entire £100,000 estate and deprive her own nephew of his share. Susan Hursthouse knew she would receive half her father's £52,000 bank funds plus a share in his

£42,000 home but, with the help of her mother, she created a forged will dated 2 years earlier than the true one. After she obtained a grant of probate, relatives became suspicious and froze all funds. At Nottingham Crown Court, Ms Hursthouse was sentenced to 12 months in prison.

In another case, Susan Taylor took control of her elderly uncle's finances and sent his family letters purporting to come from a non-existent firm of solicitors. The relatives were suspicious and began to investigate, whereupon she produced a forged will. Evidence showed that she received no financial benefit and even paid the deceased's grandson £4,000. She was charged, convicted and sentenced to imprisonment for 30 months.

Forgery of wills may be carried out by others who are not related to, or have any family connections with the deceased. Francis Fallon and Richard Carr were involved in forging Land Registry and probate documents for 3 years, which could have netted more than £2 million. They transferred Land Registry details from the genuine owners and forged signatures on probate forms and wills to steal inheritances which rightfully belonged to the deceased's next of kin. Police investigations uncovered mistakes which included forging the deceased's signature on a will dated 5 days after his death. They were convicted at Southwark Crown Court of conspiracy to defraud and to forge.

The case of Yvette Adams, a National Health Service bereavement service adviser, is another case of a non-relative seeking to obtain a benefit from a vulnerable deceased person's estate. She admitted to 11 counts of offences, including forgery of wills and falsifying probate and executor documents. She was sentenced to 5 years' imprisonment (see Joseph Curl, 'A round up of recent wills and trusts cases', *STEP Journal*, 4 May 2010).

In such cases, anyone who is or may be entitled under a valid will or intestacy may apply to the court for probate or a declaration as to validity.

Where the police are not involved in prosecuting the alleged forger, if forgery is found in a probate action, the court has the power to refer the matter to the Director of Public Prosecutions, as occurred in *Stephen Supple v Pender & Another* [2007] EWHC 829 (Ch) (see T Dumont and W Mathers *et al*, 'Are wills too easy to fake? Thomas Dumont and Wendy Mathers investigate', *New Law Journal*, 27 April 2007). In that case, the deceased, Len Supple, owned a 60-acre farm. He had two children – Stephen, his son with his wife, and a daughter, Lynda, from a short relationship. Stephen left the farm in the 1970s but was still in touch with his father. Lynda lived on the farm. Immediately following the deceased's death no will was found, but about a month later Robert Pender accompanied by Lynda attended the offices of solicitors acting for Lynda with a suitcase which Pender said was left with him for safe custody by the deceased. The solicitors found a will in an unmarked envelope in the case. The will bequeathed the whole estate to Lynda with only a derisory annual sum of £100 to Stephen. Stephen contested the will on the ground that it was a forgery. The judge found forgery proved without making any finding on why, when or how the will was forged. He discredited Lynda's evidence. He directed that the case papers be sent to the Director of Public Prosecutions for investigation.

As can be deduced from the above cases, whether the prosecution succeeds or fails, the issues may still be litigated on in the civil courts if there is sufficient cogent evidence to substantiate the allegations. The decision whether or not to proceed solely on the ground of forgery, on some other ground(s) or both will depend on the facts of the case. Where the forgery has not been referred to the police by the parties, the court may refer the papers to the Director of Public Prosecutions for investigation.

7.4 BURDEN AND STANDARD OF PROOF

The burden of proving that the will is a forgery lies on the party who makes the allegation. Since forgery is a criminal offence, a person who forges a will risks being charged with the offence of forgery. If prosecuted, the standard of proof would be that which applies to all criminal offences – that is, beyond all reasonable doubt. However, that does not imply that when the allegation is raised in a contentious probate action, which falls within civil proceedings, the standard of proof is different than the civil standard of proof, i.e. on the balance of probabilities. Forgery is, nonetheless, a serious allegation as it attacks the character and reputation of the person. As Morris LJ said in *Hornal v Neuberger Products Limited* [1957] 1 QB 247:

> In English law the citizen is regarded as being a free man of good repute. Issues may be raised in a civil action, which affect character and reputation, and these will not be forgotten by judges and juries when considering the probabilities in regard to whatever misconduct is alleged. There will be reluctance to rob any man of his good name: there will also be reluctance to make any man pay what is not due or to make any man liable who is not ... (*Hornal v Neuberger Products Limited* [1957] 1 QB 247 at 266–267)

This, however, does not mean that a higher standard of proof is required, only that the court has to be vigilant and jealous and take great care to assess the quality of the evidence adduced to establish the allegations made. The more serious the allegation, the more cogent the evidence must be before a finding on the balance of probabilities can be made. The factors which the court will consider in assessing the quality of evidence will depend on the circumstances of each case. Where the suspicion is slight it may be easily dispelled but it may be so great that it cannot be removed:

> These are all matters of ordinary experience, requiring the application of good sense on the part of those who have to decide such issues. They do not require a different standard of proof or a specially cogent standard of evidence, merely appropriately careful consideration by the tribunal before it is satisfied of the matter which has to be established. (*Re D (Secretary of State for N.I. intervening)* [2008] UKHL 33 at [28])

In *The Solicitor for the Affairs of Her Majesty's Treasury v Doveton & Anor* [2008] EWHC 2812 (Ch) at [129], the judge, in reaching the conclusion that the allegation of forgery was made out, took into account the totality of the evidence and referred to 14 significant specific factors which emerged during the evidence (see para 7.2).

In *Devas & Others v Mackay* [2009] EWHC 1951 (Ch), although the case was not pursued on forgery but on the grounds of testamentary capacity, lack of knowledge and approval and undue influence, the suspicious circumstances in which the testatrix executed her will were significant and thus the standard of proof required was very relevant. When assessing the evidence and considering the standard of proof, the judge referred to the established principles and specifically referred to some 15 factors which were so weighty that they could not be ignored (at [74]).

In *Gale v Gale* [2010] EWHC 1575 (Ch), in finding that two codicils executed were forgeries, the court was vigilant in identifying the evidence which led the court to that conclusion.

7.5 CONCLUSION

The fact that a forged will is likely to fail on the requirements of the Wills Act 1837 as to execution, such as lack of testamentary capacity, lack of knowledge and undue influence, means that the courts tend to rely on those grounds to declare a will invalid. The court's unease about a finding of forgery is best indicated in the case of *Gale v Gale* [2010] EWHC 1575 (Ch), where the judge when finding the case of forgery said:

> The law can be dealt with rather shortly. The Claimant seeks to prove the 2002 codicil and the 2004 codicil. I have held that both are forgeries. That, plainly, marks the end of her claim. Her claim must be rejected. As to the 2004 codicil, there is an additional reason why the codicil must fail and that is that the Testatrix did not have testamentary capacity at the time of its execution. If my

finding of forgery were wrong, the codicil would fail on this ground in any event. The same is not true of the 2002 codicil as I have held that testamentary capacity did exist on 21 March 2002. As to both of these codicils, however, if my finding of forgery were wrong, I would have held that neither was signed on the date it purported to be signed but was backdated from a time when the Testatrix did not retain testamentary capacity. Of course I cannot be sure, in these circumstances, when the signing would have taken place, but I infer from all the evidence I have set out that such signing would have taken place sometime after the execution of the 2005 settlement. I have the ESDA test evidence to guide me in dating the signing of the 2004 codicil in the late summer of 2004 at the earliest, when the Claimant admits the Testatrix lacked testamentary capacity. I do not have the same assistance in relation to the 2002 codicil. However, in the light of the fraudulent backdating of the 2004 codicil and the execution of the 2005 settlement, I have more than enough to infer that the signing would have taken place some period of time after January 2005. At all events, once fraud is established, all presumptions of due execution (and knowledge and approval) would cease to have any sway and the Claimant would not be able to establish that the codicil was executed at a time when the Testatrix had testamentary capacity and knew and approved its contents. (*Gale v Gale* [2010] EWHC 1575 (Ch) at [130])

Chapter 8

Burial Disputes

8.1 INTRODUCTION

It is not unusual for family conflicts to arise as to who is legally entitled to make the decision on how and where the deceased's body should be disposed of. With the increase in multiple marriages, civil partnerships and relationships, and the resulting complex arrangements, disputes can arise as to who has rights over the deceased's body. Conflicts can arise between an estranged wife and mistress, or between parents of the deceased and his/her wife/husband/civil partner/cohabitant. Disputes may also arise between parents where their views differ as to how and where to dispose of their child's body or ashes. The deceased may have indicated in his/her will his/her wishes concerning the disposal of his/her body but those wishes may not accord with the beliefs, religious or otherwise, or wishes of those who are left behind. It is thus important to have some knowledge of the law governing the disposal of the deceased's body so that informed decisions may be taken amicably rather than through a confrontational approach and litigation. Where a dispute cannot be resolved by agreement and an application is made to the court, in determining the competing interests of the parties the court must take into account the provisions of the European Convention for the Protection of Human Rights and Fundamental Freedoms 1950 (European Convention on Human Rights) and the importance given to any determination taking account of the wishes and feelings of the person who is the subject of the dispute.

8.2 OWNERSHIP OF THE BODY

The will of the testator/testatrix will usually contain a provision setting out the testator's/testatrix's wishes on the disposal of his/her body. The direction, however, does not have any effect in law and is unenforceable. This is because at common law a person has no property in his/her body after death (*Williams v Williams* (1882) 20 Ch D 659). It does not form part of his/her estate and it cannot pass under a person's will or on intestacy. With a few exceptions, any provision in a will on disposal of the deceased's body has no legal effect and cannot be enforced. This does not mean that such indications are to be ignored as irrelevant. Any expression of the testator's/testatrix's wishes or direction as to disposal will, nevertheless, be a relevant consideration along with the wishes and feelings of others, as under the European Convention on Human Rights a person's wishes and feelings are matters of relevance in any dispute, particularly under Article 8(1) (see *Borrows v HM Coroner for Preston* [2008] EWHC 1387 (QB)).

8.3 EXCEPTIONS TO THE RULE ON TESTATOR/ TESTATRIX DIRECTION OVER BODY

8.3.1 Human Tissue Act 2004

There are statutory provisions which enable specific directions given by the testator/testatrix for his/her body to be used for medical research, education and organ donation to be respected and to apply. Part 1 of the Human Tissue Act 2004 sets out the activities for medical research, education or transplantation which are authorised under the Act. Save in relation to examination of the body under the authority of a coroner, consent is necessary of the deceased, of a person nominated by him/her or of a qualifying person. A direction given by the deceased in a will or elsewhere concerning the use of his/her body for medical research, education or transplantation can thus be challenged on the grounds that the appropriate consent is invalid on the ground of non-compliance with the provisions in sections 2 and 3.

8.3.1.1 Authorisation of activities for scheduled purposes

Section 1(1) of the Human Tissue Act 2004 sets out the following activities that can be lawful if done with appropriate consent:

> (a) the storage of the body of a deceased person for use for a purpose specified in Schedule 1, other than anatomical examination;
> (b) the use of the body of a deceased person for a purpose so specified, other than anatomical examination;
> (c) the removal from the body of a deceased person, for use for a purpose specified in Schedule 1, of any relevant material of which the body consists or which it contains;
> (d) the storage for use for a purpose specified in Part 1 of Schedule 1 of any relevant material which has come from a human body;
> (e) the storage for use for a purpose specified in Part 2 of Schedule 1 of any relevant material which has come from the body of a deceased person;

Burial Disputes

(f) the use for a purpose specified in Part 1 of Schedule 1 of any relevant material which has come from a human body;
(g) the use for a purpose specified in Part 2 of Schedule 1 of any relevant material which has come from the body of a deceased person.

Under section 1(2) of the Human Tissue Act 2004, the storage of the body of a deceased person for use for the purpose of anatomical examination is lawful if done:

(a) with appropriate consent, and
(b) after the signing of a certificate—

(i) under section 22(1) of the Births and Deaths Registration Act 1953 (c. 20), or
(ii) under Article 25(2) of the Births and Deaths Registration (Northern Ireland) Order 1976 (S.I.1976/1041 (N.I. 14)),

of the cause of death of the person.

And under section 1(3) of the Human Tissue Act 2004, the use of the body of a deceased person for the purpose of anatomical examination shall be lawful if done:

(a) with appropriate consent, and
(b) after the death of the person has been registered—

(i) under section 15 of the Births and Deaths Registration Act 1953, or
(ii) under Article 21 of the Births and Deaths Registration (Northern Ireland) Order 1976.

Schedule 1 lists the following scheduled purposes referred to under Part 1 of the Human Tissue Act 2004:

1. Anatomical examination.
2. Determining the cause of death.
3. Establishing after a person's death the efficacy of any drug or other treatment administered to him.
4. Obtaining scientific or medical information about a living or deceased person which may be relevant to any other person (including a future person).
5. Public display.
6. Research in connection with disorders, or the functioning, of the human body.
7. Transplantation.

'Anatomical examination' and 'anatomical purposes' are defined in section 54 of the Human Tissue Act 2004. 'Anatomical examination' means 'macroscopic examination by dissection for anatomical purposes', and 'anatomical purposes' means 'purposes of teaching or studying or researching into, the gross structure of the human body'.

8.3.1.2 'Appropriate consent'

It will be observed that 'appropriate consent' is fundamental to the use of the body for any of the purposes set out in Schedule 1 to the Human Tissue Act 2004. Sections 2 and 3 set out what 'appropriate consent' means. In relation to a child, subject to the child being of sufficient age, maturity and understanding, 'appropriate consent' means his/her consent. To be valid, the consent must be in writing and:

(a) it must be signed by the child concerned in the presence of at least one witness who must attest the signature; or
(b) it is signed at the direction of the child in his/her presence and in the presence of at least one witness who attests the signature (section 2(4) and (6)). *Note*: whilst a child under 18 is not eligible to make a will, he/she is able to consent to his/her body/body parts being used for medical purposes on his/her death.

Where the child has not given any consent, it is open to a person who had parental responsibility for the child immediately before his/her death, or if no person had parental responsibility for the child a person who had a qualifying relationship with him/her at the time, to give consent for the use of the body for scheduled purposes (section 2(7) of the Human Tissue Act 2004).

In relation to an adult, 'appropriate consent' means consent of that person. Although the Human Tissue Act 2004 does not make any provision for a prescribed form for giving consent, it sets out the procedure which must be followed to provide valid consent. Section 3(5) states that the consent must be given in writing and it is only valid if:

(a) it is signed by the person concerned in the presence of at least one witness who attests the signature,
(b) it is signed at the direction of the person concerned, in his presence and in the presence of at least one witness who attests the signature or
(c) it is contained in a will of the person concerned made in accordance with the requirements of—

(i) section 9 of the Wills Act 1837 (c. 26), or
(ii) Article 5 of the Wills and Administration Proceedings (Northern Ireland) Order 1994 (S.I. 1994/1899 (N.I. 13)).

Where the deceased has given a valid consent, the deceased's direction cannot be overruled by family members and they cannot prevent the removal or examination or use of the body or parts of the body as the case may be. Although, in practice, the authorities consult relatives and consider their objections, the authorities are not under a duty to consult relatives or consider their objections if a valid consent has been provided by the deceased.

8.3.1.3 Nominated representatives

If the deceased has nominated a person to provide the necessary consent, the appointment of the nominee is valid only if the appointment has been made in compliance with the provisions set out in section 4 of the Human Tissue Act 2004:

(1) An adult may appoint one or more persons to represent him after his death in relation to consent for the purposes of section 1.
(2) An appointment under this section may be general or limited to consent in relation to such one or more activities as may be specified in the appointment.
(3) An appointment under this section may be made orally or in writing.
(4) An oral appointment under this section is only valid if made in the presence of at least two witnesses present at the same time.
(5) A written appointment under this section is only valid if—

    (a) it is signed by the person making it in the presence of at least one witness who attests the signature,
    (b) it is signed at the direction of the person making it, in his presence and in the presence of at least one witness who attests the signature, or
    (c) it is contained in a will of the person making it, being a will which is made in accordance with the requirements of—

        (i) section 9 of the Wills Act 1837 (c. 26), or
        (ii) Article 5 of the Wills and Administration Proceedings (Northern Ireland) Order 1994 (S.I. 1994/1899 (N.I. 13)).

(6) Where a person appoints two or more persons under this section in relation to the same activity, they shall be regarded as appointed to act jointly and severally unless the appointment provides that they are appointed to act jointly.

8.3.1.4 Qualifying relationship

If no nomination has been made, persons who have a 'qualifying relationship' can give consent. Those who are considered as having a qualifying relationship are set out in section 27(4) of the Human Tissue Act 2004 and include the following persons in ranking order:

(a) spouse or partner;
(b) parent or child;
(c) brother or sister;
(d) grandparent or grandchild;
(e) child of a person falling within paragraph (c);
(f) stepfather or stepmother;
(g) half-brother or half-sister;
(h) friend of longstanding.

In certain circumstances (set out in section 7 of the Human Tissue Act 2004), the Human Tissue Authority has power to dispense with consent where the deceased has not given consent or nominated a person to provide consent on his/her behalf and none of those qualified to give consent (see the above list) can be traced.

8.3.2 Human Fertilisation and Embryology Act 2008

8.3.2.1 Posthumous use of sperm

Following the case of *R v Human Fertilisation and Embryology Authority ex parte Blood* [1997] 2 FLR 742, where it was held that sperm taken from a donor whilst he was in a coma at the request of his wife and where no consent had been previously given for the sperm to be taken, stored and used was contrary to section 4(1) of, and Schedule 3 to, the Human Fertilisation and Embryology Act 1990, the Act was amended by the Human Fertilisation and Embryology (Deceased Father) Act 2003 to address the issue of the posthumous use of a man's sperm. The provision is now incorporated in section 39 of the Human Fertilisation and Embryology Act 2008, which permits a man to consent to the use of his sperm after his death. For the consent to be effective, the man must have consented in writing to the use of his sperm or embryo after his death and to being treated in respect of any resulting child as the child's father for the purposes of birth registration, and the consent must not have been withdrawn.

8.4 PERSONS WHO HAVE RESPONSIBILITIES FOR THE BODY AND FUNERAL ARRANGEMENTS

The executors of the deceased are under a duty to dispose of the body and thus have a right to its custody and possession until it is disposed of (*Dobson v North Tyneside Health Authority* [1996] 4 All ER 474). In the case where intestacy arises, the duty will fall on the personal representatives who will be those who have priority under the Non-Contentious Probate Rules 1987 and section 46 of the Administration of Estates Act 1925. The executors are not generally responsible for making the arrangements for the funeral but they may take on the responsibility if there is no one willing to do so. This will include the mode and place of burial and if cremated the disposal of the ashes (*Leeburn v Derndorfer* [2004] WTLR 867). Generally, the executors take on the responsibility because funeral expenses are discharged out of the estate. Any directions given by the testator/testatrix on the disposal of his/her body are not binding on the executors. This is demonstrated by the decision in *Holtham v Arnold* [1986] 2 BMLR 123. The deceased, Mr Arnold, separated from his wife and thereafter lived with Ms Holtham. Before his death in 1986 he gave Ms Holtham oral directions as to his wishes for his funeral. Although a divorce petition was filed by his wife in November 1985, 14 months after the separation, she did not proceed with it. On the deceased's death, the estranged wife as his widow had the right to administer his estate and, therefore, had the duty to undertake the arrangements for his funeral as the rightful person to be appointed as his personal representative. Ms Holtham as the deceased's cohabitant wanted the funeral arrangements to comply with the deceased's wishes, but the widow disagreed. An application by Ms Holtham to the court to appoint her as the deceased's administratrix limited to making arrangements for the burial pursuant to section 116 of the Senior Courts Act 1981 was refused because the application was not considered to fall within the 'special circumstances' for the court to exercise its discretion. The court applied the principle that the person lawfully entitled to administration had the right to possession of the body and duty to undertake the funeral arrangements.

This illustrates the point that, in law, whilst the direction given by the deceased is a factor to be taken into account and respected, it is not binding. However, this decision must now be considered alongside Article 8 of the European Convention on Human Rights and the Human Rights Act 1998.

8.4.1 Others with the right to possession and duty to dispose of a body

When a person dies in a hospital or institution, whilst in the armed forces or for example in rented premises and a dispute arises between family members concerning the disposal of the body, the person in lawful possession of the body may make the decision on the mode of disposal. In such cases it is good practice to seek the direction and sanction of the court before taking any steps. The case of *Lewisham Hospital NHS Trust v Hamuth & others* [2006] EWHC 1609 (Ch) best illustrates this point. In that case, the deceased died in hospital. In his last purported will the deceased expressed a wish to be cremated. He appointed his nurse and main carer, Hamuth, as his executor and left his estate to him. Hamuth intended to respect the deceased's wish to be cremated but the deceased's family wanted him to be buried in the family plot. They challenged the will on the grounds of lack of testamentary capacity and knowledge and approval. The hospital applied for a direction from the court. Hart J held that, as the validity of the will was in dispute and would not be determined soon, it was inappropriate to wait until the outcome of the proceedings, and that since at common law the person under whose roof the deceased died has the duty to make the arrangements for the disposal of the body (*R v Stewart* (1840) 12 Ad & El 773 at 778), the hospital was in lawful possession of the body and thus had the right to decide how the body should be disposed of. The hospital indicated that the family should make the arrangements for the burial in the family plot.

Where a body is unclaimed, the local authority for the area in which the body is found has a duty to bury the body pursuant to section 46 of the Public Health (Control of Disease) Act 1984.

8.4.2 Disposal of the body of a child

The parents of a child have the responsibility of disposing of their child's body provided they have sufficient means (*Re Vann* (1851) 169 ER 523). This duty arises as part of their parental responsibility for their child under section 3(1) of the Children Act 1989. Where the child has property, the child's parents would be the appropriate persons with priority to apply for a grant. Disputes, however, between parents both in relation to mode and place of burial, and disposal of ashes are not uncommon especially in cases where the parents are separated or divorced. The cases of *Fessi v Whitmore* [1999] 1 FLR 767 and *Hartshorne v Gardner* [2008] EWHC B3 (Ch) best illustrate the nature of the conflicts that can arise between parents and the factors which the court will take into account when determining the issues between the parents.

In *Fessi v Whitmore* [1999] 1 FLR 767, the parents were in agreement on cremation as the mode of disposal of the body of their 12-year-old son. The dispute was over where to lay the boy's ashes. The parents were divorced. The son lived with his father in the Nuneaton area, where the family had always lived until they moved to Aberystwyth a few days before the fatal accident. As he was the main carer of the boy following the breakdown of the marriage, the father wanted his wish that his son's ashes should be interred near the new home to prevail, whilst the mother's wishes were that they should be interred in Nuneaton at the church where her parents' ashes were scattered or at the crematorium where the ashes of the paternal grandfather were scattered. In the alternative, the father proposed that the ashes should be divided between the parents. As parents, both were entitled to possession of the body and to decide where the ashes should be interred. Judge Boggis dealt with the issues between the parents as trustees rather than under the provisions for the administration of an estate. The court's approach was to take into account all the circumstances and the views of both parents and to determine the issues between them on the basis of fairness and justice to both sides. The judge considered that the father had a strong case, but those facts had to be balanced against the enormous distress that would be caused to the family if the ashes were to remain in Borth, both because it was where the accident occurred and also because it was so far from the home that the son had with his parents when they lived together for 11 years. The judge directed that the ashes should be scattered at the Nuneaton Crematorium for three reasons:

> First, it is a place where all the family can have some focus. Secondly, it is the place where Mark's paternal grandfather's ashes have been scattered and, therefore, has a natural focus for Mark's father himself to attend. Thirdly, taking everything into account, it seems to me the appropriate place as one where all members of the family can come together to see a fitting memorial to Mark's life. (*Fessi v Whitmore* [1999] 1 FLR 767 at 770F)

Judge Boggis rejected the father's alternative option as he considered it to be 'wholly inappropriate'. The division of the ashes as an option was also considered by Byrne J in *Leeburn v Derndorfer* [2004] WTLR 867 but on the facts it was rejected. In that case, the dispute was between three siblings who could not reach agreement on how their father's ashes should be disposed of. The daughters wanted the ashes interred at a cemetery; their brother suggested the ashes should be divided between all three of them. The daughters disregarded their brother's wishes and interred the ashes at a cemetery of their choice. The brother applied for one-third of the ashes to be disinterred and given to him. His application was refused mainly because of the delay of 4 years since the ashes were interred – 30 months before proceedings were commenced and a further 18 months before the trial was concluded. The decision to inter the ashes at the cemetery was taken by a majority of the executors and their choice of cemetery could not be considered inappropriate.

In *Hartshorne v Gardner* [2008] EWHC B3 (Ch), the deceased was aged 44 when he died in a road traffic accident. The dispute was between his parents, who had been divorced for about 35 years, as to whether he should be buried or cremated and as to the place of the funeral or interment. The father wanted a burial in Kington; the mother wanted a cremation and the ashes to be interred in Worcester where she lived. Her other objections were that Kington was some 40 miles away and as she could not drive it would make it difficult for her to visit the grave. Both parents had an equal right to apply for administration of their son's estate, both had a right to possession of the body and, therefore, no distinction could be made between them. In the absence of an agreement between the parents, the coroner would not authorise the release of the body to either parent without order of the court. In arriving at her decision, the judge took into account the deceased's wishes and the place where he had the closest connection as relevant factors. Other factors considered relevant were the fact that the deceased's body should be disposed of with proper respect and decency and without delay. These had to be balanced against the mother's difficulties. In giving her reasons for her decision, the judge said:

> I do not underestimate the difficulty faced by the Defendant visiting her son's grave. However, it seems to me that although this is a weighty factor, the fact that the deceased made his life in Kington for the last eight years of his life and that his fiancée as well as his father and brother wish him to be buried there, accordingly, outweigh the Defendant's personal wishes and difficulties. As I have said, even on her own evidence, her contact with her son and interest in his personal life and doings was very small in his last years compared with that of Miss Housley and other members of the deceased's family. While I do not doubt the Defendant's affection for the deceased and grief at his death, in my judgment virtually all the evidence points strongly in favour of the Claimant's case. I therefore decide the issue in favour of the Claimant. (*Hartshorne v Gardner* [2008] EWHC B3 (Ch) at [24])

In *Scotch v Birching* (2008) (unreported), the deceased child was 5 years of age. The mother was charged with his murder and was in custody awaiting a trial. She wanted the child buried near her home. The father wanted the child to be buried in Milton Keynes where he was born and where he lived until his mother abducted him. The dispute was easily resolved in this case because although both parents had parental responsibility, a murderer or a person who has committed manslaughter or any other offence within the provisions of the Forfeiture Act 1982 is debarred from taking a grant over the estate of the deceased, which left the father as the only person with the duty to dispose of the body and, therefore, also the right to possession of the body. In allowing the father's application, the court exercised its powers under section 116 of the Senior Courts Act 1981 because of the 'special circumstances' which made it 'necessary or expedient' to do so.

8.4.2.1 *Child in care*

Where the child is in the care of the local authority, although the local authority shares parental responsibility with the parents, on the death of the child the local authority's parental responsibility ends. The parents have the duty to dispose of the body of their child and, therefore, the right to possession of the body. It is only when the parents are unable to undertake their responsibility that the local authority will need to step in to make arrangements for the burial or cremation. Similarly, the natural parents' rights take precedence over those of a foster carer with whom a child was placed (*R v Gwynedd CC ex parte B* [1992] 3 All ER 317).

8.4.2.2 *Adopted child*

The status of an adopted child is governed by the Adoption and Children Act 2002. An adoption order gives parental responsibility for the adopted child to the adopters (section 46(1)), i.e. all the rights and duties, powers, responsibilities and authority which by law a parent of a child has in relation to the child and his/her property (section 3(1) of the Children Act 1989). As from the date of the adoption order, the child is treated as the legitimate child of both adopters (if adopted by a couple). If the adoption order was made to one person alone, the child will be treated as the legitimate child of the person in whose favour the adoption order was made (sections 51(2) and 67(1) and (2) of the 2002 Act). The child thus is in the same position as a biological child of his adoptive parent(s). Hence, in relation to any dispute over burial rights, the rights of the adoptive parent(s) rank higher than those of the natural parents. In *Buchanan v Milton* [1999] 2 FLR 844, the court was asked by the natural mother of the adopted person to displace the adoptive parents' rights in favour of those of his natural parents on the grounds of special circumstances of the child's aboriginal heritage. In that case, the deceased was born in Queensland, Australia to Aboriginal parents who gave their consent to the child being adopted when he was 4 days old. He was placed with his adoptive family, who were English, when he was just over 2 years old and an adoption order was made. In 1979, when the deceased was 7 years old, the adoptive parents returned to England and thereafter lived in England. In 1996, at the invitation of the natural parents, the deceased visited Australia and met his birth family but returned to England. He maintained telephone contact with his mother. The deceased lived with his partner and their daughter. On his death, his birth mother requested that his body be returned to Australia for burial in accordance with the Aboriginal custom. When the adoptive parents and the deceased's partner refused to accede to this request, the birth mother applied for the adoptive parents to be displaced pursuant to section 116 of the Senior Courts Act 1981. This section permits the displacement of persons who would normally have the duty and the right to dispose of the body if, by reason of the special circumstances, it appears to the High Court to be necessary or expedient to appoint as administrator some other person. Hale J (as she then was) held that the deceased's heritage and the importance of Aboriginal burial custom, the right of the deceased's child to know of her father's cultural background and of his natural Aboriginal family's interest were all capable of amounting to 'special circumstances', but the court also had to be satisfied that it was necessary or expedient to displace the personal representatives. In determining this issue, the court had to carry out a balancing exercise between the views of the birth family, those of the adoptive parents, the wishes of the deceased, and the interests of his child. Balancing these factors, Hale J (as she then was) said:

> even if none of them is given any greater weight than the other, it is quite clear to me that this is not a case in which there are special circumstances making it necessary or expedient to displace the persons ordinarily entitled to the grant of letters of administration of the estate. (*Buchanan v Milton* [1999] 2 FLR 844 at 857G)

The adoptive parents were given the grant, and the body was released to them for them to make the appropriate funeral arrangements.

8.5 IMPACT OF THE EUROPEAN CONVENTION ON HUMAN RIGHTS

There are conflicting views on the question whether issues concerning burial rights and interment of ashes engage the rights which are enshrined under Article 8 of the European Convention on Human Rights. These issues are also likely to engage rights protected under Article 9.

Article 8 of the European Convention on Human Rights provides:

1. Everyone has the right to respect for his private and family life, his home and his correspondence.
2. There shall be no interference by a public authority with the exercise of this right except such as is in accordance with the law and is necessary in a democratic society in the interests of national security, public safety or the economic well-being of the country, for the prevention of disorder or crime, for the protection of health or morals, or for the protection of the rights and freedoms of others.

The European Court of Human Rights (ECtHR) has applied Article 8 rights when determining burial issues. In *Dodsbo v Sweden* [2006] ECtHR Application No 61564/00, for example, the appeal to the ECtHR concerned the refusal of the authorities and the County Administrative Court to permit the applicant to move her husband's urn to her family plot in Stockholm. She relied on Article 8 (right to respect for private and family life). The ECtHR found (by 4 votes to 3) that the Swedish authorities acted within the wide margin of appreciation afforded to them in balancing the interest of the individual against society's role in ensuring the sanctity of graves, and held accordingly that there was no violation of Article 8.

In *X v Germany* (1981), Application No 8741/79, 24 DR 137, Hamburg administrative authorities refused the applicant the right to have his ashes scattered on his own land on his death. The administrative court allowed his appeal but required that his ashes should be placed in an urn and buried on his land. On further appeal, the administrative authorities' decision was reinstated. A further appeal was lodged but the applicant died before the proceedings were heard and his son continued the appeal. The appellant's grounds of appeal were that the refusal to allow him to scatter his ashes was a violation of his rights under Articles 8 and 9 of the European Convention on Human Rights. On the Article 8 rights the court held that although the issue concerned arrangements after a person's death, this did not mean 'that no issue concerning such arrangements may arise under Article 8 since persons may feel the need to express their personality by the way they arrange how they are buried'. The Commission accepted that Article 8 was engaged but it went on to consider whether the legislation on cemeteries and burial constituted an interference with the right to respect for private life of the deceased. The Commission noted that the legislation gave an individual the freedom to choose the means of burial or cremation and provided that cemeteries should secure a peaceful resting place having regard to other factors such as public health to protect the public interests. The right set out under Article 8(1) must be considered with those under Article 8(2) and, on the facts, the legislation on which the refusal was based did not constitute an interference with the deceased's right to respect of his private life. The court also rejected the argument that the deceased's wish to have his ashes scattered on his own land could be considered a manifestation of one's 'religion or beliefs, in worship, teaching, practice and observance' (Article 9) (see further the human rights handbooks published by the Council of Europe).

Rights under the European Convention on Human Rights have been considered in two English cases and a Scottish case, but without a clear consensus on whether Convention rights are engaged.

In *Borrows v HM Coroner for Preston* [2008] EWHC 1387 (QB), Cranston J considered the relevance of Convention rights when determining whether the natural parents of a 15-year-old boy, L, or his paternal uncle who brought him up should have the right to make funeral arrangements when L committed suicide while he was in a young offenders' institution. The parents were both heroin addicts. When the inquest into the death concluded, the mother sought possession of the body. The coroner, on becoming aware of the conflict between the mother and uncle, offered mediation services but the mother would not compromise. The uncle made arrangements for a cremation in the district where he lived in accordance with L's wishes and was willing to let the mother have the ashes to be scattered in Liverpool. Although the mother accepted that L expressed a wish to be cremated, she wanted L to be buried in Liverpool where she lived and where her family members were buried. The coroner was advised that in law the mother had priority over the uncle to possession of L's body. The uncle, therefore, issued proceedings for judicial review, and leave to do so was given by Collins J but with an indication that the case would be better dealt with by a claim being made in the Queen's Bench Division. The judge described the relationship of the uncle and his wife with L as one of 'psychological parents' (as referred to by Baroness Hale in *Re G (Children)* [2006] UKHL 43). The judge considered the domestic law, the order of priority for a grant on intestacy, the court's powers under section 116 of the Senior Courts Act 1981 and European jurisprudence. He concluded that in view of the European Convention on Human Rights and its impact, as demonstrated by the case law on burial rights and issues, domestic law developed under common law had to be considered in that light. In relation to the relevance of the deceased's wishes, he said:

It is quite clear from the jurisprudence of the European Court of Human Rights that the views of a deceased person as to funeral arrangements and the disposal of his or her body must be taken into account. However, this aspect of Strasbourg jurisprudence is easily accommodated within domestic law: in this type of case a person's wishes can be regarded as a special circumstance in terms of Section 116 of the Act. Otherwise, the jurisprudence of the European Court of Human Rights does not cast doubt on the domestic law. Rule 22 can still apply. Special circumstances may displace the order of priority set out there although a high test has to be satisfied, whether it is necessary or expedient to do so. (*Borrows v HM Coroner for Preston* [2008] EWHC 1387 (QB) at [20])

In some cases, if Article 8(1) of the European Convention on Human Rights (the right to family life) is engaged, it may be that, apart from the deceased's wishes, there are other claims to the exercise of that right. For example, in *Borrows v HM Coroner for Preston* [2008] EWHC 1387 (QB), there was the family life which L enjoyed with the Borrows family on the one hand and his family life with his mother, Mrs McManus, on the other hand. *Boyle v The United Kingdom* (1994) 19 EHRR 179 was a case which arose in a different context involving an uncle and nephew. The Commission in that case held that the uncle/nephew relationship could fall within the scope of family life. Therefore, there is no doubt that those in Mr Borrows' position can invoke Article 8(1) (*Boyle v The United Kingdom* (1994) 19 EHRR 179 at para 21).

In applying the provisions of section 116 of the Senior Courts Act 1981, Cranston J identified the special circumstances to be: (a) the mother's addiction; (b) L's wishes to be cremated; (c) the mother's disregard for her son's wishes, although she was aware of them and of his reasons; (d) the uncle and aunt's relationship with L; and (e) L's connection with St Helens where he lived, attended school and had friends. On the issue of necessity and expediency, Cranston J was firmly of the view that the mother's addiction and her inability to assume responsibility made it necessary for the mother's rights to be displaced. Her rights were, nevertheless, protected in that she was able to attend the funeral and to have her son's ashes.

However, in *Ibuna v Arroyo* [2012] EWHC 428 (Ch), Peter Smith J disagreed with the decision of Cranston J in *Borrows v HM Coroner for Preston* [2008] EWHC 1387 (QB) that the European Convention on Human Rights and the Human Rights Act 1998 applied after death. In *Ibuna v Arroyo*, the deceased was a congressman in the Philippines. He was resident in both the Philippines and California. He was domiciled in the Philippines. He was married but separated from his wife. The deceased issued proceedings for the annulment of his marriage which were pending when he died while receiving medical treatment at a clinic in London. In his will, he appointed his daughter from his first marriage as his executrix and left his assets on trust to his cohabitant, C, for life and then to his three children. C arranged for the body to be flown to the Philippines for burial in accordance with his wishes. He told his daughter that he wished to be buried in the family mausoleum in the North Cemetery in Manila where his mother is buried. He also stated his wish to have his wake in the ancestral family home at 14 Badjao Street where his grandparents' wakes were held. He told his daughter on a number of occasions that he wished C to make the funeral arrangements but that there was no change to his wishes. Before the body could be repatriated, the deceased's widow, who had been estranged from the deceased for 6 years and had no contact with him, claimed the right to possession of his body. This resulted in the daughter and C making a without notice application for an injunction restraining the widow from disposing of the body. The widow made an application to the court in the Philippines that as the deceased widow she had rights of possession of the body. At the hearing in London, expert evidence confirmed that under Philippine law the funeral should take place in accordance with the expressed wishes of the deceased. In the absence of such expression, his religious beliefs or affiliation should determine the funeral rights. In case of doubt, the form of the funeral was be decided upon by the person obliged to make arrangements for the same after consulting the other members of the family. Peter Smith J, having considered Philippine law, the primacy of an executor under English law, the order of priority for a grant where the deceased dies domiciled overseas under rule 30 of the Non-Contentious Probate Rules 1987, and the application of the rights under the European Convention on Human Rights, referred to by Cranston J in *Borrows v HM Coroner for Preston*, disagreed with Cranston J's conclusion concerning those rights. He concluded that English law was clear that an executor has the primary duty to dispose of the body, i.e. the daughter in this case, and also that under the Non-Contentious Probate Rules 1987 she had prior rights to be granted administration. The judge then went on to state the deceased's express wishes which were supported by the Advance Health Directive amounted to special circumstances which enabled him to exercise his discretion under section 116 of the Senior Courts Act 1981. He granted a limited grant to the deceased's daughter and C, because they as the personal representatives would give effect to the deceased's wishes and that should have paramountcy as suggested in *Borrows v HM Coroner for Preston*, 'it is a factor which the personal representatives can take into account and no doubt they would bona fide consider the deceased's wishes'. Lastly, he hoped that the other parties would recognise his judgment to enable the deceased's body to be disposed of in accordance with the deceased's clearly expressed wishes, as demonstrated in evidence and the signed documents.

In the Scottish case of *Connolly v MOD* [2011] CSOH 124, the dispute was between the widow and the mother of a private in the Black Watch, who died whilst on training in Germany and hence his body was in the possession of the

Ministry of Defence (MOD). The dispute was about where he should be buried. The army intended to release the body to his mother, who was one of the executors of the deceased's will. The widow claimed that as his sole beneficiary she was entitled to possession, that the deceased had orally expressed where he wished to be buried, and that if the body was released to the mother it would be an infringement of her rights under Article 8 of the European Convention on Human Rights. The widow sought a judicial review of the MOD's decision to hand over the body to the deceased's mother. Lord Brodie determined the Article 8 issue raised by the widow in three parts, namely: (a) whether there was an interference with the applicant's rights under Article 8(1); (b) whether any interference was in accordance with the law; and (c) whether such interference was justified under Article 8(2). On the first point, Lord Brodie held that the action of the MOD would be an interference of the widow's rights under Article 8(1). On the second point, Lord Brodie considered what the legal position of the two contenders was in law. There was no direct authority under Scottish law on who had priority, but under English law the executor had priority, subject to any direction of the court. He went on to say:

> The fact that he [the executor] pays does not make him responsible for arranging the funeral. It is the surviving spouse and next of kin (not the executor) who have rights to solatium for unauthorised interference with the dead body ... Thus, in Scots law, I would see near relatives as well as the executor or prospective executor as having rights and interests in respect of the body of the deceased. The nature of these rights is not the same ... Determining what are appropriate funeral arrangements by reference to the quality of relationships within a family appears to me a task for which the court is quite unsuited. (*Connolly v MOD* [2011] CSOH 124 at [57])

However, Lord Brodie went on to say that while the MOD was in an impossible position, what it intended to do was in accordance with the law and therefore of Article 8 of the European Convention on Human Rights.

Clearly, rights under the European Convention on Human Rights have been raised and challenged in the courts. The first instance decisions in *Borrows v HM Coroner for Preston* [2008] EWHC 1387 (QB) and in *Ibuna v Arroyo* [2012] EWHC 428 (Ch) appear to be conflicting. However, that is not to say that Convention rights are irrelevant or inapplicable in burial disputes. These two decisions turned on their own facts. In *Ibuna v Arroya*, the court was able to deal with the discrete issue under section 116 of the Senior Courts Act 1981 as the case could be successfully argued on the grounds of special circumstances due to the international element, the conflict on the issue of who was entitled to the grant – under Philippine law it was the estranged widow but under English law it was the daughter, and both these were at odds with the deceased's expressed wish that his cohabitant, C, should be responsible for the funeral arrangements. Although the daughter was willing to respect her father's wishes that C should arrange the funeral, since C had no rights under Philippine law it was necessary to ensure that C was included in making the arrangements and thus give effect to the deceased's wishes, which was clearly a factor to be taken into account. In other circumstances, the deceased's wishes – which may include his religious beliefs and those of persons with whom he was closely connected and had an emotional and meaningful relationship – may impact significantly on the Article 8 rights and the right to freedom of thought, conscience and religion enshrined under Article 9 of those persons. These rights are relevant factors which the court is bound to consider, even if it decides to base its decision on section 116. Where, for example, the deceased had a strong religious belief which included the mode of burial and those who were closely related to him shared his belief, there would be considerable force for arguing that both their Article 8 rights to family life and Article 9 rights to freedom of conscience and religious beliefs should be respected. European jurisprudence appears to recognise these rights as being significant in burial disputes.

8.6 PROCEDURE

A study of the cases cited above indicates that there is no uniformity in the procedure which is adopted to issue proceedings for the court to resolve disputes concerning the possession and disposal of the deceased's body.

In an application relating to a deceased child, application has been made under section 8 of the Children Act 1989 for a specific issue order (see *Fessi v Whitmore* [1999] 1 FLR 767), under section 116 of the Senior Courts Act 1981 and under the court's inherent jurisdiction. The assumption that the application came within the provisions of the Children Act 1989 may have been made on the false premise that because parental responsibility forms the basis of the parents' duty and responsibility for the disposal of the child's body, the issue must come within the ambit of the Children Act 1989. However, this is clearly wrong as there is nothing in the Act and more specifically in section 8 to suggest that the Act applies to children beyond the grave. In *Fessi v Whitmore*, the initial application to obtain injunctions was made under the Children Act 1989. It was amended to an application pursuant to what is now Part 64 of the CPR (formerly Order 85 of the Rules of the Supreme Court (RSC)). The order was eventually made under the inherent jurisdiction of the High Court when the final hearing adjudicated on. The inappropriateness of proceeding under the Children Act 1989 and pursuant to Part 64 was referred to in the judgment of Judge Boggis, who dealt with the issue on the basis that the dispute was one akin to a dispute between trustees. With regard to proceeding under Order 85, Judge Boggis said:

It seems to me that, on analysis, the parties are rather in the nature of trustees bringing a dispute to the court and seeking the directions of the court as to the resolution of that dispute, given that there are valid contentions on both sides. It is on that basis that I propose to decide the case. I do not think that I am being asked to give directions as to the administration of an estate ... this court is well used to exercising disputes between trustees and adjudicating on the proper course to follow when no agreement can be reached by the parties concerned. (*Fessi v Whitmore* [1999] 1 FLR 767 at 770B)

In cases concerning a deceased adult, the application has been made both under what is now Part 64 of the CPR and the Senior Courts Act 1981. For example, in *Holtham v Arnold* [1986] 2 BMLR 123, the application was brought pursuant to Order 85 of the RSC and in the alternative pursuant to section 116 of the Senior Courts Act 1981. Hoffmann J (as he then was) did not consider that the use of Order 85 was appropriate. As regards proceeding under section 116, he pointed out that he could only exercise his discretion if it could be established that there were special circumstances, and that it was necessary or expedient for the court to exercise its discretion. On the facts, those conditions were not met. Similarly, in *Buchanan v Milton* [1999] 2 FLR 844, the application was made under section 116 but the court did not consider that the facts met the criteria for the court to exercise its discretion. In *Borrows v HM Coroner for Preston* [2008] EWHC 1387 (QB) and *Connolly v MOD* [2011] CSOH 124, the application was made by seeking a judicial review. The decision to use the judicial review procedure is understandable because, in both cases, the applicant was seeking to challenge an administrative decision. However, in the former case, the issue was dealt with under section 116 and, in the latter case, the Scottish court applied English law.

It is submitted that applications in burial disputes should not be brought under rule 64.2 of the CPR as it is wholly inappropriate. This rule applies to claims for the court to determine any question arising in the administration of the estate of a deceased person or the execution of a trust and for an order concerning the administration of a deceased person's estate or the execution of a trust under the direction of the court. Applications relating to burial disputes are not proceedings relating to the administration of an estate or execution of a trust.

In relation to applications concerning both a child and an adult deceased, section 116 of the Senior Courts Act 1981 and the court's inherent jurisdiction under section 19(2)(b) provide the most obvious and frequently used basis for the court's jurisdiction. Section 116 provides:

> (1) If by reason of any special circumstances it appears to the High Court to be necessary or expedient to appoint as administrator some person other than the person who, but for this section, would in accordance

with probate rules have been entitled to the grant, the court may in its discretion appoint as administrator such person as it thinks expedient.
(2) Any grant of administration under this section may be limited in any way the court thinks fit.

This gives the court an absolute discretion. The applicant would need to establish that he/she is a fit and proper person to administer the estate or if it is a limited grant, to deal with the immediate issue which, in a burial dispute, would be to make arrangements for the mode and location of the funeral and disposal of the body. The applicant would have to satisfy the court that there are special circumstances which justify the court determining the issues in dispute and that it is necessary or expedient for the court to appoint an administrator and, where necessary, to give such directions as it thinks fit.

The application should be made by using the procedure under Part 8 of the CPR and the claim form. The statement in support should include:

(a) details of the deceased and any will, with a copy of the will exhibited;
(b) details of the person entitled to a grant under the will or in the case of intestacy those entitled in priority to a grant under rule 20 or rule 22 of the Non-Contentious Probate Rules 1987;
(c) reasons for the application;
(d) any other relevant facts;
(e) details of the proposed limitation, if a limited grant is applied for.

Chapter 9

Rectification

9.1 INTRODUCTION

Rectification of a document is an equitable remedy which empowers the court to give effect to the intention of a party or parties by correcting, omitting, modifying or amending a document. The court's power to rectify a will is, in the main, statutory and fairly recent. Before 1983, if a will did not record the testator's/testatrix's intention, the remedy was to challenge the will on lack of knowledge and approval so as to exclude the will from probate or if there was a genuine mistake, to correct the error through the process of construction and so as to interpret the words or to omit a mistake. The court's use of this remedy in cases relating to wills was very limited. The need was recognised for rectification as a remedy which was appropriate and should be available to give effect to the intention of a testator/testatrix where there had obviously been an error. It was introduced, amongst other provisions which applied to wills, in section 20 of the Administration of Justice Act 1982 and came into force on 1 January 1983.

The court's power to rectify a will does not mean that it has the power to rewrite a will. This remedy is available only when there is an issue on the construction or interpretation of the terms of the will which suggests that the will is ambiguous, uncertain, obscure or meaningless, or that the intentions of the testator/testatrix have been misunderstood. The rise in the use of information technology, the availability of standard precedents in electronic form and the facility to copy and paste clauses into a client's will means that this is the first option to be considered when an error is discovered in drafting, where there is a misunderstanding of the instructions of the testator/testatrix or where a mistake is made in the execution of a will. This occurred in *Marley v Rawlings & Anor* [2011] EWHC 161 (Ch) where, by mistake, a couple executed each other's wills and neither the solicitor nor the assistant who witnessed the attestation noticed the mistake at the time. It is, therefore, not surprising that when a mistake or error is discovered, legal advisers are under pressure to advise rectification as the obvious and first choice rather than a claim in negligence against the original solicitors.

Some of the issues of construction which may arise where clarification is required are considered in Chapter 2. While section 20 of the Administration of Justice Act 1982 provides the remedy, section 21 provides the means by which the court is able to ascertain the testator's/testatrix's intentions. Section 21 gives the court power to permit extrinsic evidence to be introduced and relied on to resolve the issues and to ascertain the intentions of the testator/testatrix. The statutory provisions and the basic principles are dealt with in this chapter.

9.2 SECTION 20 OF THE ADMINISTRATION OF JUSTICE ACT 1982

Section 20(1) of the Administration of Justice Act 1982 provides:

> (1) If a court is satisfied that a will is so expressed that it fails to carry out the testator's intentions, in consequence—
>
> (a) of a clerical error; or
> (b) of a failure to understand his instructions,
>
> it may order that the will shall be rectified so as to carry out his intentions.

A person's right to seek rectification of a will is limited to the two specific grounds and then only if it can be established that the will as read in its literal sense does not give effect to the testator's/testatrix's intentions. It will be appropriate to seek rectification where the testator/testatrix or the draftsman omitted or included something in error in the will or the draftsman has misunderstood the testator's/testatrix's instructions. The court's powers of rectification are also limited to carrying out such intentions. Further limitations are imposed by way of time limits within which a claim for rectification should be made, which provide protection from liability to the personal representative if he/she distributed any part of the estate after the end of the limitation period.

Section 20(2)–(4) of the Administration of Justice Act 1982 provides that:

> (2) An application for an order under this section shall not, except with the permission of the court, be made after the end of the period of six months from the date on which representation with respect to the estate of the deceased is first taken out.
>
> (3) The provisions of this section shall not render the personal representatives of a deceased person liable for having distributed any part of the estate of the deceased, after the end of the period of six months from the date on which representation with respect to the estate of the deceased is first taken out, on the ground that they ought

to have taken into account the possibility that the court might permit the making of an application for an order under this section after the end of that period; but this subsection shall not prejudice any power to recover, by reason of the making of an order under this section, any part of the estate so distributed.

(4) In considering for the purposes of this section when representation with respect to the estate of a deceased person was first taken out, a grant limited to settled land or to trust property shall be left out of account, and a grant limited to real estate or to personal estate shall be left out of account unless a grant limited to the remainder of the estate has previously been made or is made at the same time.

9.3 CLERICAL ERROR

What is meant by a 'clerical error' is not defined in the Administration of Justice Act 1982, but a study of case law provides a useful guide. Of the earlier cases, much referred to are *Wordingham v Royal Exchange Trust Co* [1992] 1 Ch 412 and *Re Segelman Deceased* [1996] Ch 171.

Re Segelman Deceased [1996] Ch 171 provides the guidelines which the court now applies and which are likely to be the most helpful in preparing a case for rectification. In this case, Chadwick J set out three questions which a court needs to ask when rectification is being sought to remedy the terms of a will, to determine whether the application is within the requirements of section 20(1) of the Administration of Justice Act 1982:

> The subsection requires the court to examine three questions. First, what were the testator's intentions with regard to the dispositions in respect of which rectification is sought. Secondly, whether the will is so expressed that it fails to carry out those intentions. Thirdly, whether the will is expressed as it is in consequence of either (a) a clerical error or (b) a failure on the part of someone to whom the testator has given instructions in connection with his will to understand those instructions. (*Re Segelman Deceased* [1996] Ch 171 at 186D)

This test has been approved by the Court of Appeal in a number of cases, for example *Bell v Georgiou* [2002] EWHC 1080 (Ch), *Pengelly v Pengelly* [2007] EWHC 3227 (Ch) and *Sprackling v Sprackling* [2008] EWHC 2696 (Ch).

In *Re Segelman Deceased* [1996] Ch 171, the testator's wish was to set up a trust for those members of his family who were in need. The draftsman, however, added a substitution clause but omitted the words 'leaving issue' from the substitution clause which had the effect that certain members of the family could not claim the benefit during the lifetime of their parents. This was contrary to the wishes and intention of the testator as set out in the testator's schedule of names, which included the words 'and issue' and made it unnecessary to add a substitution clause. Chadwick J was satisfied that the will as drafted did not represent the testator's intention, that the draftsman inadvertently made a mistake in failing to delete the substitution clause and that it was appropriate to rectify the will so as to delete the offending words. In applying section 20(1) of the Administration of Justice Act 1982 to the facts, Chadwick J said that the court's jurisdiction:

> extends to cases where the relevant provision in the will, by reason of which the will is so expressed that it fails to carry out the testator's intentions, has been introduced, or as in the present case, has not been deleted in circumstances in which the draftsman has not applied his mind to its significance or effect. (*Re Segelman Deceased* [1996] Ch 171 at 186D)

Clearly, therefore, 'clerical error' includes where the draftsman has not applied his/her mind to the significance and effect of the clause he/she is inserting in the will in relation to the instructions given and the wishes expressed by the testator/testatrix.

In *Wordingham v Royal Exchange Trust Co* [1992] 1 Ch 412, the mistake made by the draftsman was an omission when updating a will using a new precedent. He inadvertently omitted a clause containing the exercise of a power of appointment, which appeared in two previous wills. When considering whether the mistake came within section 20(1) of the Administration of Justice Act 1982, Edward Evans-Lombe QC said that a 'clerical error' means an inadvertent error made in the process of recording the intended words as part of the drafting or transcription of the will. It can include a failure by the draftsman to follow the testator's/testatrix's instructions. It could, therefore, also be said to occur where the draftsman has failed to apply his/her mind to the words used when drafting to ensure that it reflects the intentions of the testator/testatrix. Similarly, in *Pengelly v Pengelly* [2007] EWHC 3227 (Ch), the court held that:

> where a word or words has or have been mistakenly omitted, different considerations may arise, and there may well be a greater potential for characterising the error as one of a clerical nature rather than the section 20(1)(b) situation of a failure to understand the testator's instructions ... If words have been mistakenly omitted, and the rectification sought is the insertion of a word or words, it may be possible more readily to bring oneself within the case of clerical error. The reason for that is that one is more readily able to find a clerical error where something has been omitted than where it has been inserted. (*Pengelly v Pengelly* [2007] EWHC 3227 (Ch) at [23])

(See also *Chittock v Stevens* [2000] WTLR 643, where the application was made on the basis of an omission.)

In *Price v Craig* [2006] WTLR 1873, the error was caused as a result of the variations in the instructions given by the testator. In that case, between March 2003, when the testator first gave instructions, and February 2004, during which a draft will was prepared and submitted by the solicitor for approval, the testator's original instructions concerning the disposal of the residuary estate were varied on two occasions. Subsequently, an executor on the testator's authority confirmed the testator's instructions but with one variation. He now wished the legacies to the charities to be provided from the proceeds of the matrimonial home and that 'the balance of the moneys remaining from the property realisation whether it is just my 50% share or includes Dora's 50% share as well should be divided equally amongst the following named people ...'. The named persons were the testator's children. The will, however, provided that the testator's wife was to have an interest in the income of the testator's half share of the home, which meant that the charities' legacies would only be payable on the widow's death. The draftsman when preparing the will substituted 'property fund' for 'trust fund' (which was the term used in the first draft of the will), which led to the situation where the residue of the estate not comprised in the *property fund* was not disposed of. The children who were intended to benefit sought rectification of the will. Applying the decision in *Re Segelman Deceased* [1996] Ch 171, Michael Furness QC (sitting as a deputy High Court Judge) explained that the jurisdiction under section 20(1) of the Administration of Justice Act 1982 was not limited to errors in transcribing, but extended to a situation where the person drafting the will did not appreciate the significance or effect of the introduction or deletion of a particular provision. In including the words, the draftsman did not apply his mind to the effect it would have of defeating the testator's intentions. This was clearly a clerical error rather than a misunderstanding of the deceased's intentions and wishes.

In *Clarke v Brothwood* [2006] EWHC 2939 (Ch), all sides recognised that there was a drafting error and that the will as drafted did not represent the intentions of the testatrix. The dispute between the parties was whether it was an appropriate case for rectification. On a literal construction of clause 5 of the will, 60% of the residuary estate was undisposed of and that clearly was not the intention of the testatrix. It was argued that the will should be rectified in such manner that the estate was divided not in fractional shares (which accounted for only 40% of residue) but in percentage shares which would thus account for 100% of the residue. There was clearly a mathematical error made by the testatrix in giving her instructions based on calculating the fractions of the estate to be distributed to the beneficiaries. Applying *Re Segelman Deceased* [1996] Ch 171, it was held that even if the error has been made by the deceased, the jurisdiction is open to rectify the will provided the person taking instructions and the person who drafted the will did not apply their minds to the effect of the will as drafted. On the facts, it was held that it was inconceivable that if the draftsman applied his mind to the problem rather than simply recording the fractions, he would not have appreciated that 60% of the residuary estate was undisposed of.

Thus the 'clerical error' also applies to mathematical errors.

In *Austin v Woodward & Anor* [2011] EWHC 2485 (Ch), the effect of blindly using updated precedents when drafting a new will for the testatrix in place of an earlier clause in a will made in 1993, led to an absolute bequest in favour of the testatrix's daughter in the will made in 1993 being drafted so as to pass the property into the residue, giving the daughter a life interest with the remainder to the testatrix's grandchildren. Evidence which was not challenged indicated that the testatrix did not intend to change that disposition and clearly showed that she intended the disposition made in the earlier will to remain unaltered. On the evidence, Daniel Alexander QC, sitting as a deputy High Court Judge, held that it was appropriate to grant the remedy of rectification because there had clearly been a clerical error in that, in using a new precedent clause, a provision in the will had been introduced without the draftsman applying his mind to its significance and effect on the disposition as a whole.

An attempt to seek rectification in *Marley v Rawlings & Anor* [2011] EWHC 161 (Ch), a case where a husband signed his wife's will and the wife her husband's, failed both at first instance and on appeal to the Court of Appeal. At first instance, Proudman J held that the will signed by the testator failed to give effect to the will as he signed the wrong document and did not intend by his signature to give effect to the will as required by section 9(b) of the Wills Act 1837. This rendered the whole document invalid and therefore section 20 of the Administration of Justice Act 1982 was inapplicable. Proudman J also said that 'clerical error' did not extend to cases where the wrong document is signed, as section 20 was limited to drafting errors and not where the requirements of the Wills Act 1837 have not been complied with, even if the document signed is in identical terms to the one which he should have signed. In dealing with the issue of section 20, the judge stated:

> whilst as explained in *Segelman*, the definition of clerical error bears a wide meaning, the error cannot in my view extend to something beyond the wording of the will which is sought to be rectified. I note that in s.20 there is a requirement that the court be 'satisfied that a will is so expressed' that it fails to carry out the testator's intentions. There was no error of drafting in this case, whether by inclusion or by omission or by miscasting words. The wills were both correctly expressed; the error was simply that the wrong will was tendered for signature. What if, instead of what actually happened, the solicitor had pulled a will prepared for a totally unconnected testator out of his briefcase and that one had been signed by mistake? It flies in the face of common sense to say that the court would have jurisdiction to rewrite the will in that situation, but there can be no ground of distinction in principle.

In my judgment therefore, s 20 does not provide a solution for the problem which has arisen. (*Marley v Rawlings & Anor* [2011] EWHC 161 (Ch) at [29]–[30])

On appeal to the Court of Appeal (*Marley v Rawlings & Anor* [2012] EWCA Civ 61), the court held that the will was not valid as the formalities in section 9 of the Wills Act 1837 were not complied with and that, when the testator signed the will, he intended to give effect to a will but not the one he signed. It was not:

> in the same class as a will, which is the will of the testator but contains errors which can be corrected by construction, omission or rectification. If the difference between them is a question of degree, then there is ample clear water between the two situations to justify why this one falls on the wrong side of the line and he other does not ... (*Marley v Rawlings & Anor* [2012] EWCA Civ 61 at [56])

In no way could it be said that the testator was 'authenticating the contents of the will in front of him by his signature because they were not the testamentary provisions he intended to make, he was, furthermore, in no position to execute that will because it was simply not his will'.

However, Sir John Thomas, President of the Queen's Bench Division (as he then was), stated that the power under section 20 of the Administration of Justice Act 1982 to rectify can be exercised if the document before the court is the will of the testator. If the will did not meet the requirement of section 9(b) of the Wills Act 1837, the question of rectification does not arise. But he went on to observe 'that there are powerful arguments for the section to be given a wide and generous scope'. He also stated that Parliament made very limited changes to the law in 1982 and that 'it would not be right for a court to go beyond what Parliament then decided'. On further appeal to the Supreme Court (*Marley v Rawlings & Anor* [2014] UKSC 2), it has now been held that the circumstances which arose in this case came within the scope of a 'clerical error' and, therefore, the will should be rectified. A full discussion of the reasons given by the court is set out in Chapter 3, para 3.5. The liberal and wider approach is adopted by courts in the Commonwealth and on which the appellant had relied.

In summary, therefore, a clerical error includes:

- an omission;
- inadvertent inclusion of words;
- errors in transcribing and failure by the draftsman to appreciate the effect of the words used;
- drafting and mathematical errors;
- blind use of precedents without consideration of the impact on the testator's/testatrix's instructions.

The ground of clerical error does not apply where the draftsman has misunderstood the testator's/testatrix's instructions (but see para 9.4).

9.3.1 Errors made in a DIY will

In view of the increase in DIY wills and wills drafted by those who put themselves out as will-makers, the question arises whether the ground of 'clerical error' is available if a testator/testatrix has made the error in expressing his/her intentions or assessing the value of the estate when making a home-made will. In *Re Williams (decd), Wiles v Madgin* [1985] 1 WLR 905, Nicholls J (as he then was) said:

> In passing, I note that there is no claim for rectification in the present case. It was suggested in the course of argument that s 20 could not apply to a home-made will such as the one before me, because 'clerical error' in s 20(1)(a) suggests a clerk. I do not accept this. A testator writing out or typing his own will can make a clerical error just as much as someone else writing out or typing a will for him. (*Re Williams (decd), Wiles v Madgin* [1985] 1 WLR 905 at 911–912)

Although this statement was *obiter*, it was nevertheless referred to and approved in *Wordingham v Royal Exchange Trust Co* [1992] 1 Ch 412, and in *Re Segelman Deceased* [1996] Ch 171, in which Chadwick J, when reaching his decision, applied that of Nicholls J when he said:

> In my view, the jurisdiction conferred by s 20(1), through para (a), extends to cases where the relevant provision in the will – by reason of which the will is so expressed that it fails to carry out the testator's intentions – has been introduced (or, as in the present case, has not been deleted) in circumstances in which the draftsman has not applied his mind to its significance or effect. It is to this failure to apply thought that Latey J and the editor of Mortimer attach the phrase 'per incuriam'. (*Re Segelman Deceased* [1996] Ch 171 at 186D)

As Nicholls J pointed out in *Re Williams (decd), Wiles v Madgin* [1985] 1 WLR 905 at 911–912, a testator writing out his own will can make a clerical error just as much as someone else writing out a will for him.

This was also relied on in *Clarke v Brothwood* [2006] EWHC 2939 (Ch) by Judge Behrens in reaching his conclusion:

> I am not sorry to reach this conclusion. Mr Sartin's construction would lead to a bizarre construction of the Act. It would mean that if Miss Martin made a mistake in typing the will there could be rectification; if Mr Clarke made a mistake in recording the instructions there could be rectification, but that if Miss Martin made a mistake and that mistake was faithfully typed out by Mr Clarke (without thinking about it) there could be no rectification. It is difficult to see why

Parliament should have intended such a consequence. (*Clarke v Brothwood* [2006] EWHC 2939 (Ch) at [43])

9.4 FAILURE TO UNDERSTAND THE TESTATOR'S/ TESTATRIX'S INSTRUCTIONS

Pursuant to section 20(1)(b) of the Administration of Justice Act 1982, the court has power to rectify a will where the draftsman has failed to understand the testator's/testatrix's instructions but this is likely to be limited. The few reported cases indicate that it will apply where the draftsman has failed to understand the testator's/testatrix's *intentions*. The cases of *Goodman v Goodman* [2006] EWHC 1757 (Ch) and *Sprackling v Sprackling* [2008] EWHC 2696 (Ch) best illustrate how this provision is interpreted by the court.

In *Goodman v Goodman* [2006] EWHC 1757 (Ch), the testator and his wife agreed to purchase the property of the testator's father for £390,000. It was agreed that they would redeem the mortgage and discharge the loan charged on the property and also pay monthly instalments of £3,000, which would continue even after the whole of the balance of the purchase price was discharged. The father agreed to pay monthly rent of £1,000 in respect of his occupation of the property which he held under an assured shorthold tenancy. When the couple instructed solicitors to prepare their wills, their arrangements with the father were clearly explained to the solicitors with a view of both acknowledging and recording the agreement. The draftsman, however, inserted a clause in the will, 'I give an allowance of £2,000 per month to Geoffrey Goodman until such time as he ceases to reside at the property known as 44 Denman Drive South London NW11 6RH'. On the testator's death, his widow applied for rectification of the will on the ground that the testator had never intended to create a lifetime legacy to his father. On the evidence, the court found that the solicitor failed to understand that the testator's intention was simply to record the agreement between the couple and the father rather than create a legacy.

In *Sprackling v Sprackling* [2008] EWHC 2696 (Ch), the dispute concerned the disposition of two properties made in clauses 3 and 4 of the will. Clause 3.3 of the will provided the following specific legacy, 'Provided my lovely wife Felicity survives me by 28 days to Felicity my property known as Sandilands Farm, Rogate aforesaid to include the fishing lake with access to the car park'. Clause 4 provided, 'In the event that my brother Arnold Sprackling has predeceased me I give absolutely but subject to any tax my property known as Nyewood Farm ... to Simon'. With regard to the disposition of 'Sandilands Farm', the issue was whether the deceased intended to make a bequest of the whole farm or merely the Farmhouse. The solicitor who previously took detailed instructions from the deceased and advised him was on holiday when the deceased, prior to undergoing major surgery, wished to clarify the provisions he made earlier. The solicitor, Ms K, who attended on him took his further instructions but passed on the drafting of the will to her assistant, H. There was extensive evidence on the deceased's intentions. Norris J found Ms K to be an unsatisfactory witness and the explanations she offered on her attendance note and the crucial instructions unconvincing. After assessing the evidence at length, Norris J concluded:

> 67. I am satisfied that the Deceased was unaware that there was any difference between (a) his intentions as recorded in the draft Will and the instructions as given and recorded in the attendance note that he had; and (b) the terms of the document he was signing. He did not change his mind. He overlooked a mistake in the Will – a mistake that had arisen from Victoria Kenny and Helen Gagan's failure to understand his instructions.
>
> 68. I am equally satisfied that (no doubt partly because of his own error in recording his true intentions in relation to Nyewood) he did not appreciate that Victoria Kenny had misunderstood the position in relation to Nyewood. Nobody drew to his attention his existing statement of wishes under the holding will and sought his confirmation that he wished to alter the contingency on which Simon inherited Nyewood to the exact opposite of what it currently was. Suffering from a brain tumour and on the threshold of potentially fatal or disabling surgery he may be forgiven for not noticing Ms Kenny's confusion of Thorney Island and Nyewood in the attendance note. He did not change his mind. He overlooked a mistake in the Will – a mistake that arose [from] Victoria Kenny and Helen Gagan's failure to understand his instructions. (*Sprackling v Sprackling* [2008] EWHC 2696 (Ch) at [67]–[68])

9.4.1 Situations to which section 20(1)(b) of the Administration of Justice Act 1982 does not apply

Section 20(1)(b) of the Administration of Justice Act 1982, however, does not apply where the draftsman has understood the testator's instructions but fails to understand the legal effect of the words used in the will (see Francis Barlow et al. (eds), *Williams on Wills* (LexisNexis Butterworths, 10th edn, 2014)). In such a case, the disappointed beneficiary's claim lies in professional negligence against the solicitor. A claim for rectification under section 20(1)(b) may now, however, be made where in error the wrong will is given by the solicitor for execution by the testator who also does not notice the error. The circumstances in which the error arose may be relevant (see *Marley v Rawlings & Anor* [2014] UKSC 2 (see paras 3.5 and 9.3)).

Section 20(1)(b) of the Administration of Justice Act 1982 also cannot be relied on to speculate on the testator's/testatrix's intention. In *Bell v Georgiou* [2002] EWHC 1080 (Ch) and approved by the Court of Appeal ([2002] EWCA Civ

1510), B claimed that the will as drawn did not deal with the amount of the deceased's estate equal to the nil band. By her will, the deceased gave B a legacy of £150,000, the remainder of her estate on certain trusts and the residue to the RAF Benevolent Fund. B contended that on the basis of the deceased's handwritten notes, it was clear that she intended to give him a further legacy of £223,000, a sum equal to the nil band, or that she intended to give the RAF Benevolent Fund only £11,000, resulting in a partial intestacy. B's claim was rejected both at first instance and on appeal. This was clearly a case where the beneficiary believed that the deceased should have provided him with a bequest equivalent to the nil band and he sought construction of the will to give effect to this belief, relying on notes prepared by the deceased. But it is a clear illustration of the principle that the court has no power to rewrite the deceased's will and that the relief of rectification can only be sought within the limitations set out in the statute.

The provision in section 20(1)(b) of the Administration of Justice Act 1982, by referring to a will being expressed so 'that it fails to carry out the testator's intentions, in consequence of a failure to understand the testator's instructions' clearly envisages the drawing up of a will by a person other than the testator (a third party). It will, therefore, not apply where the will was made by the testator personally.

9.5 LIMITATION PERIOD

Section 20(2) of the Administration of Justice Act 1982 provides that an application for an order for rectification under the section:

> shall not, except with the permission of the court, be made after the end of the period of six months from the date on which representation with respect to the estate of the deceased is first taken out.

As in the case of claims under the I(PFD)A 1975 (see Chapter 13), time begins to run from the grant of representation. The court does, however, have power to permit a claim to be made out of time but the criteria on which permission is granted are not set out. Since this provision is identical to that in section 4 of the I(PFD)A 1975, case law on an application made to bring a claim out of time under section 4 will be relevant to a claim for rectification where the claim is out of time. This issue was considered by David Donaldson QC in *Chittock v Stevens* [2000] WTLR 643. In that case, a widow thought that she was to receive the bulk of her husband's estate by survivorship, but did not discover that this was not the case until the 6-month time limit elapsed. She applied for leave to apply out of time to rectify the will, saying that the revocation of the necessary provision was an error. The judge held that the application should be decided on similar principles to applications for an extension of time under the I(PFD)A 1975, and applied the guidelines set out by Megarry VC in the leading case of *Re Salmon (Deceased), Coard v National Westminster Bank* [1981] Ch 167. These are:

(a) The discretion is unfettered and one that is exercised judicially in accordance with what is just and proper.

(b) The onus lies on the applicant to establish sufficient grounds for taking the case out of the general rule and depriving those who are protected by it of its benefits. Furthermore, the time limit prescribed is a substantive provision laid down in the Act itself, and is not merely a procedural time limit imposed by rules of court which may be treated with indulgence appropriate to procedural rules. The burden on the applicant is not a triviality. The applicant must make out a substantial case for its being just and proper for the court to exercise its statutory discretion to extend the time.

(c) The court must consider how promptly and in what circumstances the applicant is seeking an extension of time. The whole of the circumstances must be looked at, including the reason for the delay and how promptly the applicant gave a warning to the defendant of the proposed application.

(d) It is material whether or not negotiations were commenced within the time limit; if they were and time has run out while they are proceeding, this is likely to encourage the court to extend the time. Negotiations commenced after the time limit has expired might also aid the applicant, at any rate, if the defendants have not taken the point that time has expired.

(e) Of relevance will be the issue of whether or not the estate was distributed before the claim was notified.

(f) It will be relevant whether refusal to extend the time would leave the applicant without redress against anybody.

In *Chittock v Stevens* [2000] WTLR 643, the failure to proceed arose from a fundamental mistake as to the value of the estate. The beneficiaries operated under the same misapprehension and did not, therefore, act to their detriment because of the delay. It was thus held to be proper and just in all the circumstances to grant permission to apply for rectification out of time. See also *Price v Craig* [2006] WTLR 1873 and *Pengelly v Pengelly* [2007] EWHC 3227 (Ch), where the court ordered rectification out of time on the basis that the estate was not distributed and, therefore, to make an order would not be prejudicial to any person.

It should be noted, however, that section 20(3) of the Administration of Justice Act 1982 absolves the personal representatives from liability for distribution made of any part of the estate after the 6-month period, on the ground that they ought to have taken into account the possibility that the court might permit the making of an application for an order under this section after the end of that period. However, this does not prejudice any power to recover, by reason of the making of an order under this section, any part of the estate so distributed. The court is thus empowered to make a recovery order of any assets that may have been distributed. Personal representatives are thus entitled to seek recovery of assets so distributed.

9.6 BURDEN AND STANDARD OF PROOF

The onus is on the claimant to prove that the case falls within the ambit of section 20 of the Administration of Justice Act 1982. The standard of proof is the ordinary civil standard of balance of probabilities that the will fails to give effect to the deceased's intention. However, in view of the fact that the challenge is made of the intention expressed in the will, the court will require convincing evidence that the document does not in fact set out what the deceased intended (see Chapter 2). Cases cited in paras 9.1–9.5 indicate that the evidence adduced to establish the case for rectification includes notes written up by the deceased before the instructions are given (see *Bell v Georgiou* [2002] EWHC 1080 (Ch) and *Sprackling v Sprackling* [2008] EWHC 2696 (Ch)); evidence from the lawyers and disclosure of attendance notes and papers from the client's file (see *Sprackling v Sprackling*); evidence from accountants and financial advisers where appropriate; evidence of family members; comparisons of previous wills executed by the deceased and the circumstances in which the wills were made.

9.7 PROCEDURE

An application for rectification may be commenced in either the Family Division or the Chancery Division of the High Court, depending on whether or not the application is opposed.

9.7.1 Unopposed applications where there is no other claim

9.7.1.1 Venue

If the application is unopposed and there is no other probate claim intended, the application may be made in a probate registry under rule 55 of the

Non-Contentious Probate Rules 1987. The application for rectification of a will under section 20(1) of the Administration of Justice Act 1982 may be made to a district judge (rule 55(1)).

9.7.1.2 Form

The application must be supported by an affidavit/statement setting out the grounds of the application together with such evidence as can be adduced as to the testator's/ testatrix's intentions, and as to whichever of the following matters are in issue:

(a) in what respects the testator's/testatrix's intentions were not understood; or

(b) the nature of the alleged clerical error (rule 55(2) of the Non-Contentious Probate Rules 1987).

The affidavit should be made by someone who had knowledge of the facts relating to the instructions given by the deceased or by someone who has been involved in taking instructions and drafting the will. It must also not only set out which of the two grounds is relied on but also give details of how the error occurred, what the deceased's intentions were and the basis on which it is suggested that the will does not correctly record those intentions. The affidavit/statement should exhibit the will and a copy of the proposed draft of the will in its rectified form.

9.7.1.3 Service of the application

Unless otherwise directed, notice of the application should be given to every person having an interest under the will, whose interest might be prejudiced, or such other person who might be prejudiced, by the rectification applied for, and any comments in writing by such person should be exhibited to the affidavit/statement in support of the application.

9.7.1.4 Criteria for making the order

Unless any direction to the contrary has been given, before making the order for rectification the district judge must be satisfied that notice has been given to every person having an interest under the will whose interest might be prejudiced or such other person who might be prejudiced by the rectification and that the application is unopposed (rule 55(4) of the Non-Contentious Probate Rules 1987). Note that it is not necessary for any interested party to have given formal consent. It is sufficient if, having been given notice, no response is made opposing the application.

9.7.2 Procedure for opposed application

The procedure for a contested application for rectification is governed by Part 57 and PD 57, paragraphs 9–11 of the CPR.

9.7.2.1 Venue

An application for rectification which is opposed must be made in the Chancery Division of the High Court.

Probate claims in the county court must only be brought in:

    (a)   a county court where there is also a Chancery District Registry; or
    (b)   the Central London County Court.

9.7.2.2 Form

The application must be made using the procedure under Part 7 of the CPR. This is because the application is based on facts which are likely to be disputed (rule 57.3). The claim form must contain a statement of the nature of the claimant's and the defendant's interest in the estate, and set out the grounds on which the order for rectification is sought (rule 57.7). If the claimant is the person to whom the grant was made in respect of the will of which rectification is sought, unless the court orders otherwise, the grant of probate or letters of administration with the will annexed must be lodged with the court when the claim form is issued (rule 57.5(2)(a)). If a defendant has the probate or letters of administration in his/her possession or under his/her control, he/she must, unless the court orders otherwise, lodge it with the court within 14 days after service of the claim form on him/her (PD 57, paragraph 10.1).

9.7.2.3 Service

The claim form should be served on the personal representatives and any other person who has an interest under the will and who might be prejudiced by the rectification.

9.7.2.4 Defendant's response

The defendant who is served with the claim form must file his/her acknowledgement of service within 28 days of service of the particulars of claim if the particulars of claim are not served with the claim form and in any other case within 28 days after service of the claim form. If service is effected outside the jurisdiction under rule 6.32 or rule 6.33 of the CPR, this period is extended by 14 days from that which is specified in rule 6.35 or PD 6B. If an acknowledgment of service is filed, a defence must be filed within 28 days of service of the particulars of claim unless extended by agreement, in which case the court should be notified in writing of the agreement and of the extended time limit (see rules 15.4 and 15.5).

9.7.2.5 Orders

A copy of the order(s) made for the rectification of a will must be sent to the Principal Registry of the Family Division for filing, and a memorandum of the order must be endorsed on, or permanently annexed to, the grant under which the estate is administered (PD 57, paragraph 11 of the CPR). The effect of an order for rectification is that it will be read as if the will was executed in accordance with the will as rectified.

9.8 SUMMARY

- Rectification is a statutory remedy and is limited to the two grounds set out in section 20 of the Administration of Justice Act 1982.
- It is a discretionary remedy.
- The application must be made promptly and in any event within 6 months of the grant of representation. If made outside this period, the relevant criteria to bring a claim outside this period are those set out in *Re Salmon (Deceased), Coard v National Westminster Bank* [1981] Ch 167 and, in any event, it will be necessary to set out the reasons for the delay and that it would be proper and just in all the circumstances to extend the time limit.
- The burden of proof is on the person who seeks rectification.
- The standard of proof is the civil standard of proof, but the court will require convincing evidence that the will as drafted and executed does not accord with the deceased's intention. It is generally considered that the court's powers are too narrow and should be widened. This is one of the issues which the Law Commission will be reviewing in its project on the law of wills.
- The Law Commission's *Twelfth Programme of Law Reform*, Law Com No 354, includes a review of the law of wills. Within this review, one of the main focus points will be to consider widening the court's powers, and in particular to grant the court dispensing power to pass invalid wills to probate in order to give effect to a clear evidence-based intention to pass property that is contained in an invalid will.

Chapter 10

Revocation of a Will

10.1　INTRODUCTION

Grounds for challenging the will of a testator/testatrix are discussed in the previous chapters, based on whether the statutory formalities of making and executing a valid will were complied with when the will was made, interpretation of the testator's/testatrix's intention and the circumstances which may have affected and/or influenced the state of his/her mind. This chapter considers alleged circumstances which relate to the actions taken by the testator/testatrix himself/herself which may have the effect of revoking any will he/she has executed because a will is revocable at any time during his/her lifetime.

The circumstances in which a will may be revoked are set out in sections 18–22 of the Wills Act 1837. These include:

(a) By marriage or the formation of a civil partnership of the testator/testatrix after the will was executed.
(b) By the annulment or dissolution of the testator's/testatrix's marriage or civil partnership.
(c) By revocation and execution of a subsequent will.
(d) By destruction of a validly executed will. This includes a situation where, although a will is known or alleged to have been executed, it is not found, and cases where the will is found but it is defaced with indications that it was intended to be destroyed.

A will may also be revoked if it provides for a conditional revocation of a will on the happening of an event and the condition is satisfied.

10.2　REVOCATION BY MARRIAGE

With certain exceptions, section 18 of the Wills Act 1837 as substituted by the Administration of Justice Act 1982 provides that a will be revoked by the marriage of the testator/testatrix. This section applies to all wills executed after 1 January 1983. Wills made before 1 January 1983 continue to be governed by section 18 in its original form and section 177 of the Law of Property Act 1925. Section 18 applies to voidable marriages even if that marriage is subsequently annulled.

Section 18(3) and (4) of the Wills Act 1837 sets out two circumstances when a will is not revoked by the subsequent marriage of the testator/testatrix. These circumstances are as follows:

(1) Where it appears from a will that at the time it was made the testator/testatrix was expecting to be married to a particular person and that he/she intended that the will should not be revoked by the marriage, the will shall not be revoked by his/her marriage to that person (section 18(3)).

(2) Where it appears from a will that at the time it was made the testator/testatrix was expecting to be married to a particular person and that he/she intended that a disposition in the will should not be revoked by his/her marriage to that person:

 (a) that disposition shall take effect notwithstanding the marriage; and

 (b) any other disposition in the will shall take effect also, unless it appears from the will that the testator/testatrix intended the disposition to be revoked by the marriage (section 18(4)).

In order for these provisions to apply, two conditions must be satisfied. First, it must be evident from the content of the will that the testator/testatrix contemplated marriage to a 'particular person'. In the event that the testator/testatrix marries a person other than the person referred to in the will, the will would be revoked. Secondly, that the testator/testatrix 'intended' that the disposition in the will should not be revoked by the subsequent marriage. The subsequent marriage, however, will not defeat an exercise by the will of a power of appointment, unless the property would, in default of the exercise of the power, pass to the testator's/testatrix's personal representatives (section 18(2)).

10.3 REVOCATION BY MARRIAGE BETWEEN SAME SEX COUPLES

Pursuant to section 11 of, and Schedules 3 and 4 to, the Marriage (Same Sex Couples) Act 2013 (which received Royal Assent on 18 July 2013), the above provisions will apply to a testator/testatrix who enters into a same sex marriage. Section 11 provides:

> (1) In the law of England and Wales, marriage has the same effect in relation to same sex couples as it has in relation to opposite sex couples.
> (2) The law of England and Wales (including all England and Wales legislation whenever passed or made) has effect in accordance with subsection (1).
> (3) Schedule 3 (interpretation of legislation) has effect.
> (4) Schedule 4 (effect of extension of marriage: further provision) has effect.
> (5) For provision about limitations on the effects of subsections (1) and (2) and Schedule 3, see Part 7 of Schedule 4.
> (6) Subsections (1) and (2) and Schedule 3 do not have any effect in relation to—
>
>> (a) Measures and Canons of the Church of England (whenever passed or made),
>> (b) subordinate legislation (whenever made) made under a Measure or Canon of the Church of England, or
>> (c) other ecclesiastical law (whether or not contained in England and Wales legislation, and, if contained in England and Wales legislation, whenever passed or made).
>
> (7) In Schedules 3 and 4—
>
> "existing England and Wales legislation" means—
>
>> (a) in the case of England and Wales legislation that is primary legislation, legislation passed before the end of the Session in which this Act is passed (excluding this Act), or
>> (b) in the case of England and Wales legislation that is subordinate legislation, legislation made on or before the day on which this Act is passed (excluding legislation made under this Act);
>
> "new England and Wales legislation" means—
>
>> (a) in the case of England and Wales legislation that is primary legislation, legislation passed after the end of the Session in which this Act is passed, or
>> (b) in the case of England and Wales legislation that is subordinate legislation, legislation made after the day on which this Act is passed.

Schedule 3, Part 1, paragraph 1 of the Marriage (Same Sex Couples) Act 2013 provides:

(1) In existing England and Wales legislation—

   (a) a reference to marriage is to be read as including a reference to marriage of a same sex couple;

   …

However, it does not apply to a will made before the Marriage (Same Sex Couples) Act 2013 comes into force, as Schedule 4, Part 1, paragraph 1 provides:

(1) Section 11 does not alter the effect of any private legal instrument made before that section comes into force.
(2) In this paragraph "private legal instrument" includes—

   (a) a will,

   …

10.4 REVOCATION BY FORMATION OF CIVIL PARTNERSHIP

Pursuant to the amendments made to the Wills Act 1837 by Schedule 4 to the Civil Partnership Act 2004, similar provisions as those which apply to a marriage (see para 10.2) have been extended to a testator/testatrix who enters into a civil partnership after he/she has executed his/her will (section 18B of the Wills Act 1837).

Section 18B(3) of the Wills Act 1837 provides that if it appears from a will:

(a) that at the time it was made the testator/testatrix was expecting to form a civil partnership with a particular person, and
(b) that he/she intended that the will should not be revoked by the formation of the civil partnership,

the will is not revoked by its formation.

Section 18B(4)–(6) of the Wills Act 1837 provides that if it appears from a will:

(a) that at the time it was made the testator/testatrix was expecting to form a civil partnership with a particular person, and
(b) that he/she intended that a disposition in the will should not be revoked by the formation of the civil partnership,

the disposition made will take effect despite the formation of the civil partnership, and any other disposition made in the will also takes effect unless it appears from the will that the testator/testatrix intended the disposition to be revoked by the formation of the partnership.

10.5 EFFECT OF CONVERSION OF CIVIL PARTNERSHIP TO SAME SEX MARRIAGE

Parties to a civil partnership wherever formed will be able if they so wish to convert their civil partnership to a marriage by following the procedure under regulations made under the Marriage (Same Sex Couples) Act 2013. Section 9 provides:

(1) The parties to an England and Wales civil partnership may convert their civil partnership into a marriage under a procedure established by regulations made by the Secretary of State.

(2) The parties to a civil partnership within subsection (3) may convert their civil partnership into a marriage under a procedure established by regulations made by the Secretary of State.

(3) A civil partnership is within this subsection if—

(a) it was formed outside the United Kingdom under an Order in Council made under Chapter 1 of Part 5 of the Civil Partnership Act 2004 (registration at British consulates etc or by armed forces personnel), and

(b) the part of the United Kingdom that was relevant for the purposes of section 210(2)(b) or (as the case may be) section 211(2)(b) of that Act was England and Wales.

Hence, if a testator/testatrix makes a will in contemplation of a civil partnership which is later formed and then converted into a marriage in accordance with the provisions in the Marriage (Same Sex Couples) Act 2013, the subsequent marriage will not have the effect of revoking the will by the subsequent conversion.

10.6 REVOCATION BY ANNULMENT OR DISSOLUTION OF THE TESTATOR'S/TESTATRIX'S MARRIAGE

Section 18A of the Wills Act 1837 as amended by the Law Reform (Succession) Act 1995 now provides that in respect of a testator/testatrix dying after 1 January 1996, if the testator's/testatrix's marriage is dissolved or annulled, any provision in his/her will which appoints his/her former spouse as executor or trustee, or which confers a power of appointment upon him/her, will take effect as if the former spouse died on the date on which the marriage was dissolved or annulled, unless the will shows a contrary intention. It also provides that any property which would, but for this section, have passed to the former spouse under the will, shall now pass as if the former spouse died on the date of the divorce or annulment unless the will shows a contrary intention.

This applies also to a marriage which is dissolved or annulled elsewhere than in a court of civil jurisdiction in England and Wales, if the dissolution or annulment is entitled to be recognised in England and Wales by virtue of Part II of the Family Law Act 1986.

Similarly, in view of the provisions contained in the Marriage (Same Sex Couples) Act 2013, an annulment or dissolution of a same sex marriage will have the same effect. Pursuant to the Marriage (Same Sex Couples) Act 2013 (Commencement No 2 and Transitional Provision) Order 2014 (SI 2014/93), some provisions came into force on 21 January 2014, the majority came into force on 13 March 2014, and the remaining provisions, i.e. sections 6, 13 and 17(4), and paragraph 21 of Schedule 7 came into force on 3 June 2014.

However, these provisions do not affect the right of the former spouse to apply for financial provision under the I(PFD)A 1975.

10.7 REVOCATION BY ANNULMENT OR DISSOLUTION OF THE TESTATOR'S/TESTATRIX'S CIVIL PARTNERSHIP

Schedule 4, Part 1, paragraph 2 to the Civil Partnership Act 2004 amends the Wills Act 1837 by inserting an additional section 18C to extend the provisions in relation to annulment and dissolution of marriage to the annulment and dissolution of civil partnerships. This will also apply if the testator's/testatrix's civil partnership is dissolved or annulled elsewhere than in England and Wales and the dissolution or annulment is entitled to recognition in England and Wales by virtue of Chapter 3, Part 5 of the Civil Partnership Act 2004 (section 18C(1)(b) of the Wills Act 1837).

As in the case of a marriage, the former partner's rights to apply for financial provision under the I(PFD)A 1975 are not affected (section 18C(3) of the Wills Act 1837 as amended by the Civil Partnership Act 2004).

10.8 REVOCATION AND EXECUTION OF A SUBSEQUENT WILL

A will may be revoked at any time by a testator/testatrix making another will, provided it is made clear that all earlier testamentary dispositions are revoked. Section 20 of the Wills Act 1837 provides:

> No will or codicil, or any part thereof, shall be revoked otherwise than as aforesaid, or by another will or codicil executed in manner herein-before required, or by some writing declaring an intention to revoke the same, and executed in the manner in which a will is herein-before required to be executed.

This section clearly provides for the revocation of a will by a subsequent will or codicil validly executed or by some other declaration in writing which complies with the procedure for the execution of a will. It would seem that no particular form of words is required, provided it is made clear that the testator/testatrix intends to revoke the previous will. If general words of revocation are used, this will have the effect of revoking all previous dispositions made, including appointments made in exercise of a power (*Lowthorpe-Lutwidge v Lowthorpe-Lutwidge* [1935] P 151).

It does not, however, follow that revocation of a will necessarily revokes any codicil to it. Much depends on the form of words used to revoke the will.

Where the testator makes a valid will and then subsequently makes another will without any words of revocation, the effect of the subsequent will on the earlier will depends on whether there are any inconsistencies between the two wills and the extent of those inconsistencies. If both wills are co-extensive, the second later will has the effect of revoking the earlier will. If not, both wills can be admitted to probate and it will be for the court to determine whether effect can be given to both (see *Townsend v Moore* [1905] P 66, CA). The testator's/testatrix's intentions will be collected from all the circumstances of the case. The court will consider the contents of the instruments in dispute in order to ascertain the intentions of the testator/testatrix, but by virtue of section 21 of the Administration of Justice Act 1982 the court is entitled to consider extrinsic evidence in ascertaining the testator's/testatrix's intentions.

Even where a second will indicates a revocation of a previous will, disputes may still arise on the issue of what the testator/testatrix intended, and in such cases the court may consider not only the contents of the wills in question but also other evidence to ascertain the testator's/testatrix's intention. However, where the revocation clause is clear in its terms, the burden of proving that the testator/testatrix did not intend to revoke an earlier will is on the party who seeks to override this clause. Disputes are more likely to arise where the testator/testatrix had connections with more than one country and properties in jurisdictions other than England and Wales. *Re Wayland* [1951] 2 All ER 1041 and *Lamothe v Lamothe* [2006] EWHC 1387 (Ch) are examples of cases which demonstrate the circumstances which can give rise to disputes where there are two wills.

In *Re Wayland* [1951] 2 All ER 1041, the testator had properties in England and Belgium. He made two wills. The first will was made in accordance with

Belgium law and dealt with property in Belgium. The second, later, will was made in England. It contained a revocation clause but also a clause which clearly stated that the testator intended to deal only with his estate in England. Both wills were admitted to probate, the court having determined that there was clear and unequivocal evidence to indicate that the testator intended the revocation clause to apply only to the dispositions of the testator's English estate and not his estate in Belgium.

In *Lamothe v Lamothe* [2006] EWHC 1387 (Ch), the court, having considered extrinsic evidence to ascertain the testatrix's intentions, took a different view. In that case, the testatrix, Catherine Lamothe, was born in Dominica and emigrated to England in the 1960s. She lived in England until her death on 13 December 1996. On 8 January 1993, she executed a will in England (the 1993 will) naming her son, Ronald Lamothe, and Albert Augustine, who was a friend of the family, as executors. On 18 February 1998, the executors obtained probate of that will. The testatrix, however, executed another will in Dominica on 30 May 1995 naming her son Ronald and Maria Wallace (another family friend) as executors (the 1995 will). That will was proved in Dominica on 28 July 1998. It contained a revocation clause revoking all former wills and it gave all the Dominican lands to her two children, Beverley and Ronald; divided her bank accounts equally between her two children and one of her grand-daughters; and divided the residue of all her real and personal property, whatsoever and wheresoever situated, equally between her two children. The will did not make any reference to a property at 89 Dunlace Road in England, so it fell into the residue. Beverley the testatrix's daughter was unaware of the existence of the 1995 will. Not having received any distribution of her mother's estate, she issued proceedings in 2001 for an account of the administration of the 1993 will and the removal of the executors. It was when accounts were submitted by Ronald that the existence of the 1995 will became known. As a result, the claimant Beverley issued proceedings for the revocation of the grant in relation to the 1993 will and to obtain a grant in relation to the 1995 will. She contended that in determining the issue, the court was only entitled to look at the two wills and to construe them. The application was opposed on the grounds that the 1995 will was intended only to affect the disposition of the estate in Dominica. In determining the dispute, the issue of the court's jurisdiction to consider extrinsic evidence of the testatrix's intention was raised.

Deputy Judge Roger Wyland having considered the earlier cases of *In the Goods of Oswald* (1874) LR 3 P & D 162, *O'Learly v Douglass* (1878) 1 LR IR 45, *In Resch's Will Trusts* [1969] 1 AC 514 and *Re Morris deceased* [1971] P 62, concluded:

it is clear that prior to the Administration of Justice Act 1982 it was open to the court, when considering which will or wills of a testator to admit to probate, to consider the intention of the testator and for that purpose to consider evidence outside the confines of the wills in question. There is nothing in the relevant provisions of the Administration of Justice Act 1982 which would indicate that this power was to be removed and replaced by the more limited powers to consider evidence given by that Act, nor was I referred to any case which gave such an indication. For those reasons I find that it is open to me, and indeed my duty in a case such as this, to consider all the evidence as to the surrounding circumstances of the drafting and execution of the 1995 Will to determine whether Mrs Lamothe intended thereby to revoke the 1993 Will. (*Lamothe v Lamothe* [2006] EWHC 1387 (Ch) at [32])

The judge, applying the decision in *Lowthorpe-Lutwidge v Lowthorpe-Lutwidge* [1935] P 151, also stated that the burden of proof lies on the party seeking to prevent an express clause of revocation from having the effect that would follow from the plain meaning of the words used, and that where the revocation clause is expressed in clear and unambiguous terms the burden of proof is a heavy one. The judge took into account the evidence of the lawyer who drafted the 1995 will that the effect of the revocation clause was explained to the testatrix and understood by her, and the evidence of the son that his mother was advised that the 1993 will would be revoked and that she thought about it and decided that was what she wanted to do. Taking into consideration all the circumstances and evidence, the judge found that far from being clear and unequivocal evidence that revocation was not intended, there was clear and unequivocal evidence that it was intended (at [52]).

However, if the evidence shows that the revocation clause was included in the will without the testator's knowledge and approval, it will be excluded and the court will then have to determine whether the two wills are co-extensive or they can be admitted to probate and to what extent they can stand together.

Section 19 of the Wills Act 1837 also provides that no will shall be revoked by any presumption of an intention on the ground of an alteration in circumstances.

10.8.1 Presumption of revocation

Where a will is last traced as having been in the testator's/testatrix's possession and cannot be found at his/her death, a presumption arises that the testator/testatrix has destroyed the will with the intention of revoking it. This presumption can be rebutted if there is clear evidence to show that the testator/testatrix did not intend to revoke the will or that he/she maintained his/her intention to dispose of his/her property in accordance with the will he/she was known to have made. Once the presumption arises, it is for the party who seeks to rebut it to establish that the testator/testatrix did not deliberately revoke the will by destroying it or that the will was in existence immediately before the testator's/testatrix's death. The cases of *Rowe v Clarke* [2005] EWHC 3068 (Ch) and *Re Zielinski, Korab-Karpinski v Lucas Gardiner* [2007] WTLR 1655 demonstrate the nature of the extrinsic evidence that will be admitted by the court to establish that revocation of the will was not intended by the testator/testatrix where the will cannot be found.

In *Rowe v Clarke* [2005] EWHC 3068 (Ch), the testator, Barrie Clarke, and Rowe lived together in Barrie's house for a number of years before Barrie's death in January 2005. Barrie made a will on 28 June 2000 in favour of Rowe. He then sent a copy of the will to Rowe's mother. On Barrie's death, his brother came to the house and removed a number of documents from the house and then obtained a grant of administration of Barrie's estate. It was suspected that the brother removed the will from the testator's house and destroyed it, but there was no direct evidence of this. The judge considered all the surrounding circumstances, including the fact that Barrie was not well organised in relation to keeping important documents secure; that he and Rowe continued to live together and that there was no evidence to suggest that his affection for Rowe waned; that his relationship with his brother was distant and that he previously took steps to disinherit him. On the facts, the judge found that the will was lost, pronounced in favour of the copy will in the possession of Rowe's mother and revoked the grant issued to the brother.

In *Re Zielinski, Korab-Karpinski v Lucas Gardiner* [2007] WTLR 1655, the evidence established that a will was validly executed. There was no evidence to suggest either that a later will was executed or that the testator destroyed the original will. The evidence produced, however, established against the presumption. This included evidence that the testatrix recently made a will; that she was sent a copy of the will; that she did not indicate that she changed her mind, nor was there any evidence to suggest a change of mind; and that in all legal matters she would have consulted and instructed solicitors.

In *Wren v Wren* [2006] EWHC 2243 (Ch), the claimant lived with his father until the father died. The defendants, who were the claimant's brother and sister, obtained letters of administration on the basis that the father died intestate. Subsequently, they obtained an order for possession against the claimant. In his claim, the claimant asserted that his father made a will on 9 September 1999 and that he found a copy of it concealed under a floorboard on about 25 March 2005. Under the will, stocks and shares were left to the brother and sister, and the residuary estate to the claimant. He also asserted that his father repeatedly promised to leave him the house. This was supported by evidence from friends and acquaintances to whom his father expressed this intention. The brother and sister alleged that the will was a forgery or, alternatively, they relied on the presumption that the will was revoked as the original could not be found. Evidence called from a handwriting expert was not conclusive. Rimer J found that the claimant's evidence was credible and that his evidence that his father promised to leave him the house was sufficient to rebut the presumption that the will was revoked. The grant of letters of administration was revoked and the copy will was admitted to probate.

It can be seen from the above cases that much will depend on the strength of the circumstantial evidence produced to show that the will was not revoked and that there were other reasons for the will not being found.

10.9 APPLICATION FOR THE ADMISSION TO PROOF OF A COPY WILL OR CODICIL WHERE ORIGINAL IS MISSING

Rule 54 of the Non-Contentious Probate Rules 1987 provides that an application for an order to admit to proof a will or codicil contained in a copy or some other reconstruction of it, for example a draft of it, should be made to a district judge supported by an affidavit setting out the grounds of the application and such other evidence on affidavit as the applicant can adduce:

        (i)   as to the will's existence after the death of the testator or, where there is no such evidence, the facts on which the applicant relies to rebut the presumption that the will has been revoked by destruction;

        (ii)   in respect of an oral will, as to the contents of that will;

        (iii) in respect of a reconstruction of a will, as to the accuracy of that reconstruction; and

  (b)   such further evidence as the court may require as to due execution of the will.

Where the original of a will is not available, the court may order that a copy of the will be proved if it is satisfied that exhaustive attempts have been made to obtain it and no person might be adversely affected by the failure to prove the original. If the person who is holding the original will is overseas and is refusing to deliver up the will, an application should be made as above. Where the person is in the UK a subpoena under rule 50 of the Non-Contentious Probate Rules 1987 should be issued for the will to be lodged in the court. If this proves unsuccessful, an application should be made to prove a copy.

10.10 REVOCATION BY DESTRUCTION

Section 20 of the Wills Act 1837 provides that a will is revoked by 'the burning, tearing or otherwise destroying the same by the testator or by some other person in his presence and by his direction, with the intention of revoking the same'.

Although short and drafted in plain language, this section gives rise to a number of issues which need to be considered carefully.

First, the section refers to two specific ways in which a will may be destroyed but also provides for the destruction to occur by other means which have the effect of destroying the will.

Secondly, it also provides for the destruction to be carried out not only by the testator/testatrix but also by a third party. However, where the destruction is carried out by a third party, the destruction will only have the effect of revoking the will if it is carried out: (a) in the presence of the testator/testatrix; and (b) at his/her direction. If the testator/testatrix is not present when the will is destroyed, the destruction will be ineffective to revoke the will even if the testator/testatrix has given instructions for its destruction. Nor will a subsequent ratification by the testator/testatrix of an unauthorised destruction result in the revocation of the will (*Gill v Gill* [1909] P 157).

Thirdly, two elements must be proved to establish that a will was revoked as a result of the testator/testatrix destroying the original will executed by him/her, namely, the physical and the mental element, that is the *actus reus* – the act of destruction – and the *mens rea* – the intention to revoke. Either one of these two elements by itself will not suffice. A will cannot be revoked simply by change of circumstances (see section 19 of the Wills Act 1837). There must be some evidence of the testator's/testatrix's intention to revoke the will. The evidence may suggest that the testator/testatrix by his/her actions destroyed his/her will but that he/she did not have the relevant intention. For example, where the revocation was in fact an act of inadvertence or a mistake, as occurred in *Re Phelan* [1971] 3 All ER 1256, or where the will was destroyed when the testator/testatrix was drunk, as in *In the Goods of Brassington* [1902] P 1. In *Re Phelan*, the testator used a printed will form to make a will, leaving a legacy and his residuary estate to his landlord and the landlord's wife. Subsequently, in the mistaken belief that he had to make separate wills in relation to his stocks and shares, he used three further printed will forms leaving certain block units of his stocks and shares in trust to his landlord and the landlord's wife but did not delete the standard revocation clause from any on the three wills he executed. There was no evidence to show which of these documents was the last to be signed. The beneficiaries sought to admit all four will to probate. Given the circumstances, the court permitted all four wills to be admitted to proof, omitting the revocation clauses from the last three wills which were all executed on the same day, on the basis that whereas the court could not remake the will 'it can omit words which have come in by inadvertence or by misunderstanding if their omission gives effect to the true intention of the testator'.

10.10.1 Partial destruction

The destruction need not be complete as long as the evidence establishes that what was destroyed formed the material part of the disposition, or the evidence establishes that the testator/testatrix could not have intended what remains to have effect. Writing on the will or defacing part of it will not have the effect of revoking the will unless what remains invalidates the will or does not adequately indicate the disposition which the testator/testatrix intended to make. The facts in *Re Adams (Deceased)* [1990] Ch 601 demonstrate how a partial defacing or intended destruction may invalidate a will. In that case, the testatrix made a will after obtaining legal advice. Her solicitors retained the original will. Subsequently, she instructed them to destroy the will. The solicitors returned the will to her for destruction as any destruction by them at her instructions but without her presence would not have been effective to revoke the will. On her death, the will was found but it was defaced with a ball point pen. In particular, the attestation clause and the signatures of the testatrix and the witnesses were so heavily obliterated that it was impossible to read them. The executors of the will, who were also the beneficiaries, sought to admit the will for probate. Their application was refused as the material part of the will was obliterated to such an extent that it could not be deciphered even by experts without physically interfering with the document. The court held that the will was revoked within the meaning of section 20 of the Administration of Justice Act 1982 as the attestation clause and the signatures which established its validity, and thus which formed a material part of the will, were destroyed.

There may, however, be instances of partial destruction which will result in only that part being revoked and the rest being upheld. In cases where only part of the will has been destroyed, revocation of the whole will may result if the destroyed part is sufficiently material so as to make it impossible to administer the remaining dispositions or make it impossible to salvage the will. The inference may be drawn unless the contrary is proved that the testator/testatrix intended only to revoke that part which was destroyed and not the whole. The facts in *Re Everest (Deceased)* [1975] Fam 44 serve as a good illustration of how the parts of the will which have not been destroyed may still remain effective. In that case, the testator having made a will altered some of the provisions in it. Two days later he died. When the widow found the will, the lower half of the first page was cut away. In the will, the testator gave certain chattels to his widow for life with directions that after her death they were to form part of his residuary estate. The rest of his estate and the residue of his personal estate he left on certain trusts. The trusts could not be identified as they were set out in the part that was cut away. In all other respects, the will was complete and validly executed. It was held that the mutilation was not such as to give rise to an inference that the testator intended to

revoke his will in its entirety. Although there was no evidence as to the nature of the trusts he intended to set up, the court found that there was sufficient remaining of the will to indicate that the testator intended that what remained of the will should remain effective. In those circumstances, the court ruled that it would be wrong to refuse to give effect to his wishes in so far as they were determinable.

Hence, before embarking on challenging the will on the ground of revocation by destruction, careful consideration should be given to the manner in which the destruction is alleged to have occurred, whether the act of destruction was complete and whether the intent to revoke can be established. Where only partial destruction of the will has occurred, the danger is that the court may hold only that part which has been destroyed as having been revoked and give effect to the remainder of the will in order to give effect to the wishes of the testator/testatrix.

10.11 CONDITIONAL REVOCATION

If a testator/testatrix revokes his/her will conditionally, the will remains in effect until the condition has been satisfied. Where, however, the condition relates to another will of the testator/testatrix and depends upon that will being valid, then if that will turns out to be invalid, the revocation will not be effective as it is dependent upon the validity of the subsequent will and the provisions contained in it. This type of conditional revocation is known as 'dependent relative revocation'. The doctrine applies where a testator/testatrix destroys a will in the mistaken belief that its revocation will have the effect of reviving an earlier will (*Powell v Powell* (1866) LR 1 P & D 209). Similarly, where a testator/testatrix destroys a will with the intention of making a new will, but does not in fact make a new will or makes an ineffective new will, provided there is clear evidence to establish that when he/she revoked the old will his/her intention was to revoke the old will only in order to make another will, i.e. that it was conditional upon the making of the new and effective new will, the old will remains effective (*Dixon v Treasury Solicitor* [1905] P 42).

10.12 PREPARATION AND EVIDENCE

Before a will is challenged on the ground that it was revoked on any of the bases referred to above, it is essential to ensure that all the facts initially relied on are scrutinised and investigated, as are all the surrounding circumstances including those of the testator/testatrix when the original and subsequent wills were made or, where it is alleged that a will was never made, cannot be found or has been defaced or destroyed, the circumstances which led to the loss of the will or its mutilation. In all cases, it is both the actions of the testator/testatrix in making a will or destroying the will and his/her intention at the relevant time which are crucial. The court's power to consider extrinsic evidence in order to determine the issues before it and, in particular, in ascertaining the intention of the testator/testatrix should not be underestimated.

Chapter 11

Lifetime Agreements and Gifts

11.1 INTRODUCTION

Family relationships, obligations and dependence may lead a person to enter into an agreement with a family member or a third party on the basis that he/she will ensure that on his/her death the third party will receive an interest in the estate or a specific property. These agreements take different forms but can be enforceable against the estate in a claim for a declaration of the third party's rights over the property or damages. Such a claim may also be challenged wholly or in part by the estate and or the beneficiaries.

Such an agreement may take different forms. The agreement may be that the testator/testatrix will make a will in which he/she will ensure that a specific property or fund is bequeathed to the other party or for his/her benefit. This agreement is commonly known as a contract to make a will which is enforceable against the estate. The validity of the agreement may be challenged by the personal representatives of the estate of the testator/testatrix. The property or fund may also be subject to an application under section 11 of the I(PFD)A 1975.

The testator/testatrix may by his/her conduct have encouraged the third party to believe that he/she would acquire an interest in the testator/testatrix's estate, thereby inducing the third party to act to his/her detriment. This type of arrangement is usually made in a parent/child relationship where a parent may encourage a daughter or son to work in the family business in the belief that he/she will receive an interest in the parent's estate. If the testator/testatrix then fails to make the provision, the party who was encouraged to act to his/her detriment may sue the estate on the ground of proprietary estoppel.

Two or more persons, usually a couple in a relationship, for example a husband and wife, a couple living together or a couple in a same sex relationship, may enter into an agreement to execute joint or mutual wills disposing of property belonging to each of them to the other on his/her death and then proceed to make their joint will or mutual wills. These arrangements or agreements often lead to a challenge on whether the wills made can validly be regarded as mutual wills and whether the survivor can validly dispose of the property acquired by him/her in breach of the agreement reached between them.

A person may also make a gift to another in contemplation of his/her death which is not intended to, nor does it, come into effect until the death of the donor. This type of arrangement is known as *donatio mortis causa*. Certain conditions must be fulfilled in order for there to be a valid *donatio mortis causa* and, therefore, this arrangement is open to challenge if a claim is made against the estate of the donor on his/her death.

These arrangements are discussed in detail in this chapter.

11.2 CONTRACTS TO LEAVE PROPERTY BY WILL

Under this arrangement the testator/testatrix in his/her lifetime enters into a contract by which he/she agrees to leave by his/her will a sum of money or other property to any person, or by which he/she agrees that a sum of money or other property will be paid or transferred to the named person out of his/her estate. Provided that the agreement clearly identifies the property which is to pass on the death of the testator/testatrix, the promisee is entitled to make a claim against the estate for a declaration of his/her right or for damages in lieu. Where appropriate, an injunction may be obtained to prevent the disposition of the property (*Synge v Synge* [1894] 1 QB 466). In order to be enforceable, the agreement must be validly executed. There must be an intention to enter into a binding agreement with an offer being made by one party and accepted by the other. There must be some consideration given and accepted, and the subject of the contract, be it property or money, must be identified.

On the death of the testator/testatrix, if a claim is made the claimant must prove the existence of a valid contract between the claimant and the testator/testatrix. The validity of the contract, however, may be challenged. For example, if the agreement was for a transfer of property it must comply with section 2 of the Law of Property (Miscellaneous Provisions) Act 1989 and must be in writing. Prior to 27 September 1989, when this Act came into force, agreements relating to land had to comply with section 40 of the Law of Property Act 1925 which required a contract for the sale of land to be made in writing or evidenced by a note or memorandum signed by the deceased or a person authorised by him/her to sign on his/her behalf.

Irani v Irani & Others [2006] EWHC 1811 (Ch) (a case where the agreement came within section 40 of the Law of Property Act 1925 above) provides a good example of a contract to make a will, a challenge made on its validity and the evidence which the court will take into account when determining whether a valid contract was concluded. In that case, an agreement was reached between a husband and wife during negotiations in an application made by the wife for financial remedy following the dissolution of their marriage. During negotiations, the husband through his solicitors made an offer in the following terms:

> In order to compromise this matter, may we put forward the following suggestion:-
> Our client undertakes not to sell, mortgage or otherwise deal with or dispose of the property and to execute a will leaving the property in equal shares to the children of the family Xerxis, Mahnaz and Rushna together with a further quarter share to Florine Da Costa. (*Irani v Irani & Others* [2006] EWHC 1811 (Ch) at [9])

The offer was accepted by the wife through her solicitors and as part of the agreement she agreed to discontinue her application but neither she nor her solicitors took any further action in the proceedings. On 6 August 1984, pursuant to the agreement reached, the husband signed an un-witnessed document in which he purported to leave the property to the four children in the following terms:

> To Whom It May Concern
> I Kaikhushroo Boman Irani in accordance with my divorce settlement dated 23.7.84 do here by leave my property at 62 Macfarlane Road Shepherds Bush London W12 7JZ in equal shares to Xerxis Irani, Mahanaz [sic] Irani, Rushna Irani and Florine Da Costa.
> K B Irani (*Irani v Irani & Others* [2006] EWHC 1811 (Ch) at [13])

Clearly, this was not a valid will but he intended to execute, and believed that he executed, a valid will. He did not make any other will. He died intestate in September 1996. Under the intestacy rules the deceased's illegitimate son, Edward, his former wife and the three children were entitled to a share in the estate. The former wife and children claimed that a valid contract was made between her and the deceased. Edward challenged this by issuing a claim for declarations that he was entitled to an equal one-quarter share in the deceased's estate (which was admitted) and that the property formed part of the deceased's estate (which was in dispute). Mrs Irani thereupon made a third party claim in the proceedings (to which her three children, Florine and Edward were defendants) in which she claimed that she orally accepted unconditionally the terms proposed in the letter dated 19 July 1994, and that this thereby constituted a contract between her and the deceased. The terms of the contract were that, in consideration of Mrs Irani not proceeding with her application for a lump sum payment order and a property adjustment order in respect of the property, the deceased would not sell, mortgage or otherwise deal with or dispose of the property and would execute a will leaving the property in equal shares to her three children and Florine. Edward contended that although the deceased made an offer it was not validly accepted by the wife and that it was unenforceable as it was not evidenced in writing as required by section 40 of the Law of Property Act 1925.

Applying *Tiverton Estates Ltd v Wearwell Ltd* [1975] Ch 14, Lightman J found that a valid and enforceable contract was made as the written offer made by the deceased was orally accepted. Lightman J referred to the following facts as evidence of a valid agreement. He said:

> (1) the execution by the Deceased of what he evidently considered was a valid will in the form agreed; (2) the assurances he gave to Mrs Irani and Rushna that he had done so; and (3) the discontinuance by Mrs Irani of the ancillary proceedings. I am not deterred from reaching this conclusion by the choice by the Deceased of the puzzling date of 23.7.84 as the date of the 'divorce settlement': why he chose that date does not matter. Nor am I concerned that no valid will was executed: the Deceased clearly thought that the Will was a valid will and that its execution constituted fulfilment of his contractual obligation ... (*Irani v Irani & Others* [2006] EWHC 1811 (Ch) at [19])

11.2.1 Court's powers under the Inheritance (Provision for Family and Dependants) Act 1975 in relation to contracts to leave property by will

Where a person is entitled to property on the death of the deceased pursuant to a contract to leave property by will, it may nevertheless be subject to be brought into the pool of assets to make financial provision for a person who is entitled to, and does, make a claim for an order under section 2 of the I(PFD)A 1975 for financial provision to be made out of the estate of the deceased. The claimant may apply to the court for it to make an order or orders under section 11, but only if the conditions set out in that section are met.

Section 11(2) of the I(PFD)A 1975 provides that where the court is satisfied that the conditions are met, then subject to the provisions of section 11 and of sections 12 and 13, the court may make any one or more of the following orders:

> (i) If any money has been paid or any other property has been transferred to or for the benefit of the donee in accordance with the contract an order directing the donee to provide, for the purposes of the making of the financial provision, such sums of money or other property as may be specified in the order;
> (ii) If the money or all of it has not been paid or the property or all the property has not been transferred in accordance with the contract, an

order directing the personal representatives not to make any payment or transfer any property, or not to make any further payment or transfer any further property, as the case may be, in accordance therewith or directing the personal representatives only to make such payment or transfer such property as may be specified in the order. The court may also give such consequential directions as it thinks fit (including directions requiring the making of any payment or the transfer of property) for giving effect to the order or for securing a fair adjustment of the rights of the persons affected thereby.

However, in order for the court to make an order under section 11 of the I(PFD)A 1975, the applicant must establish that a valid and enforceable contract to make a will was entered into by the deceased; that full valuable consideration was not provided by the donee or other person on his/her behalf; that the deceased entered into the contract with the intention of defeating an application for financial provision under the Act or reducing the amount of the provision which might otherwise be granted (although this may not have been his/her sole intention); and that the exercise of the court's power under section 11 would facilitate the making of financial provision.

The court, when determining the application under section 11 of the I(PFD)A 1975 must, therefore, have regard to all the circumstances in which the contract was entered into, the relationship between the deceased and the donee and any other relevant circumstances. Furthermore, even if it is satisfied that the conditions set out in section 11 are met, the court will only exercise its powers to the extent that it considers the amount of money paid or the value of the property transferred to the donee exceeds the value of the consideration given for the contract.

11.3 PROPRIETARY ESTOPPEL

Claims for proprietary estoppel have become more common in commercial, family and contentious probate cases. Following the House of Lords' decision in *Yeoman's Row Management Ltd and Anor v Cobbe* [2008] UKHL 55, it was suggested that the decision narrowed the scope for a successful claim to be made based on proprietary estoppel (see Kate Chambers, 'Has Yeoman narrowed the scope for a successful claim of proprietary estoppel?', *New Law Journal*, 21 November 2008, p 1629). However, in *Thorner v Major* [2009] UKHL 18, the House of Lords acknowledged that in family and probate cases a different and more flexible approach than the approach in commercial cases was necessary. Where it is raised and the requirements to establish the claim are satisfied, it does not follow that the claimant will succeed in obtaining the relief which he seeks. The court, in such cases, will consider the position of others who have a legitimate claim in law to the deceased's estate and will make such award as is sufficient to satisfy the equity and do justice between the parties (*Evans v HSBC Trust Co* [2005] WTLR 1289).

The test to be applied for the doctrine to operate was set out in *Re Basham (Deceased)* [1986] 1 WLR 1498 as follows:

> Where one person (A) has acted to his detriment on the faith of a belief, which was known to and encouraged by another person (B), that he either has or is going to be given a right in or over B's property, B cannot insist on his strict legal rights if to do so would be inconsistent with A's belief. The principle is commonly known as proprietary estoppel, and since the effect of it is that B is prevented from asserting his strict rights it has something in common with estoppel. But in my judgment, at all events, where the belief is that A is going to be given a right in the future, it is properly to be regarded as giving rise to a species of constructive trust, which is the concept employed by a court of equity to prevent a person from relying on his legal rights where it would be unconscionable for him to do so. The rights to which proprietary estoppel gives rise, and the machinery by which effect is given to them are similar in many respects to those involved in cases of secret trusts, mutual wills and other comparable cases in which property is vested in B on the faith or an understanding that it will be dealt with in a particular manner. (*Re Basham* [1986] 1 WLR 1498 at 1503H–1504A and B)

The key elements which must be satisfied to establish a case of proprietary estoppel are, therefore:

(a) There must be a representation or assurance given to the claimant that the claimant would acquire certain property on the deceased's death.

(b) The representation may be made by conduct or partly by conduct and must be clear and unequivocal.

(c) The representation must appear to have been taken seriously and must be intended to be relied on or reasonably taken to be so intended.

(d) The claimant must have relied on the representations made or assurances given to his/her detriment.

(e) The representations made or assurances given to the claimant, whether expressly or impliedly should relate to identified property owned by the defendant (*Thorner v Major* [2009] UKHL 18).

The essential elements to establish a claim based on proprietary estoppel are best illustrated by reference to some cases where the claim has succeeded. In *Evans v HSBC Trust Co* [2005] WTLR 1289, two brothers, who were not related to the deceased, claimed that they were entitled to the whole of the deceased's estate as she treated them as her grandchildren and expressly and repeatedly gave them assurances that they would inherit the whole of her estate. They maintained that, relying on those assurances, they acted to their detriment in incurring liabilities which they would otherwise not have incurred. On the facts, the court found that it would be unconscionable not to act upon those assurances. However, the court took into account the fact that the deceased was survived by three blood relatives, and adjusted the claim to make provisions for them.

In *Thorner v Major* [2009] UKHL 18, the deceased was a farmer. The claimant was his cousin who worked for him on the farm for about three decades but for which he received no remuneration. The deceased, however, made representations which led the claimant to believe that he would inherit the farm. Relying on those representations, the claimant turned down a job that was offered to him by a friend and thus he acted to his detriment. In allowing his appeal, the House of Lords held on the facts that the continuing conduct of the deceased over a long period was a relevant factor. Lord Neuberger emphasised that when considering the requirement that an assurance had to be 'clear and unequivocal' before it can be relied on, three other factors had to be taken into account. These were (at [84]), first, that the effect of words or actions had to be assessed in their context so that just as a sentence could have one meaning in one context and a very different meaning in another context, so could an assurance, which would be ambiguous or unclear in one context but be a clear and unambiguous assurance in another context:

> 85. Secondly, it would be quite wrong to be unrealistically rigorous when applying the 'clear and unambiguous' test. The court should not search for ambiguity or uncertainty, but should assess the question of clarity and certainty practically and sensibly, as well as contextually. Again, this point is underlined by the authorities, namely those cases I have referred to in para 78 above, which support the proposition that, at least normally, it is sufficient for the person invoking the estoppel to establish that he reasonably understood the statement or action to be an assurance on which he could rely.
> 86. Thirdly, as pointed out in argument by my noble and learned friend Lord Rodger of Earlsferry, there may be cases where the statement relied on to found an estoppel could amount to an assurance which could reasonably be understood as having more than one possible meaning. In such a case, if the facts otherwise satisfy all the requirements of an estoppel, it seems to me that, at least normally, the ambiguity should not deprive a person who reasonably relied on the assurance of all relief: it may well be right, however, that he should be accorded relief on the basis of the interpretation least beneficial to him. (*Thorner v Major* [2009] UKHL 18 at [85]–[86])

Lord Neuberger distinguished between a written contract and one made orally thus:

82. ... This shows that (a) the interpretation of a purely written contract is a matter of law, and depends on a relatively objective contextual assessment, which almost always excludes evidence of the parties' subjective understanding of what they were agreeing, but (b) the interpretation of an oral contract is a matter of fact (I suggest inference from primary fact), rather than one of law, on which the parties' subjective understanding of what they were agreeing is admissible.

83. The reason for this dichotomy is partly historical. Juries were often illiterate, and could therefore not interpret written contracts, whereas they could interpret oral ones. But it also has a good practical basis. If the contract is solely in writing, the parties rarely give evidence as to the terms of the contract, so it is cost-effective and practical to exclude evidence of their understanding as to its effect. On the other hand, if the contract was made orally, the parties will inevitably be giving evidence as to what was said and done at the relevant discussions or meetings, and it could be rather artificial to exclude evidence as to their contemporary understanding. Secondly, and perhaps more importantly, memory is often unreliable and self-serving, so it is better to exclude evidence of actual understanding when there is no doubt as to the terms of the contract, as when it is in writing. However, it is very often positively helpful to have such evidence to assist in the interpretation of an oral contract, as the parties will rarely, if ever, be able to recollect all the details and circumstances of the relevant conversations. (*Thorner v Major* [2009] UKHL 18 at [82]–[83])

Moving on from that decision, in *Revenue and Customs v Benchdollar Ltd* [2009] EWHC 1310 (Ch) (although not a family case), the court referred to a number of principles which may be of relevance when considering whether to pursue a claim on proprietary estoppel. These are:

(a) It was not enough that the common assumption was understood by the parties. It had to be expressly shared between them.

(b) The expression of the common assumption by the party alleged to be estopped must be such that he/she may properly be said to have assumed some responsibility for it, in the sense of conveying to the other party an understanding that he/she expected the other party to rely upon it.

(c) The other party must have relied upon the common assumption to a sufficient extent.

(d) Reliance must have occurred in connection with some subsequent dealings between the parties.

(e) The person alleging the estoppel must have acted upon and suffered some detriment or some benefit thereby must have been conferred on the person alleged to have been estopped. The benefit must be sufficient to establish that it would be unjust or unconscionable for that person to assert his/her legal position.

In *Re Basham (Deceased)* [1986] 1 WLR 1498, the claimant was the step-daughter of the deceased. She worked without pay for the deceased on the understanding that she would inherit his estate. The doctrine of proprietary estoppel was applied. Similarly, the doctrine was applied in *Wayling v Jones* [1995] 2 FLR 1029, CA, where the claimant had been in a same sex relationship with the deceased over a long period and worked for the deceased on the assurance given to him that he would inherit the deceased's estate (see also *Kinane v Mackie-Conteh* [2005] EWCA Civ 45).

Conversely, it may be useful to give an illustration of cases where the court has dismissed a claim based on proprietary estoppel, such as *MacDonald v Frost* [2009] EWHC 2276 (Ch) and *Shirt v Shirt* [2012] EWCA Civ 1029.

In *MacDonald v Frost* [2009] EWHC 2276 (Ch), the claim was brought by the deceased's two daughters. They each made monthly payments to their father and each received money and property worth about £20,000 from him. When his wife died and he remarried, they continued to make the payments to him. In his will the deceased left his entire estate to his second wife. The daughters brought a claim against the estate asserting that the deceased repeatedly assured them that they would benefit from his estate. The court dismissed their claim as the evidence did not disclose that there was any express assurance or promise given to the daughters after the deceased remarried, and there was no other reason for the deceased to have made such promises.

In *Shirt v Shirt* [2012] EWCA Civ 1029, a father and son were in a farming partnership but the farm property was registered in the father's name. After about 10 years, their relationship broke down and they went their separate ways. About 25 years later, the son claimed that he had a beneficial interest in the farm. He alleged that representations were made to him by his father between 1976 and 1986 that he would have an interest in the farm and, therefore, he had a claim under the doctrine of proprietary estoppel. His claim was dismissed as the trial judge found that the father did not make any representations to his son. His appeal was also dismissed.

In *Smith v Bottomley* [2013] EWCA Civ 953 (although not a probate case or a claim brought under the I(PFD)A 1975), the unmarried couple, Ms Smith and Mr Bottomley, had been in a relationship since 1990. Ms Smith worked for Mr Bottomley's company and they cohabited for a period. They had one child together and were engaged. In 2002, Mr Bottomley promised to marry Ms Smith and they purchased a property in joint names, conveyed as tenants in common and accompanied by a formal declaration of trust. Ms Smith gave up her rented accommodation with the intention that they would live together as a family in the new property. Mr Bottomley and his company owned other properties. He assured Ms Smith that although the properties were not held jointly in their names, all of their assets were equally owned by them. When the couple separated, Ms Smith sought a declaration and quantification of her beneficial interest in the other properties owned by Mr Bottomley and/or the company on the basis of a constructive trust or proprietary estoppel. At first instance, the judge found Ms Smith was entitled to a half share of one of the properties and that she was underpaid by £21,000 in relation to her share in a second property. Mr Bottomley appealed. On the specific facts of the case, the Court of Appeal ruled that it was not possible to say that her agreement to marry Mr Bottomley constituted some kind of continuing detrimental reliance which continued in relation to any later promise made in relation to the other property. The Court of Appeal did not give any guidance on whether a promise to marry could, in principle, constitute sufficient detrimental reliance to found a claim to a constructive trust, as it considered that it was not necessary to do so on the facts in this case. It held that the answer is likely to depend upon the particular factual circumstances: for instance, did acceptance of one offer of marriage preclude acceptance of another, competing offer which foreclosed the offeree from protecting his/her financial position more fully by accepting the competing offer?

In relation to the argument that by surrendering her rented accommodation Ms Smith acted to her detriment again, on the facts the Court of Appeal found that the primary reason Ms Smith gave up her own accommodation was that she was provided with accommodation rent free by Mr Bottomley at Treetops, then at Cropredy, then in Spain. Further, the court did not consider that Ms Smith's giving up rented accommodation in her own name to move to shared accommodation with Mr Smith, for which she did not have to pay, could in the circumstances of this case constitute material detrimental reliance sufficient to generate any form of equitable claim against the company (at [62] and [63]).

If a statement is made in a deed, for example in a recital, that statement is capable of giving rising to an estoppel. The interpretation of the document will involve looking at the meaning that it would convey to a reasonable person having all the background knowledge which would reasonably have been available to the parties (see *Brudenell-Bruce, Earl of Cardigan v Moore and Anor* [2012] EWHC 1024 (Ch) and the cases cited therein).

In conclusion, and by way of summary therefore, the cases show that in order to found a claim of proprietary estoppel, the claimant must adduce evidence to establish:

(a) assurances or representations made by the deceased;
(b) reliance placed on them by the claimant;
(c) detriment to the claimant as a consequence thereof.

Even if such a claim is established, the relief that will be granted will be limited to that which is equitable and just in the circumstances.

11.4 MUTUAL WILLS

A challenge may be made where it is alleged that the deceased entered into a mutually binding will, the result of which is to prevent him/her from disposing of his/her estate other than on the basis agreed and set out in that will. The will executed in consequence of such an agreement is known as a mutual will. This occurs when two or more persons agree to execute their respective will in substantially the same terms and confer benefits to each other following an agreement between them to make such wills and not to revoke the wills without the consent of the other.

It is thus essential to establish that there was an agreement between the persons concerned for each of them to make a will in a particular form and not to revoke that will without the other's consent or without first giving notice to the other (see *Olins v Walters* [2008] EWCA Civ 782). It is not enough to show that both wills are in identical terms. Although it may be preferable to incorporate the agreement in the will, it is not necessary to do so as long as there is clear evidence of the agreement, whether in written form or expressed orally. If neither is available, extrinsic evidence may be adduced to prove the terms of the agreement reached between the parties and their intentions, but in such a case the evidence must be both clear and convincing. The case of *Re Goodchild (Deceased), Goodchild v Goodchild* [1996] 1 All ER 670 illustrates some of the practical difficulties which can arise. The court referred to the principle of constructive trust or 'floating trust' which would be applied to cases of mutual wills where there was a clear agreement that the wills were to be mutually binding. On the death of the first testator, the trust would become irrevocable and crystallise on the death of the second testator. The remarriage of the second surviving testator does not affect the validity of the 'floating trust' or destroy the trust. In *Goodchild*, the court found that the wills were not mutually binding. The court, however, overcame the problem of the deceased's exclusion of his son from his will on the basis that when the deceased's first wife made her will, she did so on the understanding that the deceased would give effect to what they agreed and was their mutual intention. That gave rise to a moral obligation on the deceased which did not entitle him to feel free to disinherit their son at least in relation to that part of his property which he derived from his first wife.

In *Olins v Walters* [2008] EWCA Civ 782, the husband and wife made wills and codicils in identical terms by agreement. On the death of the wife, the husband sought to challenge the fact that the wills were mutually binding. Both at first instance and on appeal, the court found that mutual wills were made, as the facts confirmed that the wills were executed as a result of the advice given to them by their solicitor, who was their grandson, to allay the concerns the couple had that the survivor of them would come under pressure from family members to vary the arrangement that the couple jointly reached. The agreement was also confirmed in codicils.

A more recent example where the court confirmed that mutual wills were made is the case of *Charles v Fraser* [2010] EWHC 2154 (Ch). Two elderly sisters agreed to and made wills bequeathing their estate to each other and thereafter to certain beneficiaries. Neither will made any reference to the agreement, nor did the wills contain a statement against revocation. It was, however, apparent from the terms of both wills that the sisters carefully discussed the matter and agreed the terms set out in the wills. Eleven years after the first sister died, the survivor made a new will leaving her estate to her friend. The will was challenged. The court found that the detailed division of the estate and the calculations of the interest that each beneficiary was to receive and that were incorporated in both wills indicated their intentions. The court held that the estate was to be held on trusts set out in the original will. The case is also relevant in that the judge outlined in his judgment the principles which apply to mutual wills. He said:

> The law
> I take the law on mutual wills to be as follows:
> (i) Mutual wills are wills made by two or more persons, usually in substantially the same terms and conferring reciprocal benefits, following an agreement between them to make such wills and not revoke them without the consent of the other.
> (ii) For the doctrine to apply there has to be what amounts to a contract between the two testators that both wills will be irrevocable and remain unaltered. A common intention, expectation or desire is not enough.
> (iii) The mere execution of mirror or reciprocal wills does not imply any agreement either as to revocation or non-revocation
> (iv) For the doctrine to apply it is not necessary that the second testator should have obtained a personal financial benefit under the will of the first testator (albeit that in the present case Ethel had, of course, done so).
> (v) It is perfectly possible for there to have been an agreement preventing revocability as to part of the residuary estate only, in which case the doctrine only applies to that part.
> (vi) The agreement may be incorporated in the will or proved by extraneous evidence. It may be oral or in writing.
> (vii) The agreement must be established by clear and satisfactory evidence on the balance of probabilities.
> (viii) The agreement is enforced in equity by the imposition of a constructive trust on the property which is the subject matter of the agreement. The beneficiaries under the will that was not to be revoked may apply to the Court for an order that the estate is held on trust to give effect to the provisions of the old will.
> (ix) The action relates only to the dispositive part of the will. The new will is fully effective to deal with non-dispositive matters, such as the appointment of Executors. Accordingly where the doctrine applies the Executors appointed under

the final will hold the assets of the estate on trust to give effect to the earlier will. (*Charles v Fraser* [2010] EWHC 2154 (Ch) at [59])

Where the agreement is not clear, but the arrangement between the parties is that of a constructive trust, it can be argued that it attaches to the property which the survivor received from the estate of the first to die; or that it attaches to the property of the first to die and the survivor, at the date of the first to die; or to the whole of the property at the date of death of the survivor. It has also been suggested that where the property includes the disposition of land, the agreement must comply with the requirement of section 2 of the Law of Property (Miscellaneous Provisions) Act 1989 which requires such an agreement to be in writing and signed by both parties (see *Healey v Brown* [2002] EWHC 1405 (Ch)). One can argue, however, that a will is a bequest of land and since the agreement is mutually binding the two wills should be read together as one document and, therefore, it complies with the section.

It will be observed that the subject of mutual wills is fraught with difficulties. The lesson to learn from the decided cases is to ensure that a written statement is made and signed by both parties, recording clearly the terms of the parties' agreement. In the absence of such a statement or some other form of record of the agreement, the execution of identical wills by two or more persons is open to challenge.

11.5 DONATIO MORTIS CAUSA

Donatio mortis causa is a gift made by a person in contemplation of death but the gift does not take effect until death has occurred. The requirements for an effective *donatio mortis causa* were set out in *Sen v Headley* [1991] Ch 425. For there to be an effective gift under this doctrine the following conditions must be satisfied:

(a) The gift must be in contemplation of death.
(b) The gift must be made on condition that it becomes absolute and irrevocable only on the death of the donor.
(c) The subject matter of the gift, or something which represents the gift, must have been delivered to the donee or someone on his behalf with the intention of parting with it.
(d) The property must be capable of passing by *donatio mortis causa*. The property must be transferred by delivery or by executing an appropriate document.

A challenge may be made to such a gift on the basis that one or more of the above conditions was not satisfied at the time the gift was made. It can also be challenged on the ground that the donor of the gift lacked the mental capacity to make the gift. In this case, it will be for the donee to prove that the donor had capacity. A gift of *donatio mortis causa* may be challenged in proceedings under the I(PFD)A 1975 if it can be established that it was made with the intention of defeating a claim for financial provision under the Act (see Chapter 13).

In the recent case of *King v Chiltern Dog Rescue and Redwings Horse Sanctuary* [2015] EWCA Civ 581, when reversing the decision of the High Court ([2014] EWHC 2083 (Ch)), the Court of Appeal narrowed the first requirement. The deceased was an animal lover. She had made a will in 1998 leaving the bulk of her estate to seven charities. The claimant, Mr King, was her nephew and he had had a close relationship with her. Between 2006 and 2007, he agreed to move into her house because she had told him that she was getting old and found it difficult to cope and live on her own. He claimed that she had promised that the property would be his on her death. In 2010, she had written a note to that effect. About 4 or 6 months prior to her death, she had handed him the deeds to the property and said that, 'this will be yours when I go' or words to that effect. He claimed that two further documents had been made expressing similar sentiments. She died on 21 April 2011. At first instance, the court found that there had been a *donatio mortis causa* in his favour. On appeal, however, Jackson LJ ruled that the first requirement of *donatio mortis causa*, i.e. 'in contemplation of death' meant that the donor must have anticipated death in the 'near future and for a specific reason'. He stated that *Vallee v Birchwood* [2013] EWHC 1449 (Ch), [2014] Ch 271 had been wrongly decided and should not be relied on. Applying *Sen v Headley* where death occurred within 3 days and *In Re Craven's Estate* [1937] Ch 423 within 5 days, 'near future' should be measured in days rather than weeks or months.

11.6 CONCLUSION

In relation to all the above lifetime agreements and gifts, they will be effective only if the conditions which attach to them are satisfied. They are open to challenge if the conditions are not satisfied. If they are satisfied, and a claim is made under the I(PFD)A 1975, a contract to make a will and *donatio mortis causa* may be challenged under sections 8 and 11 provided it can be established that the agreement was made or the gift was given with the intention of defeating such a claim.

Chapter 12

Jointly Owned Assets and Assets Held on Constructive Trust

12.1 JOINTLY OWNED ASSETS

12.1.1 Introduction

Any reference to joint property or jointly owned assets includes both a beneficial interest in real property and all other property, such as shares and bank accounts. Jointly owned property may raise issues relating to ownership, the extent of the deceased's and the third party's interest in the property and, consequently, whether the deceased was free to dispose of the property or his/her interest in it in his/her will and whether it forms part of his/her estate. It follows, therefore, that how the beneficial ownership passes will depend on how the assets were held.

Where real property is held in joint names, the parties' interest in the property and how the property passes on death will depend on whether their respective interest was identified by deed, declaration of trust or otherwise, when the property was acquired and whether it was transferred into their joint names as joint tenants or tenants in common. If the property was transferred and held by them as joint tenants, on the first death, the beneficial interest in the property will automatically pass by survivorship to the survivor, unless it can be established that the joint tenancy was severed during the lifetime of the deceased. Where the joint tenancy is severed, the deceased and the third party will hold the property thereafter as tenants in common and each of them will be free to dispose of their respective beneficial interest in the property by will or it will pass in accordance with the rules of intestacy if either or both die intestate.

In the case of property held by the deceased and a third party as tenants in common, each will not necessarily hold an equal beneficial interest in the property. The interest each will have in the property will depend on what was agreed between them. Their respective beneficial interest will pass under their will or intestacy.

12.1.2 Property held as joint tenants

Where property is held in joint names, it is important to ascertain whether the property is held by the deceased and the third party as joint tenants or tenants in common. If the property is held by them as joint tenants, the presumption is that the beneficial entitlement of each follows the title and they hold the property jointly in equal shares. If this is challenged, it is for the person who seeks to claim that the beneficial interest is different from that shown on the title deeds to establish his/her claim. Where bank or other accounts are held jointly in the name of the deceased and a third party, for example the deceased and her daughter, issues may be raised regarding whether the deceased alone was entitled to the monies in the account or whether it was intended that both the deceased and the third party were entitled to it. Where the circumstances indicate that the account was held in joint names for convenience, it will form part of the estate of the deceased. In deciding the issue, the court will need to examine the arrangements between the parties and the reason and purpose for which it was set up, to what extent the money was available to the third party, what the parties intended and whether the intention was for the deceased only to have sole rights and control of the use of money. If it is contended that it was not, it will be for the party who asserts this to establish that it was not. *Drakeford v Cotton* [2012] EWHC 1414 (Ch) provides a good example. In that case, following a lottery win, a couple made mirror wills leaving their property to each other and then to their three children, L, M and R, in equal shares. After her husband's death, the wife transferred two of her accounts into the joint names of herself and her daughter, M. About 4 months later, L, who was estranged from her family, apologised to her mother and accepted that her behaviour towards her mother had been hurtful and had caused distress to her mother. Following this contrition, the mother made statements indicating that she intended to make an immediate gift of the money held in the joint accounts to M so that the full legal and beneficial ownership of the money held in the accounts passed to M by survivorship on the mother's death. L claimed that the money formed part of the mother's estate and passed under her will to the three children in equal shares. On the facts, the court held that the mother clearly indicated her intention that M should have the money, and that she formed a settled intention, expressed her intention and the agreement between them created a declaration of trust.

Similar issues may arise in the case of life insurance policies as to whether the interest that the deceased and the third party had in the policy was genuinely held by them as joint tenants or whether each had a sole right to the sum assured on death (see *Holland v Murphy* [2003] EWCA Civ 1862, where it was held that the policy was held by the policyholders as joint tenants).

Where property is owned jointly by the deceased and another, the deceased may have taken steps to sever the joint tenancy. Whether steps taken to sever the joint tenancy will in fact have the effect of severing the joint tenancy will depend on the circumstances of the case and the actions taken to sever the tenancy.

12.1.3 Severance of joint tenancy

A joint tenancy may be severed by written notice, mutual agreement, a course of dealings between the parties or actions taken by one or both of them during or within proceedings or by court order. The effect of severance is that it removes the right of survivorship, and the deceased's share in the property remains as part of his/her estate and does not automatically pass to the survivor as in the case of joint tenancy.

Severance will normally occur by written notice of severance in accordance with section 36(2) of the Law of Property Act 1925. Where written notice is not available, reliance may be placed on the nature and extent of any agreement reached between the parties and their intentions or their conduct during litigation.

12.1.3.1 Severance as a consequence of actions taken in proceedings

Actions taken by a joint tenant during the course of proceedings may have the effect of severing the joint tenancy. Whether the steps taken: (a) before proceedings are issued; or (b) in issuing proceedings; or (c) during the course of proceedings, will have the effect of severing the joint tenancy will depend on the nature of the actions taken and the intention of the party at the time. The mere filing of a divorce petition *per se* will not result in severance (*Harris v Goddard* [1983] 3 All ER 242) because one of the parties may seek the transfer of the whole or part of the joint asset to himself/herself or seek a sale with the transfer of the whole of the net proceeds to himself/herself (see *Marshall v Marshall* [1998] EWCA Civ 1467).

However, difficulties may arise where there is no direct evidence of a written notice of severance. In such cases, the surrounding circumstances will have to be relied on to ascertain whether a mutual agreement was reached between the parties and resulted in severance and/or whether their conduct indicates that the parties intended to sever the joint tenancy. Two cases issued in different Divisions of the High Court and with different factual situations best illustrate how severance of a tenancy can effectively occur, where no written notice of severance has been given, as a result of the action taken by the parties concerned or those acting on their behalf during the course of court proceedings.

In *Quigley v Masterson* [2011] EWHC 2529 (Ch), M and P jointly owned a house in which they lived. When their relationship broke down, P's solicitors made attempts to sever the joint tenancy by written notice to M but subsequently P was found to lack capacity. P's daughter applied to the Court of Protection for appointment as a deputy for P and for authorisation to sell the house. M applied to be joined as a party in the proceedings. She conceded that the property was jointly owned in equal shares. However, before the issues could be determined, P died, at which point the issue arose whether on his death the property passed to M by survivorship or whether there was a severance of the joint tenancy and she was entitled to only one half of the interest in the property. On appeal, it was held that the action taken by M in the proceedings before the Court of Protection and in seeking a sale of the property and the division of the net proceeds of sale in equal shares was a clear indication that M was treating and accepting that the joint tenancy was severed. P's daughter who was appointed to act as P's deputy was authorised to receive notice of severance on P's behalf.

In *Davis v Smith* [2011] EWCA Civ 1603, a married couple purchased a property in their joint names. When the marriage broke down, the husband vacated the property. During the divorce proceeding that ensued, an agreement was reached between the parties that the property should be sold and the net proceeds of sale and the surrender value of an endowment policy should be shared between them equally with appropriate adjustments. The endowment policy was surrendered and the proceeds divided as agreed. The property was put on the market for sale. Before the wife could sign the notice of severance, she died. It was held that the course of conduct between the parties clearly indicated not only an agreement that their jointly owned assets would be realised and divided between them, but also that they put into action their intention and thereby severed the joint tenancy. Therefore, on the wife's death the property did not pass to the husband by survivorship.

12.1.3.2 Severance by the court in a claim under the Inheritance (Provision for Family and Dependants) Act 1975

Section 9(1) of the I(PFD)A 1975, as amended by section 6 of, and Schedule 2 to, the Inheritance and Trustees' Powers Act 2014, now provides that:

> where a deceased person was immediately before his death beneficially entitled to a joint tenancy of any property, then if an application is made for an order under section 2 of this Act, the court for the purpose of facilitating the making of financial provision for the applicant under this Act may order that the deceased's severable share of that property, shall, to such extent as appears to the court to be

just in all the circumstances of the case, be treated for the purposes of the Act as part of the net estate of the deceased.

Where such a claim is intended to be made or is made, the issues to consider are as follows:

- To ensure that the application for an order under section 9 of the I(PFD)A 1975 is made within the main claim for financial provision, because the court will be able to exercise its discretionary powers to permit an application under section 9 to be made, notwithstanding that it was made after the grant of representation is first taken out but only in cases where it extends the time for bringing the substantive application.
- Did the deceased hold the property as joint tenant with another party immediately before his/her death?
- On what grounds may it be appropriate to seek such an order?
- What criteria will the court apply when determining whether to order severance?
- The valuation of the deceased's severable share immediately before his/her death.

12.1.4 Limitation period

Any application for an order under section 9 of the I(PFD)A 1975 made before 1 October 2014 had to be made before the end of 6 months from the date on which representation with respect to the estate of the deceased was first taken out. The court did not have the power to extend this time limit even if an extension of time had been granted in respect of the substantive application. Amendments made to the Act by the Inheritance and Trustees' Powers Act 2014 remove this restriction and tie it in with any application made for an extension of time for bringing the substantive claim. It is thus essential where the deceased's estate consists of property held jointly to include an application for a section 9 order in the main claim.

12.1.5 Meaning of property

Property for the purposes of relief under section 9 of the I(PFD)A 1975 includes a chose in action (section 9(4)) and therefore includes both real property and other forms of property such as monies in a joint account (see *Powell v Osborne* [1993] 1 FLR 1001), a joint insurance policy or other joint investments. It applies only to property that was jointly held at the date of the deceased's death. If the joint tenancy was severed before the deceased's death, relief under section 9 cannot be relied on.

12.1.6 Circumstances which will lead to an order being considered

This is a discretionary remedy. The court will only exercise its discretion if it considers it is necessary to facilitate the making of an order for financial provision for the claimant(s), for example because the estate is inadequate to meet the claim(s) made, or to honour the wishes of the deceased in his/her will or on his/her intestacy.

12.1.7 Criteria which the court will apply

There are four factors which the court will take into account when determining an application made under section 9 of the I(PFD)A 1975. These are:

(a) To what extent does it appear to be just in all the circumstances to exercise its discretion?
(b) Is it necessary to facilitate the making of financial provision for the claimant?
(c) What was the value of the asset immediately before the death of the deceased?
(d) Any inheritance tax payable in respect of the severed share (section 9(2)).

Regard must be had to any inheritance tax payable in respect of the severed share. In exercising its discretion, the court must be satisfied that an order under section 9 of the I(PFD)A 1975 would facilitate an award of financial provision for the claimant. The court will also need to balance the needs of the claimant with those of any other party who would be entitled to a benefit under the deceased's will or on his/her intestacy and other claimants under the Act. Where severance is considered to be appropriate, it does not follow that it will relate to the whole of the deceased's interest in the asset. It will be limited to such amount as is necessary to order reasonable financial provision. The value of the property is that given immediately before the death of the deceased. This provision, however, does not mean that the court can or should disregard any fall in values between death and the hearing of an application under the Act or a rise in the value at the trial date (see *Dingmar v Dingmar* [2006] EWCA Civ 942 and *Jessop v Jessop* [1992] 1 FLR 591).

12.2 CONSTRUCTIVE TRUST

A claim may be made against the estate of the deceased where the deceased entered into an arrangement or agreement with another party under which he held the property which formed part of his estate in trust for the claimant.

Staden v Jones [2008] EWCA Civ 936 is an example of how a deceased may appear to be the owner of property when he, in fact, holds the property on constructive trust and only as a trustee for a third party. In that case, the appellant, who was the daughter of the deceased, sought to enforce a trust arising from an agreement reached between her parents on their divorce which led her mother to agree to transfer her share in the property to her father, on the basis that it would pass to the daughter. On the basis of the agreement in which the father gave a signed undertaking to that effect, the mother executed the transfer for no consideration. The father subsequently remarried and transferred the property into the joint names of himself and his second wife, who on his death acquired the beneficial interest in the property by survivorship. The Court of Appeal in allowing the appeal held that it was clear from the intention of the parties that the deceased was to hold the property on the basis that he would hold half the beneficial interest in the property for the daughter subject to his right to occupy it. The daughter's interest did not lie only in the proceeds of the sale of the property.

In *Q v Q* [2008] EWHC 1874 (Fam), the court held that the deed of gift in relation to the property, which was the subject of the dispute, gave rise to a constructive trust in favour of the husband. See also the case of *Hameed v Qayyum* [2009] EWCA Civ 352, where the court approached the issue on the basis of what the approach of equity would have been if there was a claim for rescission of the agreement by the wife for innocent misrepresentation.

Ownership on the basis of a constructive trust may also be raised by a third party, usually a cohabitant, where the property was held solely in the name of the deceased but the third party contends that it was held jointly in trust for the deceased and the third party. In such cases, the court will have to determine if a constructive trust was created and, if so, also determine their respective interests in the property.

Although it is a commercial case, *Bieber & Others v Teathers Ltd (In liquidation)* [2012] EWCA Civ 1466 set out a summary of the principles which apply in determining whether or not the arrangements or agreement between parties created a trust, by reference to the decision of the House of Lords in *Twinsectra Ltd v Yardley* [2002] UKHL 12, [2002] AC 164 as follows:

> 16. First, the question in every case is whether the payer and the recipient intended that the money passing between them was to be at the free disposal of the recipient: *Re Goldcorp Exchange* [1995] 1 AC 74 and *Twinsectra* at [74].
> 17. Second, the mere fact that the payer has paid the money to the recipient for the recipient to use it in a particular way is not of itself enough. The recipient may have represented or warranted that he intends to use it in a particular way or have promised to use it in a particular way. Such an arrangement would give rise

to personal obligations but would not of itself necessarily create fiduciary obligations or a trust: *Twinsectra* at [73].

18. So, thirdly, it must be clear from the express terms of the transaction (properly construed) or must be objectively ascertained from the circumstances of the transaction that the mutual intention of payer and recipient (and the essence of their bargain) is that the funds transferred should not be part of the general assets of the recipient but should be used *exclusively* to effect particular identified payments, so that if the money cannot be so used then it is to be returned to the payer: *Toovey v Milne* (1819) 2 B&A 683 and *Quistclose Investments* at 580B.

19. Fourth, the mechanism by which this is achieved is a trust giving rise to fiduciary obligations on the part of the recipient which a court of equity will enforce: *Twinsectra* at [69]. Equity intervenes because it is unconscionable for the recipient to obtain money on terms as to its application and then to disregard the terms on which he received it from a payer who had placed trust and confidence in the recipient to ensure the proper application of the money paid: *Twinsectra* at [76].

20. Fifth, such a trust is akin to a 'retention of title' clause, enabling the recipient to have recourse to the payer's money for the particular purpose specified but without entrenching on the payer's property rights more than necessary to enable the purpose to be achieved. It is not as such a 'purpose' trust of which the recipient is a trustee, the beneficial interest in the money reverting to the payer if the purpose is incapable of achievement. It is a resulting trust in favour of the payer with a mandate granted to the recipient to apply the money paid for the purpose stated. The key feature of the arrangement is that the recipient is precluded from misapplying the money paid to him. The recipient has no beneficial interest in the money: generally the beneficial interest remains vested in the payer subject only to the recipient's power to apply the money in accordance with the stated purpose. If the stated purpose cannot be achieved then the mandate ceases to be effective, the recipient simply holds the money paid on resulting trust for the payer, and the recipient must repay it: *Twinsectra* at [81], [87], [92] and [100].

21. Sixth, the subjective intentions of payer and recipient as to the creation of a trust are irrelevant. If the properly construed terms upon which (or the objectively ascertained circumstances in which) payer and recipient enter into an arrangement have the effect of creating a trust, then it is not necessary that either payer or recipient should intend to create a trust: it is sufficient that they intend to enter into the relevant arrangement: *Twinsectra* at [71].

22. Seventh, the particular purpose must be specified in terms which enable a court to say whether a given application of the money does or does not fall within its terms: *Twinsectra* at [16].

23. It is in my judgment implicit in the doctrine so described in the authorities that the specified purpose is fulfilled by and at the time of the application of the money. The payer, the recipient and the ultimate beneficiary of the payment (that is, the person who benefits from the application by the recipient of the money for the particular purpose) need to know whether property has passed. (*Bieber & Others v Teathers Ltd (In liquidation)* [2012] EWCA Civ 1466 at [14])

Patten LJ also emphasised that in deciding whether particular arrangements involved the creation of a trust and with it the retention by the paying party of beneficial control of the monies, proper account needed to be taken of the structure of the arrangements and the contractual mechanisms involved. It was then necessary to be satisfied not merely that the money when paid was not at the free disposal of the payee but that, objectively examined, the contractual or other arrangements properly construed were intended to provide for the preservation of the payer's rights and the control of the use of the money through the medium of a trust. Critically, this involved the court being satisfied that the intention of the parties was that the monies transferred by the payer should not become the absolute property of the payee but should continue to belong beneficially to the payer unless and until the conditions attached to their release were complied with (at [15]).

Cases decided in domestic proceedings and the principles formulated in those cases have been clarified by the Supreme Court in *Jones v Kernott* [2011] UKSC 53 and *Stack v Dowden* [2007] UKHL 17. In the latter case, the court concluded that where a conveyance is taken into the joint names of a married or unmarried couple without any express declaration of their beneficial interests, there is a presumption that the intention of the parties is to own both the legal and beneficial interests in the property jointly until the contrary is proved. The fact that the parties contributed to the purchase in unequal shares would not generally be sufficient to rebut the presumption. Attempts to show that the parties intended their beneficial interests to be different from their legal interests should not be 'lightly embarked upon' but when this is shown to be the case, the court's task will be to ascertain the parties' intention from their subsequent conduct in relation to the property. Where there is no clear evidence available from which the intention can be deduced, the court may impute or infer the appropriate intention.

The Supreme Court in *Jones v Kernott* [2011] UKSC 53 made it clear that, in a domestic context where a property is purchased in joint names, there is no presumption of a resulting trust arising from the parties having contributed to the deposit or the rest of the purchase in unequal shares. The Supreme Court said:

> the assumptions to human motivation, which led courts to impute particular intentions by way of resulting trust are not appropriate to the ascertainment of beneficial interest in a family home. Whether they remain appropriate in other contexts is not the issue in this case. (*Jones v Kernott* [2011] UKSC 53 at [53])

Allowing the appeal, the Supreme Court set out the following principles which should be applied 'where a family home is bought in the joint names of a cohabiting couple who are both responsible for any mortgage, but without any express declaration of their beneficial interests':

(1) the starting point is that equity follows the law and they are joint tenants, both in law and equity.
(2) That presumption can be displaced by showing (a) that the parties had a different common intention at the time when they acquired the home, or (b) that they later formed the common intention that their respective shares would change.
(3) Their common intention is to be deduced from their conduct: 'the relevant intention of each party is the intention which was reasonably understood by the other party to be manifested by that party's words and conduct notwithstanding that he did not consciously formulate that intention in his own mind or even acted with some different intention which he did not communicate to the other party' (Lord Diplock in *Gissing v Gissing* [1971] AC 886, 906). Examples of the sort of evidence which might be relevant to drawing such inferences are given in *Stack v Dowden*, at para 69.
(4) In those cases where it is clear either (a) that the parties did not intend joint tenancy at the outset, or (b) had changed their original intention, but where it is not possible to ascertain by direct evidence or by inference what their actual intention was as to the share in which they would own the property, 'the answer is that each is entitled to that share which the court considers fair having regard to the whole course of dealing between them in relation to the property': Chadwick LJ in *Oxley v Hiscock* [2005] Fam 211, para 69. In our judgment, 'the whole course of dealing ... in the property' should be given a broad meaning, enabling a similar range of factors to be taken into account as may be relevant to ascertaining the parties' actual intentions.
(5) Each case will turn on its own facts. Financial contributions are relevant but there are many other factors which may enable the court to decide what shares were either intended, as in case (3), or fair as in case (4). (*Jones v Kernott* [2011] UKSC 53 at [51])

Three specific points arise from the judgments in relation to property which is jointly owned, as follows:

(a) It seems that the difference between inference and imputation has to some extent been eroded. The judges differed on the issue of whether there was any difference between inference and imputation of intention from that which recognised that there may be a difference which was largely terminological and conceptual, (see judgment at [34] and Lord Collins at [58]).

(b) Where it is not possible to ascertain the parties' intentions, the court will resolve the issue by what it considers is fair, having regard to the whole course of dealings between them in relation to the property.

(c) The decision in each case will depend on the particular facts and circumstances in each case.

Where the property is transferred into the sole name of one party only, the Supreme Court's decision was as follows:

> The starting point is different. The first issue is whether it was intended that the other party have any beneficial interest in the property at all. If he does, the second issue is what that interest is. There is no presumption of joint beneficial ownership. But their common intention has once again to be deduced objectively from their conduct. If the evidence shows a common intention to share beneficial ownership but does not show what shares were intended, the court will have to proceed as at para 51(4) and (5) above (*Jones v Kernott* [2011] UKSC 53 at [52])

This decision will be relevant in particular to a claim made by a cohabitant where there is joint ownership of a property which was the parties' family home with presumption in favour of equal shares. Where the property is in the deceased's sole name the focus will be:

- first, to ascertain the parties' intention deduced objectively from their conduct;
- secondly (if it is found on the facts that there was an intention to share the beneficial interest in the property), the extent of share of the beneficial interest; and
- thirdly, if the evidence fails to show a common intention to share the beneficial ownership, the court will consider the issue on the basis of fairness having regard to their conduct in relation to the property.

An example of the application of these principles is best provided in *Thompson v Hurst* [2012] EWCA Civ 1752. See also *Gallorotti v Sebastianelli* [2012] EWCA Civ 865, where the parties were two friends who bought a property together with one of them paying a larger share of the deposit and the other agreeing to make up the difference by making a larger contribution towards the mortgage but failing to do so. Allowing the appeal, the Court of Appeal held that on the facts the only inference that could be drawn was that the parties intended the beneficial ownership should reflect their respective financial contributions. It was implausible that where the parties were two people who were living together for convenience, one should make a substantial gift to the other person. See also *Southwell v Blackburn* [2014] EWCA Civ 1347, where the claim based on constructive trust failed, but an alternative claim that the claimant had an equitable interest in a property owned in the sole name of the defendant under the doctrine of proprietary estoppel was upheld. In relation to sham transactions, a useful summary is provided by Mostyn J in *Bhura v Bhura* [2014] EWHC 727 (Fam).

In such cases, a disposition in the will may be challenged on the basis that the deceased was not in a position to dispose of the property as his/her own and as he/she willed. Additionally, if the claimant falls within the categories of applicants who are eligible to make a claim under the I(PFD)A 1975, the claim under the Act can be included in the probate proceedings (see Chapter 13).

12.3 CONCLUSION

Issues relating to joint tenancies, constructive trust and severance of a joint tenancy raise complex legal issues. The issues can become more complicated where death of one of the parties occurs and a dispute arises between a survivor who claims an interest or benefit in the asset in question and the estate of the deceased and the beneficiaries. In such circumstances, the risk is that things can get very fractious and go wrong. In the absence of clear and strong evidence, every attempt should be made to resolve the dispute by mediation rather than litigation, and an attempt should be made at least to narrow the issues in order to avoid the cost of litigation, and an order for costs including costs on the indemnity basis (see *Dharamshi & Others v Velji & Others* [2013] EWHC 3917 (Ch), where reasons given for failure/refusal to mediate were found to be unacceptable by the judge).

Chapter 13

Claims under the Inheritance (Provision for Family and Dependants) Act 1975

13.1 INTRODUCTION

In general, under English law, as long as the testator/testatrix has testamentary capacity when he/she makes his/her will and he/she validly complies with all the formalities relating to the making of a will, he/she has complete freedom to dispose of his/her estate as he/she chooses. On the testator's/testatrix's death, the personal representatives are under a duty to distribute his/her estate in accordance with the terms of his/her will. If a person has not made a will or made an invalid will, the estate will be distributed in accordance with the intestacy rules. Where, however, the will or the laws of intestacy fail to make reasonable financial provision for the testator's/testatrix's dependants, a claim may be made under the I(PFD)A 1975 as amended by a certain category of dependants for financial provision, and the court is empowered to order provisions to be made out of the estate. The power includes power to bring within the estate property which has been disposed of by the deceased during his/her lifetime if the estate is insufficient to meet the claims of the beneficiaries and the applicant(s).

Hence, a claim under the I(PFD)A 1975 is not a challenge of the testator's/testatrix's capacity to make the will or to the non-compliance of the formalities. It is a statutory remedy available only to a limited category of dependants who qualify to make the claim provided the deceased died domiciled in England and Wales, the criteria set out in the Act are met and the claim is made within the time limit prescribed in the Act. The statutory powers given to the court under the Act, however, do not permit the court to rewrite the will. The powers may only be exercised if the conditions set out in the Act are met.

The remedies available under the I(PFD)A 1975 are included in this book for completeness so that in addition or as an alternative to challenging the will, consideration is also given to ascertaining whether the client is entitled to relief under the Act. This chapter, therefore, provides only an overview of the provisions under the Act.

13.2 WHO MAY APPLY?

Those who qualify to make a claim under the I(PFD)A 1975 are:

(a) the spouse (including same sex couples from 13 March 2014) or civil partner of the deceased;
(b) a former spouse or civil partner of the deceased but no one who has formed a subsequent marriage or civil partnership;
(c) a cohabitant of the deceased;
(d) a child of the deceased;
(e) any person (not being a child of the deceased) who in relation to any marriage or civil partnership to which the deceased was at any time a party, or otherwise in relation to any family in which the deceased at any time stood in the role of a parent, was treated by the deceased as a child of the family;
(f) any person (not being a person included in the foregoing classes) who, immediately before the death of the deceased, was being maintained, whether wholly or partly, by the deceased (section 1(1) as amended).

13.2.1 Spouse or civil partner of the deceased

Pursuant to the Marriage (Same Sex Couples) Act 2013, this now includes a marriage between same sex couples. Section 11(1) provides that a marriage has the same effect in relation to same sex couples as it has in relation to opposite sex couples. The law of England and Wales (including all England and Wales legislation whenever passed or made) has effect in accordance with section 11(1) (section 11(2)). Schedule 3, Part 1, paragraph 1(a) and (b) provides that in existing legislation a reference to marriage is to be read as including a reference to marriage of a same sex couple and that reference to a married couple is to be read as including a reference to a same sex couple.

Schedule 3, Part 2, paragraph 5(2) of the Marriage (Same Sex Couples) Act 2013 defines the meaning which applies to the expressions 'husband', 'wife', 'widow' and 'widower' as follows:

(2) The following expressions have the meanings given—
  (a) "husband" includes a man who is married to another man;
  (b) "wife" includes a woman who is married to another woman;

(c) "widower" includes a man whose marriage to another man ended with the other man's death;
(d) "widow" includes a woman whose marriage to another woman ended with the other woman's death;

and related expressions are to be construed accordingly.

Same sex couples who have entered in to a civil partnership have the same rights as those enjoyed by heterosexual couples and same sex couples who enter into a marriage under the Civil Partnership Act 2004. However, this situation may change in the future as, pursuant to section 15 of the Marriage (Same Sex Couples) Act 2013, the Secretary of State is under a duty to arrange for the operation and future of the Civil Partnership Act 2004 in England and Wales to be reviewed, and for a report on the outcome of the review to be produced and published.

Also included in this category are a judicially separated spouse or civil partner, a party to a voidable marriage or civil partnership which was not annulled before the deceased died and those who have entered into a polygamous marriage. The rights of a party to a void marriage are also preserved by section 25(4) of the I(PFD)A 1975, provided that the person entered into the marriage in good faith unless the marriage of the deceased and that person was dissolved or annulled during the lifetime of the deceased and the dissolution or annulment is recognised by the law of England and Wales; or that person has during the lifetime of the deceased formed a subsequent marriage or civil partnership.

13.2.2 Former spouse or civil partner

A 'former spouse' in section 25(1) of the I(PFD)A 1975 means a person whose marriage or civil partnership with the deceased was during the lifetime of the deceased:

(a) dissolved or annulled by a decree of divorce or a decree of nullity of marriage granted under the law of any part of the British Islands, or
(b) dissolved or annulled in any country or territory outside the British Islands by a divorce or annulment which is entitled to be recognised as valid by the law of England and Wales.

A 'former civil partner' in section 25(4) of the I(PFD)A 1975, as amended by the Civil Partnership Act 2004, means a person whose civil partnership with the deceased was during the lifetime of the deceased:

(a) dissolved or annulled by an order made under the law of any part of the British Islands, or
(b) dissolved or annulled in any country or territory outside the British Islands by a dissolution or annulment which is entitled to be recognised as valid by the law of England and Wales.

Where a decree nisi has been granted but a party to the marriage dies before the decree has been made absolute, the marriage is regarded as subsisting and the widow/widower is entitled to make a claim as the spouse of the deceased. Any financial settlement reached between the parties or ordered by the court will be taken into consideration by the court in determining a claim under the Act. (For overseas divorce, see section 46(1) and (2) of the Family Law Act 1986 and, in relation to European Union Member States, see Council Regulation (EC) No 1347/2000 of 29 May 2000.)

13.2.3 Person living as husband or wife or civil partner of the deceased

This category was added to the I(PFD)A 1975 by the Law Reform (Succession) Act 1995 and the Civil Partnership Act 2004. This provision is now to be read with the provision contained in Schedule 3, Part 1 to the Marriage (Same Sex Couples) Act 2013 which in paragraph 2 provides:

(1) In existing England and Wales legislation—

(a) a reference to persons who are not married but are living together as a married couple is to be read as including a reference to a same sex couple who are not married but are living together as a married couple;
(b) a reference to a person who is living with another person as if they were married is to be read as including a reference to a person who is living with another person of the same sex as if they were married.

(2) Where sub-paragraph (1) requires a reference to be read in a particular way, any related reference (such as a reference to persons formerly living together as a married couple) is to be read accordingly.
(3) For the purposes of sub-paragraphs (1) and (2) it does not matter how a reference is expressed.

(1) This paragraph applies to existing England and Wales legislation which deals differently with—

(a) a man and a woman living together as if married, and
(b) two men, or two women, living together as if civil partners.

(2) If two men, or two women, are living together as if married, that legislation applies to them in the way that it would apply to them if they were living together as civil partners.

A person who comes within this category of claimants is only eligible to apply for financial provision under the I(PFD)A 1975 if the deceased died on or after 1 January 1996 and during the whole of the period of 2 years immediately preceding the date when the deceased died, the person was living in the same household as the deceased and as the husband or wife or civil partner of the deceased. This implies that there must have been continuous cohabitation for the full 2 years. However, in view of the societal and economic conditions which lead to couples living apart temporarily, for example posting overseas or due to illness and admission to hospital, it is likely that as long as it can be established that the couple's relationship was continuing and their home was being maintained as a single unit, it will be possible for a claim to be made under this head (see *Gully v Dix* [2004] EWCA Civ 139, *Re Watson* [1999] 1 FLR 878 and *Lindop v Agus, Bass and Hedley* [2009] EWHC 14 (Ch)). Whether the claim can be made, and if made whether it will succeed, will depend upon the factual circumstances, the evidence to support the claim and the evidence of those who may wish to challenge the claim.

13.2.4 Child of the deceased

A 'child' includes an illegitimate or legitimated and an adopted child and a child *en ventre sa mere* (i.e. a child who is conceived before the deceased's death but is born after the death). It also includes a child who is the subject of a parental order under section 30 of the Human Fertilisation and Embryology Act 1990. An adult child may also be eligible provided there is evidence to show that the deceased maintained him/her or was under an obligation to provide for him/her. For the status of a child born to same sex female civil partners, see the Legitimacy Act 1976 as amended by the Human Fertilisation and Embryology Act 2008. Issues relating to the parentage of a child born as a result of reproductive treatment are set out in the Family Law Reform Act 1987, the Human Fertilisation and Embryology Acts 1990 and 2008 and the Human Fertilisation and Embryology (Deceased Fathers) Act 2003.

13.2.5 Child who is treated as a child of the family

A person who is not the child of the deceased but who has been treated by the deceased as a child of the family in connection with a marriage or civil partnership to which the deceased was a party or otherwise in relation to any family in which the deceased at any time stood in the role of a parent, was treated by the deceased as a child of the family is eligible to make a claim under the I(PFD)A 1975 (section 1(1)(d), as amended by the Civil Partnership Act 2004 and the Inheritance and Trustees' Powers Act 2014). Note, however, that to qualify the deceased's treatment of and behaviour towards such a child must stem from a marriage or civil partnership or otherwise as a result of the deceased standing in the role of a parent. In this respect, it will be necessary to consider whether the relationship between the deceased and the applicant was a parent/child relationship. The provision as amended is wide enough to include a one-parent situation (see subsection 2A) as from 1 October 2014 when the Inheritance and Trustees' Powers Act 2014 came into force. Unlike the position under the Matrimonial Causes Act 1973, a child includes one who is an adult. Where grandparents or other relatives take on the responsibility of a child who is related to them, the child may become a child of the family within both the Matrimonial Causes Act 1973 and the I(PFD)A 1975 (see *Re A (A Child of the Family)* [1998] 1 FLR 347, CA).

13.2.6 Any other person who immediately before the death of the deceased was being maintained either wholly or partly by the deceased

For deaths occurring after 1 October 2014, in order to qualify within this category, a person must establish that immediately before the death of the deceased, the deceased was making a substantial contribution in money or money's worth towards the reasonable needs of that person, other than a contribution made for full valuable consideration pursuant to an arrangement of a commercial nature (section 1(3) of the I(PFD)A 1975).

The I(PFD)A 1975 does not make any other reference to the meaning of 'being maintained', but section 3(4) requires the court when determining such a claim to have regard:

(a) to the length of time for which, and the basis on which, the deceased maintained the applicant, and to the extent of the contribution made by way of maintenance;
(b) to whether and, if so, to what extent, the deceased assumed responsibility for the maintenance of the applicant.

13.3 TIME LIMIT FOR MAKING THE CLAIM

Prior to 1 October 2014, a claim under the I(PFD)A 1975 for financial provision had to be made within 6 months from the date on which representation with respect to the estate of the deceased is first taken out. Proceedings could not be issued before probate had been granted. Following the amendments made to section 4 by the Inheritance and Trustees Powers' Act 2014, although the time limit for bringing a claim remains at 6 months from the date on which representation is taken out, an application may now be made before such representation is first taken out. Schedule 3 to the 2014 Act also amends a number of enactments relating to the determination of the date on which representation in respect of the estate is first taken out, in so far as they affect, and to accord with, these amendments, section 23 of the I(PFD)A 1975 is consequently amended to take account of these changes. The court may, however, give permission to bring a claim outside this period (section 4 of the I(PFD)A 1975). The Act does not set out any criteria which should be applied when an application is made to extend the time limit. Two leading cases provide some guidance on the factors which the court is likely to take into account. In *Re Salmon (Deceased) Coard v National Westminster Bank* [1981] Ch 167, Megarry VC set out the following principles:

(a) The discretion is unfettered and one that is exercised judicially in accordance with what is just and proper.
(b) The onus is on the applicant to establish sufficient grounds for taking the case out of the general rule and depriving those who are protected by it of its benefits. The prescribed time limit is not merely a procedural one which may be treated with indulgence. The applicant must make out a substantial case for it being just and proper for the court to exercise its statutory discretion.
(c) The court must consider how promptly and in what circumstances the applicant is seeking an extension of time. The court must consider all the circumstances of the case including the reasons for the delay and how promptly the applicant gave a warning to the defendant of the proposed application.
(d) A material factor is whether or not negotiations have been commenced within the time limit. Negotiation commenced after expiration of the time limit may also be relevant at any rate where the defendants have not taken the point that the claim is out of time.
(e) Of relevance also is to ascertain whether the estate has been distributed before the claim was notified.
(f) The court should also consider whether refusal to give permission to apply out of time would leave the applicant without redress against any third party, for example a claim against the solicitors in negligence.

Two further factors were introduced by Browne-Wilkinson J in *Re Dennis (Deceased) Dennis v Lloyds Bank* [1981] 2 All ER 140:

(a) The applicant must show that 'he has an arguable case, a case fit to go to trial and that in approaching that matter the court's approach is rather the same as it adopts when considering proceedings for summary judgment' (see Part 24 of the CPR).

(b) Where, after a full understanding of the nature of the claim and the prospect of success, the applicant makes a conscious decision not to make a claim and then later changes his/her mind, the court ought not to permit the claim to be made irrespective of the length of time which has elapsed, save only that no distribution has taken place.

Unlike section 28 of the Limitation Act 1980, the I(PFD)A 1975 does not make any provision to safeguard those who are under a disability. It is submitted that a person under disability should not be disadvantaged or prejudiced by the absence of such a provision in the Act. Since the court's power to grant permission is discretionary, this necessarily involves consideration of the individual circumstances of each case and the protection of rights preserved under the European Convention on Human Rights.

13.3.1 Procedure for an application out of time

An application for permission under section 4 of the I(PFD)A 1975 to make a claim out of time must be made in the claim form of the substantive claim and must be supported by evidence to establish that there are good grounds for the delay and that the interests of justice justify leave being granted.

13.4 GROUNDS FOR MAKING A CLAIM FOR FINANCIAL PROVISION UNDER THE INHERITANCE (PROVISION FOR FAMILY AND DEPENDANTS) ACT 1975

There is only one ground upon which a claim for financial provision under the I(PFD)A 1975 may be made. It is that 'the disposition of the deceased's estate effected by his will or the law relating to intestacy, or the combination of his will and that law, is not such as to make reasonable financial provision for the applicant'. What is 'reasonable financial provision' varies depending on whether the claim is made by a surviving spouse or civil partner or by an individual who falls into the other categories of eligible claimants.

13.4.1 Meaning of 'reasonable financial provision' in relation to a surviving spouse or civil partner

In respect of a surviving spouse or civil partner, 'reasonable financial provision' means:

> such financial provision as it would be reasonable in all the circumstances of the case for a husband or wife (which includes a surviving spouse of a same sex marriage) or civil partner to receive, whether or not that provision is required for his maintenance.

Sections 14 and 14A of the I(PFD)A 1975 extend this wider provision to a former spouse or civil partner of the deceased where the deceased dies within 12 months of the decree absolute, dissolution of the civil partnership, nullity, decree of judicial separation or separation order, but only to cases where an application for a financial provision order under section 23 of the Matrimonial Causes Act 1973 or a property adjustment order under section 24 of that Act or in the case of civil partners, under Schedule 5, Parts 1 and 2 to the Civil Partnership Act 2004, has not been made by the other party to the marriage or civil partnership or such an application has been made but the proceedings have not been determined at the time of the deceased's death. However, a judicially separated person is excluded from receiving this wider provision unless, despite the judicial separation or separation order, the parties were living together at the time of the deceased's death. In such cases, the court is given a discretion to treat the former surviving spouse or civil partner as a surviving spouse or a surviving civil partner if it thinks it is just to do so.

13.4.2 Meaning of 'reasonable financial provision' in relation to all other cases

In all other cases, 'reasonable financial provision' means 'such financial provision as it would be reasonable in all the circumstances of the case for the applicant to receive for his maintenance'. The term 'maintenance' is not defined in the I(PFD)A 1975. Some insight may be obtained from decided cases but this is only a guide. Much will depend on the factual circumstances in each case, for example any reasons given by the testator for not having made any provision or any disability suffered by the claimant or a member of his family.

13.5 MATTERS WHICH THE COURT MUST TAKE INTO ACCOUNT

Section 3 of the I(PFD)A 1975 sets out the matters to which the court must have regard in determining whether the disposition of the deceased's estate effected by his/her will or the law of intestacy or the combination of this will and that law is such as to make reasonable financial provision for the applicant, and if reasonable provision has not been made how it should exercise its powers. They vary according to the status of the claimant but some factors are common to all the categories of claimants.

The factors which are common to all claimants are:

(a) the financial resources and the needs which the applicant, any other applicant and the beneficiaries has or is likely to have in the foreseeable future;
(b) the obligations and responsibilities which the deceased had towards any applicant or towards any beneficiary of his/her estate;
(c) the size and nature of the net estate of the deceased;
(d) any physical or mental disability of any applicant or any beneficiary of the estate of the deceased;
(e) any other matter including the conduct of the applicant or any other person which, in the circumstances of the case, the court may consider relevant.

Additionally, in the case of a surviving spouse or civil partner, the court must consider:

(a) the age of the applicant and the duration of the marriage or civil partnership;
(b) the contribution made by the applicant to the welfare of the family of the deceased, including any contribution made by looking after the home or caring for the family;
(c) the provision which the claimant might reasonably have expected to receive if, on the day on which the deceased died, the marriage or civil partnership, instead of being terminated by death, was terminated by a decree of divorce or dissolution of the partnership; but nothing requires the court to treat such provision as setting an upper or lower limit on provision which may be made by an order under section 2 of the I(PFD)A 1975 (section 3 as amended by the Inheritance and Trustees' Powers Act 2014).

In the case of an application by a former spouse, civil partner or cohabitant, the court must also consider:

(a) the age of the applicant and the duration of the marriage or civil partnership, or in the case of a cohabitant, the length of the period during which the claimant and the deceased lived together as a married couple or civil partners in the same household; and

(b) the contribution made by the applicant to the welfare of the family of the deceased, including any contribution made by looking after the home or caring for the family.

The relevant factors which the court must consider in respect of a child of the deceased and a child treated as a child of the family include those which apply to all other applicants and the manner in which the claimant was being or in which he/she might have expected to be educated or trained. As regards a child treated as a child of the family, additional factors for consideration are:

(a) whether the deceased maintained the applicant and, if so, to the length of time for which, and the basis on which, the deceased did so, and to the extent of the contribution made by way of maintenance;

(b) whether and, if so, to what extent, the deceased assumed responsibility for the maintenance of the applicant;

(c) whether in maintaining or assuming responsibility for maintaining the applicant the deceased did so knowing that the applicant was not his own child; and

(d) the liability of any other person to maintain the applicant.

In relation to any other person who was being maintained by the deceased, the court must, in addition, have regard:

(a) to the length of time for which, and the basis on which, the deceased maintained the applicant, and to the extent of the contribution made by way of maintenance;

(b) to whether and, if so, to what extent, the deceased assumed responsibility for the maintenance of the applicant (section 3(4) of the I(PFD)A 1975).

13.6 POWERS OF THE COURT TO MAKE ORDERS

If the court is satisfied that the deceased's will, the rules of intestacy or a combination of the two fail to make reasonable financial provision for the applicant, the court may make any one or more of the following orders out of the net estate (see para 13.7) of the deceased (sections 2, 5, 6 and 7 of the I(PFD)A 1975):

(a) such periodical payments and for such term as may be specified in the order;

(b) a lump sum order including payment of lump sums by instalments;

(c) an order for the transfer to the applicant of such property comprised in the net estate;

(d) an order for the settlement for the benefit of the applicant of such property comprised in the net estate;
(e) an order for the acquisition of property out of the net estate and its transfer to the applicant or its settlement for the benefit of the applicant;
(f) variation of any ante-nuptial or post-nuptial settlement or settlement made during the subsistence of a civil partnership formed by the deceased or in anticipation of the formation of such a partnership;
(g) interim orders for periodical payments or lump sum out of the net estate;
(h) variation for the applicant's benefit of the trusts on which the deceased's estate is held (whether arising under the will, or the law of intestacy or both);
(i) variation or discharge of orders for periodical payments or lump sum orders;
(j) such other consequential or supplemental orders as the court thinks necessary or expedient for the purpose of giving effect to the order or for the purpose of securing that the order operates fairly as between one beneficiary of the estate of the deceased and another and may in particular:

> (i) order any person who holds any property which forms part of the net estate of the deceased to make such payment or transfer such property as may be specified in the order;
> (ii) vary any disposition of the deceased's estate effected by his/her will, the law relating to intestacy or a combination of the two in such manner as the court thinks fair and reasonable having regard to the provisions of the order and all the circumstances of the case;
> (iii) confer on the trustees of any property which is the subject of the order such powers as appear to the court to be necessary and expedient.

In assessing the extent (if any) to which the net estate is reduced by any debts or liabilities (including any inheritance tax paid or payable out of the estate), the court may assume that the order has already been made (section 3A of the I(PFD)A 1975 inserted by the Inheritance and Trustees' Powers Act 2014).

13.7 PROPERTY TREATED AS PART OF THE NET ESTATE AND AVAILABLE FOR FINANCIAL PROVISION

Section 25 of the I(PFD)A 1975 defines the 'net estate' as comprising:

(a) all property of which the deceased had power to dispose by his/her will (otherwise than by virtue of a special power of appointment) less the amount of his funeral, testamentary and administration expenses, debts and liabilities, including any inheritance tax payable out of his/her estate on his/her death;

(b) any property in respect of which the deceased held a general power of appointment (not being a power exercisable by will) which has not been exercised;

(c) any sum of money or other property which was nominated by the deceased to any person under a statutory nomination or received by a person as a result of a *donatio mortis causa* less any inheritance tax payable in respect thereof by the nominee or the donee by virtue of section 8;

(d) the deceased's severable share of a joint tenancy by virtue of an order made under section 9. Any application for the severance of the joint tenancy to facilitate the making of financial provision for the applicant must be made before the end of the period of 6 months from the date on which representation with respect to the estate of the deceased was first taken out. The court does not have any powers to extend this time limit (see also Chapter 12);

(e) any sum of money or other property which is by reason of a disposition or contract made by the deceased with a view to defeating a claim under the Act ordered to be provided for the purpose of the making of financial provisions (sections 10 and 11, and see Chapters 11 and 12).

13.8 CONCLUSION

The claim that can be made under the I(PFD)A 1975 and the court's powers under it are not regarded as contentious probate issues but can arise within contentious probate proceedings as an alternative to or in addition to any challenge which is made to the validity of the deceased's will. The procedure which governs proceedings under the Act is set out in Part 57 of the CPR and, therefore, the Pre-Action Protocol must be followed before proceedings are commenced.

Chapter 14

Procedure

14.1 INTRODUCTION

Prior to 2006, in the majority of cases the validity of a will was not challenged and the court's role was limited to issuing the grant of probate or letters of administration. In recent years, however, there has been an increase in probate disputes. The 2012 statistics showed a rise in probate and trust disputes of almost 14% between 2010 and 2011. Wills which are not challenged are known as non-contentious or common form probate, and have been governed by the Non-Contentious Probate Rules 1987 as amended. Where there are contentious matters relating to the application for a grant of probate of the will, letters of administration of the estate of a deceased person or the revocation of a grant or the validity of a will, the claim made is known as a probate claim (rule 57.1(2) of the CPR). As from 15 October 2001, these disputes have been and continue to be governed by Part 57 of the CPR as amended and PD 57, but Part 1 applies to probate cases as it does to all civil proceedings in the county court, High Court and the Court of Appeal and pursuant to rule 1.2 the court has a duty to give effect to the overriding objective when it exercises any power given to it by the Rules and the parties are required to help the court to further the overriding objective (rule 1.3). In addition, the Pre-Action Protocols also apply generally to all contentious proceedings, and these should be followed implicitly, as should the *Chancery Guide* (HM Courts & Tribunals Service, 7th edn, 2013) on probate and inheritance claims.

14.2 PART 1 OF THE CIVIL PROCEDURE RULES – 'THE OVERRIDING OBJECTIVE'

The overriding objective referred to in rule 1.1 of the CPR is the cornerstone for all procedural and case management issues and decisions in all civil proceedings. Its objective is to enable the court to deal with cases justly.

Rule 1.1(2) of the CPR provides that dealing with a case justly includes, so far as is practicable:

   (a) ensuring that the parties are on an equal footing;
   (b) saving expense;
   (c) Dealing with the case in ways which are proportionate—

      (i) to the amount of money involved;
      (ii) to the importance of the case;
      (iii) to the complexity of the issues; and
      (iv) to the financial position of each party;

   (d) ensuring that it is dealt with expeditiously and fairly;
   (e) allotting to it an appropriate share of the court's resources, while taking into account the need to allot resources to other cases; and
   (f) enforcing compliance with rules, practice directions and orders.

The court has a duty to further the overriding objective by actively managing cases. Active case management includes:

   (a) encouraging the parties to co-operate with each other in the conduct of the proceedings;
   (b) identifying the issues at an early stage;
   (c) deciding promptly which issues need full investigation and trial and accordingly disposing summarily of the others;
   (d) deciding the order in which issues are to be resolved;
   (e) encouraging the parties to use an alternative dispute resolution procedure if the court considers that appropriate and facilitating the use of such procedure;
   (f) helping the parties to settle the whole or part of the case;
   (g) fixing timetables or otherwise controlling the progress of the case;
   (h) considering whether the likely benefits of taking a particular step justify the cost of taking it;
   (i) dealing with as many aspects of the case as it can on the same occasion;
   (j) dealing with the case without the parties needing to attend at court;
   (k) making use of technology, and giving directions to ensure that the trial of the case proceeds quickly and efficiently.

Although this list is not exhaustive, it gives the practitioner an overview of what the court will be looking to achieve and, therefore, it is well to take heed of these elements at the outset and to be prepared.

14.3 VENUE

Non-contentious probate matters are assigned to the Family Division of the High Court. All contentious claims are assigned to the Chancery Division of the High Court (rule 57.2(2) of the CPR). If, in addition to a probate claim, it is intended to apply for financial provision under the I(PFD)A 1975, this can be dealt with in the probate proceedings. All probate claims are allocated to the multi-track.

The county court has jurisdiction to deal with a probate claim only where an application for a grant has been made through the Principal Registry or a county court where there is also a Chancery District Registry and the value of the net estate does not exceed the county court limit. The reason for this is obvious in that probate issues require specialist chancery knowledge. The county courts with a Chancery District Registry are: Birmingham, Bristol, Caernarfon, Cardiff, Leeds, Liverpool, Manchester, Mold, Newcastle-upon Tyne, Preston and Central London County Court. If proceedings are commenced in the High Court because the local county court does not have jurisdiction, the High Court may, if it considers it appropriate to do so, transfer the proceedings to a county court where there is a Chancery District Registry pursuant to section 40(2) of the County Courts Act 1984.

14.4 FIRST STEP TO TAKE – ENTER A CAVEAT

Where there is any dispute as to the validity of a will or who is entitled to administer the estate, a caveat should be entered to ensure that the person lodging the caveat is informed of any application for the issue of a grant. A caveat should also be entered where time is required to obtain further information or evidence to:

(a) oppose proof of a will;
(b) obtain evidence to challenge the validity of a will;
(c) oppose the issue of the grant to the person entitled;
(d) ascertain the eligibility of the person entitled under an intestacy.

14.4.1 What is a caveat?

A caveat is a notice in writing issued out of the Principal Registry of the Family Division of the High Court or a district probate registry to show cause against the issue of a grant to anyone other than the caveator (objector). It requires the court not to permit a grant of representation to be issued in relation to the deceased's estate without first giving notice to the caveator (objector).

14.4.2 Procedure for entering a caveat

Currently, rule 44 of the Non-Contentious Probate Rules 1987 sets out the procedure to be followed when applying to enter a caveat/objection. Any person wishing to enter a caveat/objection or a solicitor acting on his behalf, may enter a caveat/objection by completing the prescribed Form 3 (see Appendix B1). The caveat/objection is entered by lodging the completed form, either personally or by post, in any registry or sub-registry and paying the prescribed fee. An official acknowledgment of the entry of the caveat/objection is provided by the registry. All caveats/objections are now entered into the registries' computer system, known as *Probateman*.

14.4.3 Duration and renewal of 'caveat'/'objection'

Once entered, a caveat/objection is effective for 6 months from the date of entry. This period may be extended by written application, which may be made by letter, to the registry or sub-registry where the caveat was entered within the last month of the period of 6 months. The application should request an extension of 6 months and must be accompanied by the prescribed fee. Further extensions may be applied for in the same way for periods up to 6 months, until the caveat/objection is removed or a probate claim is issued in the Chancery Division (rule 44(3) of the Non-Contentious Probate Rules 1987). A caveat/objection is removed by an application made on notice to a district judge or by consent.

If a probate action is commenced, the caveat/objection remains in force until the claim has been determined.

14.4.4 Warning to a caveat/response to an objection

Upon receipt of an application for a grant, the registry or sub-registry at which the application is made must cause a search to be made of the national electronically monitored index. If a caveat/objection has been entered, the registry to which the application is being made is notified of the caveat/objection. The applicant is likewise notified and the application for the grant is stayed.

The applicant for the grant, or any person having an interest in the estate, may issue a warning, in Form 4 (see Appendix B2) against the caveat/objection. The warning must be issued at the Leeds District Probate Registry. The person giving the warning must state his interest in the estate of the deceased whether under a will or on intestacy, as the case may be, and his address for service in

England and Wales and must require the caveator/objector to give particulars of his interest within 8 days (inclusive of the day of service) of service of the warning. Service may be effected by post, document exchange or fax in accordance with Order 5 of the RSC (note: not the CPR).

On service of the warning, the caveator/objector has two options namely:

(a) to enter an appearance within 8 days of service; or
(b) if the caveator/objector has no contrary interest, but wishes to show cause against the sealing of a grant to that person, he/she must issue and serve a summons for directions within 8 days of the service of the warning.

14.4.5 Entering an appearance

Under the Non-Contentious Probate Rules 1987, where the caveator/objector has a contrary interest, he must, within 8 days of service of the warning enter an appearance in Form 5 (see Appendix B3), by lodging the form at the Leeds District Probate Registry (rule 44(10)). The appearance must show that the caveator/objector has an interest contrary to that of the person applying for the grant, otherwise the entry of appearance will be refused by the court. An appearance may be entered after the prescribed 8 days provided that the person serving the warning has not filed an affidavit of service (rule 44(12)). If an appearance is entered within the 8 days, no grant may issue, except to the caveator/objector, without the order of the court.

Where the caveator/objector neither enters an appearance nor issues a summons for directions within the prescribed 8 days, the person serving the warning may file an affidavit of service of the warning, and the caveat/objection thereupon ceases to have effect (see Appendix B4 for a form of affidavit of service).

If an appearance has been entered, a stamped copy must be served immediately on the person who lodged the warning. Where an appearance has been lodged and an agreement has not been reached between the parties, either party may commence proceedings in the Chancery Division for the issues to be determined by the court.

14.4.6 Withdrawal of caveat/objection

A caveat/objection may be withdrawn at any time by the caveator/objector. When a warning is issued the caveator/objector must give notice of withdrawal to the person who issued the warning. The caveat/objection is withdrawn at the registry at which it was entered, but notice of withdrawal must be accompanied by the acknowledgement of receipt of the caveat/objection issued by that registry. The Leeds District Probate Registry is notified and the grant is then issued. No fee is payable on an application to withdraw the caveat/objection.

14.4.7 Powers of the court

Under the Non-Contentious Probate Rules 1987, where a summons for directions is issued, the application will be listed before a district judge at the Principal Registry or a district judge of the district probate registry where the application for a grant is pending. The summons must be supported by an affidavit. At the hearing, if the court is not satisfied that the caveator/objector has shown sufficient reason for his/her objections to the issue of a grant, it will direct that the caveat/objection shall cease to have effect and that the application for the grant should proceed. The court may give such other directions as may be necessary relating to any further proceedings or the application for the grant.

14.4.8 Further caveat/objection

Under the Non-Contentious Probate Rules 1987, unless the court grants permission, no further caveats/objections may be entered by the caveator/objector whose caveat/objection has been withdrawn or has ceased to have effect under the rules or by order of the court.

14.5 PROBATE CLAIMS

14.5.1 Parties

The claimant in a probate claim must have an interest in the estate of the deceased (see *Randall v Randall* [2014] EWHC 3134 (Ch)). The claimant is usually the executor of a will, or a beneficiary or other person who has an interest in the estate and seeks to challenge the validity of the will.

Any person who may be adversely affected by the claim should be made a defendant but, in any event, the person should be given notice of the proceedings so that he/she may apply to be joined as a party to the claim. If in doubt, an application should be made to the court for directions under Part 19 of the CPR and PD 57, paragraph 4.1 which both require the court as part of its case management duties to consider the issue of joinder of parties and to give necessary directions.

In a probate claim for the revocation of a grant or letters of administration, every person who is entitled, or claims to be entitled, to administer the estate under that grant must be made a party to the claim (rule 57.6(1) of the CPR).

Any person who may be affected by the court's decision in the probate proceedings may apply to the court under rule 19.4 of the CPR to be joined as a defendant to the proceedings.

14.5.2 How to start a probate claim

Before issuing proceedings, it is essential to follow the general Pre-Action Protocol and attempt to resolve the dispute by agreement or through mediation or other form of alternative dispute resolution.

Where proceedings are inevitable, it is also important in all contentious probate proceedings to familiarise oneself with the *Chancery Guide*, Chapter 24 which applies to probate and inheritance claims.

A probate claim must be commenced in accordance with the procedure set out in Part 7 of the CPR and PD 57, paragraphs 2.1 and 7.2. The claim must be commenced by using the Part 7 claim form. The claimant must provide additional copies of the claim form for the court and for each of the defendants. The claim form may be issued personally or it may be posted. On issue of the claim form, the claimant must pay the issuing fee of £465.

14.5.3 Venue

The claim must be issued out of:

(a) the Chancery Chambers at the Royal Courts of Justice;
(b) a county court where there is also a Chancery District Registry; or
(c) the Central London County Court.

All probate claims are allocated to the multi-track (rule 57.2(3) of the CPR).

Section 32 of the County Courts Act 1984 identifies which probate claims may be heard in the appropriate county court. There are Chancery District Registries at Birmingham, Bristol, Caernarfon, Cardiff, Leeds, Liverpool, Manchester, Mold, Newcastle-upon-Tyne, Preston and Central London County Court

14.5.4 Contents of the claim form

A probate claim form and any subsequent court documents relating to the claim must be marked at the top 'In the estate of [name] deceased (Probate)' (PD 57, paragraph 2.1 of the CPR). It must set out the names of the parties.

The claim form must contain a statement of the nature of the interest of the claimant and of each defendant in the estate of the deceased (rule 57.7 of the CPR). If the party disputes another party's interest in the estate, this must be set out in the statement of claim, with reasons.

If it is alleged that at the time when a will was executed the testator/testatrix did not know of and approve its contents, particulars of the facts and matters relied on must be set out.

Where it is alleged that the will was not duly executed, that at the time of execution of the will the testator/testatrix did not have testamentary capacity or that the will was obtained by undue influence or fraud, the allegation made and the particulars of the facts and matters relied upon must be pleaded (rule 57.7(3) and (4) of the CPR). For a specimen form of particulars of claim asserting undue influence, see Appendix B6.

14.5.5 Documents which must be filed with the claim form

The claimant must also file the testamentary documents of the deceased and written evidence of the testamentary documents. The written evidence about the testamentary documents should be in the form annexed to PD 57 of the CPR. The written evidence must be signed by the party personally and not by his/her solicitor or other representative. Where the party is a child or a protected person, the written evidence must be signed by his/her litigation friend (PD 57, paragraph 3.2). Where the probate claim seeks the revocation of a grant or letters of administration, if the claimant is the person to whom the grant was made, he/she must lodge the probate or letters of administration in the relevant court office when the claim form is issued. If the grant is not lodged at the time of issue, it must be lodged within 7 days of issue of the claim form. Where the defendant has the probate or letters of administration under his/her control, he/she must lodge it when he/she acknowledges service (rule 57.6(1) and (2)).

Where there is an urgent need to commence proceedings, for example in order to apply immediately for the appointment of an administrator pending the determination of the claim, and it is not possible for the claimant to lodge the testamentary documents or the written evidence at the time when the claim form is issued, application should be made to the court for permission to issue the claim form on the claimant undertaking to the court to lodge the documents and file the evidence within such time as the court directs (PD 57, paragraph 3.3 of the CPR).

14.6 WHAT THE COURT OFFICE MUST DO

When the claim form is issued, the court will stamp all the copies of the claim form, one of which will be marked as the original. The relevant office will then send a notice to Leeds District Probate Registry requesting that all testamentary documents, grants of representation and other relevant documents currently held at any probate registry are sent to the relevant office (PD 57, paragraph 2.3 of the CPR).

Rule 45 of the Non-Contentious Probate Rules 1987 provides that upon being advised of the commencement of a probate claim, the senior district judge must give notice of the action to every caveator/objector other than the claimant in the action in respect of each caveat/objection which is in force. The senior district judge must also give notice of the existence of the action to any caveator/objector who enters a caveat/objection subsequent to the commencement of the probate claim. The commencement of the action has the effect of preventing the sealing of a grant other than a grant under section 117 of the Senior Courts Act 1981 until application for a grant is made by the person shown to be entitled thereto by the decision of the court in the action. Following a grant being given, any caveat/objection entered will cease to have effect (see also PD 57, paragraph 2.4 of the CPR).

14.7 SERVICE

Service may be effected by the court or by the claimant personally, by post, document exchange or fax, in accordance with the provisions of Part 6 of the CPR. Where the defendant is outside the jurisdiction, rules 6.17–6.31 apply and care should be taken that those provisions are complied with.

14.8 ACKNOWLEDGEMENT OF SERVICE AND DEFENCE

A defendant within the jurisdiction must file the appropriate form of acknowledgement of service with the court within 28 days after service of the claim form. If the particulars of claim are not served at the same time as the claim form, the acknowledgement of service must be filed within 28 days of receipt of the particulars of claim (rule 57.4(2) of the CPR).

Where the defendant is outside the jurisdiction and the claim form is served on him/her outside England and Wales under rule 16.9 of the CPR, the period for filing the acknowledgment of service is 14 days longer than the period set out in rule 6.35 or PD 6B which supplements Part 6 (i.e. 6 weeks) (rule 57.4(3)).

The defendant's defence must also be filed within the above time limits. A defendant may give notice in his/her defence that he/she does not raise any positive case, but insists on the will being proved in solemn form and, for that purpose, intends to cross-examine the witnesses who attested the will. The advantage of giving such a notice is that the court will not make an order for costs against him/her unless it considers that there was no reasonable ground for opposing the will (rule 57.7(5) of the CPR).

14.8.1 Documents to be served with acknowledgement of service

When the defendant acknowledges service, he/she must lodge with the court any testamentary document of the deceased which is in his/her possession or control. He/she must also in written evidence describe any testamentary document of the deceased of which he/she has knowledge. If he/she does not have any such document, he/she must state that fact.

If any testamentary document of which the defendant has knowledge is not in his/her possession or under his/her control, the defendant must give the name and address of the person who has such possession or control. If the defendant does not know the identity and location of the person in whose possession or control the document is, the defendant must state that fact (rule 57.5(3) of the CPR). A form of witness statement or affidavit relating to testamentary documents is annexed to PD 57, and the use of this form is advised. The form must be signed by the defendant personally (PD 57, paragraph 3.2) or in the case of a child or a protected person, by the litigation friend.

A form for a witness statement concerning testamentary documents is set out in Appendix B5. Forms of limited defence are set out in Appendix B7 and Appendix B8.

14.9 COUNTERCLAIM

A defendant who wishes to make a claim or to seek any remedy relating to the grant of probate or letters of administration must serve a counterclaim setting out his/her contention (i.e. a Part 20 claim) with his/her defence. Where the claimant has failed to serve particulars of claim within the prescribed time, the defendant may with the permission of the court serve a counterclaim. In this event, the action will continue as if the counterclaim (Part 20 claim) were the particulars of claim and the defendant is then regarded as the claimant (rule 57.8 of the CPR).

14.10 CONTENTS OF DEFENCE/COUNTERCLAIM

The particulars of claim/defence and counterclaim must comply with rule 16.4 of the CPR. The particulars of claim must include a concise statement of the facts on which the claimant relies.

The defence must state which of the statements and allegations in the particulars of case are admitted or denied by the defendant or that he/she is unable to admit or deny them and put the claimant to proof of them. Where any allegation is denied, reasons for so doing must be set out. The defendant must also set out his/her own version of events if it differs from that pleaded by the claimant (rule 16.5(1) and (2) of the CPR). Where undue influence or fraud is alleged, it is essential to plead the case as fully as possible, with detailed particulars of all facts and matters relied on, with dates. The more serious the allegation, the higher is the burden of proof. Where valuations are disputed, the defendant must state the reason for disputing the valuation and, if he/she is able, he/she must give his/her own statement of the value (rule 16.5(6)).

14.11 FAILURE TO ACKNOWLEDGE SERVICE OR FILE A DEFENCE

Where any of several defendants does not file an acknowledgement of service or a defence, the claimant cannot in a probate action, apply for a default judgment (rule 57.10(1) of the CPR). In this instance, the claimant, provided the time for filing the acknowledgement has expired, may file written evidence of service on the defendant, of the claim form and of the particulars of case, and seek to proceed with the claim as if the defendant acknowledged service (rule 57.10(2)).

Where no defendant acknowledges service or files a defence, the claimant may, after the time for filing the acknowledgment of service and defence has expired, apply to the court for an order either that the claim should be discontinued or that the claim should proceed to trial (rule 57.10(3) of the CPR). The claimant must support such an application with written evidence of service of the claim form and the particulars of claim. The court hearing the application may direct that the claim should proceed and that the final hearing should take place on written evidence only. This allows the court to continue its supervisory role, including its role in approving any compromise and ensuring that every person who may be affected by the claim has had notice and consents to the proposals.

14.12 DISCONTINUANCE OR DISMISSAL OF A CLAIM

Pursuant to rule 57.11 of the CPR, the court has power to allow the claim to be discontinued or dismissed, on terms as to costs or otherwise, and to grant probate of the will or letters of administration to the person entitled to the grant. PD 57, paragraph 6.1 also provides that where the parties have agreed to settle a probate claim the court may:

(a) order the trial of the claim on written evidence, which will lead to a grant in solemn form;
(b) order that a claim be discontinued or dismissed under rule 57.11, which will lead to a grant in common form;
(c) pronounce for or against the validity of one or more will(s) under section 49 of the Administration of Justice Act 1985.

14.13 EXTENSION OF TIME LIMITS

Rule 2.11 of the CPR provides that the time specified by a rule or by the court may be varied by written agreement of the parties, unless the rules or practice direction provide otherwise or the court orders otherwise. Where the court has listed a case for a case management conference, a pre-trial directions hearing or a final hearing, the parties cannot agree to adjourn the hearing. Where it is sought to adjourn a listed hearing, an application must be made and supported by written evidence setting out good reasons for the application. The court may accede to the application subject to further directions and the listing of a review hearing.

14.14 DISCLOSURE

14.14.1 Pre-action disclosure

In probate claims, as in all civil action, advantage can be taken of rule 31.16 of the CPR which provides for pre-action disclosure. Pursuant to this rule an application for pre-action disclosure may be made. The application must be supported by written evidence, which should address the matters which the court is likely to take into consideration when determining the application. These include the following:

(a) whether the party against whom the disclosure is sought is likely to be a party to subsequent proceedings;
(b) whether the applicant is also likely to be a party to those proceedings;
(c) whether the documents of which disclosure is sought are of a nature which, if the proceedings were commenced, the defendant would be under a duty to disclose by way of standard disclosure;
(d) whether disclosure is desirable in order to dispose fairly of the anticipated proceedings, or to assist in resolving the dispute without resort to proceedings and to save costs.

The application for pre-action disclosure should identify the documents or class of documents of which disclosure is sought. It should also request a direction that the respondent should be required, when making the disclosure, to specify which documents are no longer in his/her possession or under his/her control, and to indicate what has happened to them. The application should also apply for inspection.

14.14.2 Disclosure under the Senior Courts Act 1981

Sections 122 and 123 of the Senior Courts Act 1981 provide for a person who is interested in the estate of the deceased to apply to the court for an order that a document in the possession of another, which may be relevant to any issue in question, should be brought before the court for examination, and for a witness summons (*subpoena*) to be issued against the person.

Section 122 of the Senior Courts Act 1981 provides:

(1) where it appears that there are reasonable grounds for believing that any person has knowledge of any document which is or purports to be a testamentary document, the High Court may, whether or not any legal proceedings are pending, order him to attend for the purposes of being examined in open court.
(2) The court may—

(a) require any person who is before it in compliance with an order under subsection (b) to answer any question relating to the document concerned; and
(b) if appropriate, order him to bring in the document in such manner as the court may direct.

Any person who, having been required by the court to do so under this section, fails to attend for examination, answer any question or bring in any document, is guilty of contempt of court.

Where it appears that any person has in his/her possession, custody or power any document which is or purports to be a testamentary document, the High Court may, whether or not any legal proceedings are pending, issue a *subpoena* requiring him/her to bring in the document in such manner as the court may in the *subpoena* direct (section 123 of the Senior Courts Act 1981).

14.14.3 Disclosure under Part 31 of the CPR

Part 31 of the CPR applies to all issues relating to disclosure which a party is under a duty to give. Where specific disclosure is sought, a request should initially be made in writing giving the other party a reasonable time within which to provide the disclosure. If such disclosure is not forthcoming, an application may be made for specific disclosure to be ordered. Pursuant to rule 31.12, the court may on such an application make an order for specific disclosure which is an order that a party must do one or more of the following things:

(a) disclose documents or classes of documents specified in the order;
(b) carry out a search to the extent stated in the order;
(c) disclose any documents located as a result of that search.

An application for specific disclosure should be supported by evidence setting out the reasons why disclosure is sought, why the documents are relevant and why it is reasonable for the court to direct such disclosure. Part 31 of the CPR provides a comprehensive set of rules for disclosure and inspection of documents, including electronic documents, with practice directions to supplement the rules, which should be followed and relied on.

14.14.4 Obtaining further information under Part 18 of the CPR

By its very nature, a probate claim concerns a situation where the party seeking to pursue or defend the claim may not have all the relevant information, for example the particulars of claim may leave many questions unanswered. In such instances, the further facility to seek information under Part 18 of the CPR is useful. A written request for such information should always be made before making any application to the court. It is only when the information is inadequate or not forthcoming that an application for an order should be made.

Lastly, it must be stressed that the general Pre-Action Protocol and the *Chancery Guide* must be consulted and followed at every step of the proceedings.

14.15 INSPECTION OF TESTAMENTARY DOCUMENTS

Except with the permission of the court, a party to a claim is not permitted to inspect the testamentary documents or the written evidence lodged or filed with the court by any party until he/she has lodged his/her testamentary documents and filed his/her evidence. Where access to the documents is required, an application must be made to the court setting out the reason, for example that the documents are required for forensic examination.

14.16 RECTIFICATION OF WILLS

Section 20 of the Administration of Justice Act 1982 provides for the rectification of a will. Where the only remedy sought is the rectification of a will and there are no other contentious probate proceedings issued or contemplated, the application for the rectification of a will is governed by rule 55 of the Non-Contentious Probate Rules 1987 and PD 57, paragraphs 9–11 of the CPR.

Rule 55 of the Non-Contentious Probate Rules 1987 provides:

> **Application for rectification of a will**
> 55. (1) An application for an order that a will be rectified by virtue of section 20(1) of the Administration of Justice Act 1982 may be made to a registrar, unless a probate action has been commenced.
> (2) The application shall be supported by an affidavit, setting out the grounds of the application, together with such evidence as can be adduced as to the testator's intentions and as to whichever of the following matters as are in issue:—
>
> > (a) in what respects the testator's intentions were not understood; or
> > (b) the nature of any alleged clerical error.
>
> (3) Unless otherwise directed, notice of the application shall be given to every person having an interest under the will whose interest might be prejudiced by the rectification applied for and any comments in writing by any such person shall be exhibited to the affidavit in support of the application.
> (4) If the district judge or registrar is satisfied that, subject to any direction to the contrary, notice has been given to every person mentioned in paragraph (3) above, and that the application is unopposed, he may order that the will be rectified accordingly.

An application for rectification can, therefore, be summarised as follows:

> (a) It is made to a district judge or district registrar of any district probate registry.

(b) It must be supported by a sworn statement setting out the grounds of the application and any other supporting evidence.

(c) Unless the court otherwise directs, if the claimant is the person to whom a grant was made in respect of the will, the probate or letters of administration must be lodged with the application (PD 57, paragraph 10.1 of the CPR); if the defendant has the grant of probate or letters of administration in his/her possession or under his/her control, he/she must, unless the court orders otherwise, lodge it within 14 days after service of the claim form on him/her (PD 57, paragraph 10.2).

(d) Notice of the application must be given to every person who has an interest under the will whose interest might be prejudiced, and to any other person who might be prejudiced by the rectification applied for.

(e) An order will be made only if the court is satisfied that the application is unopposed.

(f) If an order is made, a copy of every order made must be sent to the Principal Registry of the Family Division for filing, and a memorandum of the order must be endorsed on, or permanently annexed to, the grant under which the estate is administered (PD 57, paragraph 11.1).

14.17 COSTS

The general rule in probate actions is the same as that which applies in any civil action, namely that costs follow the event. However, where the proceedings disclose that a serious issue arose which needed to be resolved, the court has a discretion to order that the costs be met by the estate. Whether or not the claimant was justified in challenging the validity of the will depends very much on the facts of the individual case and the conduct of the parties in bringing, pursuing or defending the case. A mistaken belief on factual matters, which if not mistaken would lead to the will being pronounced invalid or the grant being revoked, may amount to a reasonable ground for opposing a will (*Wylde v Culver* [2006] EWHC 923 (Ch)). The extent to which the parties sought to negotiate the dispute will also be relevant. In this respect, following the Pre-Action Protocol and the *Chancery Guide* will be very relevant. So will any offer made for a meeting to resolve issues which is not taken up (see *Jarrom v Sellars* [2007] EWHC 1366 (Ch)). Where the fault lies with the testator/testatrix or a residuary beneficiary, the court has a discretion to order costs out of the estate (see *Rowe v Clarke (No 2) (Probate: Costs)* [2006] EWHC 1292 (Ch)).

The fact that a serious issue arose is the usual ground for seeking a no order for costs or that the costs should be borne by the estate. The following cases illustrate situations which have justified the court exercising its discretion.

In *Rowe v Clarke (No 2) (Probate: Costs)* [2006] EWHC 1292 (Ch), the grant of letters of administration to the deceased's brother was challenged by the claimant who asserted that the deceased did not die intestate. On the facts, the judge found that the deceased's will was lost or destroyed without an intention to revoke the will. The court ordered that both parties' costs should be paid out of the estate because the deceased was disorganised in the way he secured the custody of documents and his will. Those circumstances were not known to his brother when he obtained a grant and it was, therefore, reasonable for him to have contested the action by reference to the presumption of intentional destruction. In the circumstances, it was held that it would be unjust to make an order for costs leaving the defendant to bear his own costs.

In *Wylde v Culver* [2006] EWHC 923 (Ch), the testatrix made a will in 2003 in which she excluded the claimant. The claimant brought an action seeking revocation of the grant in relation to that will and a pronouncement of an earlier will on the grounds that the later will was not made by the testatrix and, therefore, was made without the deceased's knowledge and approval. His claim was based on the facts (amongst others) that the will was written by a principal beneficiary, that one of the witnesses was an unlikely choice and that the deceased's signature did not seem genuine. Having commenced the action, the claimant sought to discontinue it pursuant to rule 57.11(1) of the CPR. The issue of whether the claimant should be permitted to discontinue the action was in the discretion of the court and depended on whether the issues raised were serious and required further investigation. The issue of whether costs should be ordered against the claimant was thus linked with whether permission would be granted. If the issues raised were found not be serious enough to require investigation, there would be insufficient grounds for the claimant to resist an order for costs against him. On the facts, the court found that the deceased, the defendant or anyone connected with the action did nothing to justify an order for costs being made against them. The court in this case followed the provisions of rule 57.7(5) which provides that:

(a) A defendant may give notice in his defence that he does not raise any positive case, but insists on the will being proved in solemn form and, for that purpose, will cross-examine the witnesses who attested the will.
(b) If a defendant gives such a notice, the court will not make an order for costs against him unless it considers that there was no reasonable ground for opposing the will.

Applying these provisions, the court on the facts held that the situation in this case led the claimant to the mistaken belief that the will was not validly executed and, therefore, it amounted to a reasonable ground for opposing the will. His wish to withdraw the proceedings was the fact that he 'got cold feet' and was worried about costs. His action in commencing proceedings and pursuing the claim was done in good faith. On the facts, the claimant acted reasonably.

In *Jarrom v Sellars* [2007] EWHC 1366 (Ch), the deceased executed a will in 1990 appointing her daughter, S, and S's husband as executors, and in which the residuary estate passed to S. The deceased then made another will in which she appointed her son and a solicitor to act as executors and trustees, and the residuary estate was left to her four grandchildren in equal shares. S entered a caveat (objection) to the grant of probate. She did not issue any proceedings but attempts were made to negotiate her claim. Not having succeeded in resolving the issues, the executors issued proceedings, whereupon S agreed to remove the caveat (objection), allowing the later will to be admitted to probate and she made proposals for a meeting. The executors did not take up the offer of a meeting, notwithstanding that the estate was not liquid and had a meeting taken place matters may have been resolved or narrowed. The issue, therefore, which remained between the parties was who should pay the costs of the discontinued probate action. The executors maintained that, in accordance with the general rule that costs follow the event, S should pay the costs. The court took into account the failure of the executors in taking up the offer for a meeting and did not accept their argument that the offer lacked any agenda or detailed proposals. It was held that this was a proper case which justified the court departing from the normal rule, and made an order that S should not have to pay the costs.

In relation to discontinuance of a claim, it should also be noted that Part 38 of the CPR does not apply to probate claims (see rule 57.11), but it does apply to a claim under the I(PFD)A 1975. The issue of costs in claims under this Act is governed by Parts 36 and 44. In considering whether or not to make any order for costs, the court will have regard to any Part 36 offers. The court, however, also has a discretion to disapply the normal consequences if it considers that to do so would result in injustice. In exercising its discretion, the court will have regard to the factors set out in Part 44 and to the overriding objective (see *Lilleyman v Lilleyman* [2012] EWHC 821 (Ch), where the court, when making an order against the claimant after the Part 36 offer was made, took into account the defendant's conduct).

14.18 CONCLUSION

In all cases, it is advisable to take full and detailed instructions to ensure that there are reasonable grounds for founding any claim, and then to seek to attempt to resolve the issue, or, in the case of multiple issues, as many of them as is possible, by requesting the relevant information and disclosure, and by following the Pre-Action Protocol and the *Chancery Guide*. If these steps are not taken, the risk is that costs will be awarded against the losing party unless the court finds that there were serious issues which needed to be investigated, and that there were reasonable grounds for opposing a will or defending the claim.

Chapter 15

Statutory Wills

15.1 INTRODUCTION

The preceding chapters show that at common law, where a will is duly executed by a person who is aged 18 or over and the will appears rational on the face of it, the presumption is that the testator/testatrix had testamentary capacity unless a real doubt is raised as to capacity. Where the will is challenged on the basis that the testator/testatrix lacked testamentary capacity, the burden of rebutting the presumption falls on the person who seeks to assert lack of testamentary capacity. Section 1(2) of the MCA 2005 confirms this position by providing that a person must be assumed to have capacity unless it is established that he/she lacks capacity. The burden thus remains on the party who challenges capacity to establish lack of capacity.

If, therefore, there is real doubt about the testator's/testatrix's capacity, it is advisable to seek a determination on this issue by making an application to the Court of Protection under the provisions of the MCA 2005. If lack of capacity is established, it is advisable to ask the court to make a will on behalf of the testator/testatrix.

15.2 COURT'S STATUTORY POWERS TO MAKE A STATUTORY WILL

The court's power to make a statutory will is now governed by sections 16(2)(a) and 18(1)(i) of the MCA 2005. Section 16(2)(a) provides that the court may, by making an order, make the decision or decisions on behalf of the person lacking capacity, P, in relation to the matter or matters, and section 18(1)(i) extends the court's powers to enable it to execute a will on P's behalf.

The approach which the court should adopt under the MCA 2005 was set out in *Re P* [2009] EWHC 163 (COP), with the emphasis being on 'the overarching principle that any decision made on behalf of P must be in P's best interests' and 'the goal of the inquiry is not what P "might be expected" to have done; but what is in P's best interests'. This is more like the 'balance sheet' approach than the 'substituted judgment' approach.

The MCA 2005 thus provides a structured decision making process and as Lewison J stated in *Re P* [2009] EWHC 163 (COP), it:

> … expressly directs the decision maker to take a number of steps before reaching a decision. These include encouraging P to participate in the decision. He must also 'consider' P's past and present wishes and his beliefs and values and must 'take into account' the views of third parties as to what would be in P's best interests.
> 39. Having gone through these steps, the decision maker must then form a value judgment of his own giving effect to the paramount statutory instruction that any decision must be made in P's best interests. (*Re P* [2009] EWHC 163 (COP) at [38(vi)] and [39])

Further guidance is provided in *NT v FS* [2013] EWHC 684 (COP) at [8].

15.3　BEST INTERESTS

The criteria to be applied in assessing the best interests of P are set out in section 4 of the MCA 2005, which provides that the person making any decision on P's behalf must consider all the relevant circumstances and in particular:

(a) he/she must consider whether it is likely that P will at some time have capacity in relation to the matter in question and if it appears likely that he/she will, when that is likely to be;

(b) he/she must consider as far as is reasonably ascertainable:

 (i) P's past and present wishes and feelings (and in particular, any written relevant statement made by him/her when he/she had capacity);

 (ii) the beliefs and values which would be likely to influence P's decision if he/she had capacity, and the other factors that he/she would be likely to consider if he/she were able to do so;

(c) he/she must take into account, if it is practicable and appropriate to consult them, the views of:

 (i) anyone named by P as someone to be consulted on the matter in question or on matters of that kind;

(ii) anyone engaged in caring for P or interested in his/her welfare;
(iii) the donee of a lasting power of attorney granted by P;
(iv) any deputy appointed for P by the court;

as to what would be in P's best interests.

The decision maker must also, so far as is reasonably practicable, permit and encourage P to participate or improve his/her ability to participate, as fully as possible, in any act done for him/her and any decision affecting him/her.

P's wishes and feelings are only one of the matters which the court will take into account. In making a statutory will, the court will consider the overall picture and take into account the fact that what will live on after P's death is his/her memory, and that for most people it is in their best interests that they be remembered with affection by their family (see *Re P* [2009] EWHC 163 (COP) at [44]).

15.4 PRE-ACTION PREPARATION

Before making an application for a statutory will, it is important that as much information as possible is obtained on P's life. This will include:

- his/her interests;
- his/her relationships;
- any moral obligations that he/she may have;
- values which are important to him/her or were important to him/her when he/she had capacity;
- any charities he/she supported;
- any changes in his/her personal or marital status and financial assets;
- whether he/she executed a valid will when he/she had capacity and, if so, evidence to establish that his/her circumstances have changed so drastically since that will was executed that it would not be in his/her interests for the will to stand or, at least, there is a need for the will to be reviewed.

15.5 PROCEDURE

The procedure for making an application for a statutory will is set out in Part 9 and PD 9F of the Court of Protection Rules 2007 (SI 2007/1744).

15.5.1 Who may apply

Section 50 of the MCA 2005 and rules 51(1) and 52(2) of the Court of Protection Rules 2007 set out the list of people who are eligible to apply for a statutory will without first seeking permission from the court. Those who are not included in the list must apply for permission to issue an application for an order for a statutory will to be made.

15.5.2 Respondents to the application

The following people must be joined as respondents to the application:

(a) any beneficiary under an existing will or codicil who is likely to be materially or adversely affected by the application;
(b) any beneficiary under a proposed will or codicil who is likely to be materially or adversely affected by the application;
(c) any prospective beneficiary under P's intestacy where there is no existing will (PD 9F(9) of the Court of Protection Rules 2007).

15.5.3 People who must be notified of the application

Rule 70 of the Court of Protection Rules 2007 sets out the notification procedure, and PD 9B lists those who should be notified of the application.

15.5.4 Application form

The application must be made in Form COP 1, with supporting evidence of P's incapacity in Form COP 3 completed by a medical practitioner who has examined P and who can certify that he/she has applied the legal test for testamentary capacity. Where a will needs to be made as a matter of urgency, assistance should be sought from the Judicial Support Unit at the court and, depending on the urgency, it would be advisable to make provision for the will to be executed by a person who is available to act on the making of an order, for example the Official Solicitor.

15.5.5 Information to accompany the application form

Additional information which needs to be provided is set out in PD 64F of the Court of Protection Rules 2007. This includes:

(a) a copy of the draft will or codicil with a copy;
(b) a copy of any existing will or codicil;
(c) any consents to act by the proposed executors;

- (d) details of P's family, preferably in the form of a family tree, including details of the full name and date of birth of each person included in the family tree;
- (e) a schedule showing details of P's current assets, with an up-to-date valuation;
- (f) a schedule showing P's estimated net yearly income and spending;
- (g) a statement showing P's needs, both current and future estimates, and his/her general circumstances;
- (h) if P is living in NHS accommodation, information on whether he/she may be discharged to local authority accommodation, to other fee paying accommodation or to his/her own home;
- (i) if the applicant considers it relevant, full details of the resources of any proposed beneficiary, and details of any likely changes if the application is successful;
- (j) details of any capital gains tax, inheritance tax, or income tax which may be chargeable in respect of the subject matter of the application;
- (k) an explanation of the effect, if any, that the proposed changes will have on P's circumstances, preferably in the form of a 'before and after' schedule of assets and income;
- (l) if appropriate, a statement of whether any land would be affected by the proposed will or settlement and, if so, details of its location and title number, if applicable;
- (m) where the application is for a settlement of property or for variation of an existing settlement or trust, a draft of the proposed deed, plus one copy;
- (n) a copy of any registered enduring power of attorney or lasting power of attorney;
- (o) confirmation that P is a resident of England and Wales; and
- (p) an up-to-date report of P's present medical condition, life expectancy, likelihood of requiring increased expenditure in the foreseeable future, and testamentary capacity.

15.5.6 Execution of the will

Where a court makes an order or gives directions requiring or authorising a person to execute the will on behalf of P, the will must state that it is signed by P acting by the authorised person. The will must be signed by the authorised person with P's name and his/her own name in the presence of two or more witnesses present at the same time. The witnesses must attest the will in the presence of the authorised person and, lastly, the will must be sealed with the official seal of the court.

15.6 EFFECT OF EXECUTION

Where the will is executed as a statutory will, it has the same effect as if P had capacity to make a valid will and the will was executed by him/her as required by the Wills Act 1837, with the exceptions set out in Schedule 2, paragraph 4(3)–(5) to the MCA 2005.

Once the will is executed on behalf of P, the applicant must send the original and two copies of the will to the Court of Protection for sealing. The court will seal the original and the copies and return both documents to the applicant.

15.7 CONCLUSION

Although the material set out above does not fall within the context of contentious probate or a testamentary challenge, it is included in this book in order to raise awareness of the remedy which is available to overcome the difficulty that may arise where it is believed that a person lacks capacity, and to avoid an intestacy arising in such cases.

Appendices

A1 Wills Act 1837

1 MEANING OF CERTAIN WORDS IN THIS ACT

... the words and expressions herein-after mentioned, which in their ordinary signification have a more confined or a different meaning, shall in this Act, except where the nature of the provision or the context of the Act shall exclude such construction, be interpreted as follows; (that is to say,) the word "will" shall extend to a testament, and to a codicil, and to an appointment by will or by writing in the nature of a will in exercise of a power, [and also to an appointment by will of a guardian of a child], [and also to an appointment by will of a representative under section 4 of the Human Tissue Act 2004,] ... and to any other testamentary disposition; and the words "real estate" shall extend to manors, advowsons, messuages, lands, tithes, rents, and hereditaments, ... whether corporeal, incorporeal, or personal ... and to any estate, right, or interest (other than a chattel interest) therein; and the words "personal estate" shall extend to leasehold estates and other chattels real, and also to monies, shares of government and other funds, securities for money (not being real estates), debts, choses in action, rights, credits, goods, and all other property whatsoever which by law devolves upon the executor or administrator, and to any share or interest therein; and every word importing the singular number only shall extend and be applied to several persons or things as well as one person or thing; and every word importing the masculine gender only shall extend and be applied to a female as well as a male.

AMENDMENTS

Repealed in part, in relation to Northern Ireland, by the Statute Law Revision (Northern Ireland) Act 1954, the Statute Law Revision (Northern Ireland) Act 1976, and Wills and Administration Proceedings (NI) Order 1994, SI 1994/1899, art 38, Sch 3.

First words omitted repealed by the Statute Law Revision Act 1893, s 1, Sch.

Words "and also to an appointment by will of a guardian of a child" in square brackets substituted by the Children Act 1989, s 108(5), (6), Sch 13, para 1.

Children Act 1989 (Commencement and Transitional Provisions) Order 1991, SI 1991/828, art 3(2) (with Sch 14 para 1(1)).

Words "and also to an appointment by will of a representative under section 4 of the Human Tissue Act 2004," in square brackets inserted by the Human Tissue Act 2004, s 56, Sch 6, para 1.

Second and third words omitted repealed by the Statute Law (Repeals) Act 1969, s 1, Sch, Pt III.

Final words omitted repealed by the Trusts of Land and Appointment of Trustees Act 1996, s 25(2), Sch 4 (with s 25(4), (5)).

2 ...

AMENDMENTS
Repealed by the Statute Law Revision Act 1874.

3 ALL PROPERTY MAY BE DISPOSED OF BY WILL

... it shall be lawful for every person to devise, bequeath, or dispose of, by his will executed in manner herein-after required, all real estate and all personal estate which he shall be entitled to, either at law or in equity, at the time of his death, and which, if not so devised, bequeathed, or disposed of, would devolve ... upon his executor or administrator; and ... the power hereby given shall extend ... to all contingent, executory or other future interests in any real or personal estate, whether the testator may or may not be ascertained as the person or one of the persons in whom the same respectively may become vested, and whether he may be entitled thereto under the instrument by which the same respectively were created, or under any disposition thereof by deed or will; and also to all rights of entry for conditions broken, and other rights of entry; and also to such of the same estates, interests, and rights respectively, and other real and personal estate, as the testator may be entitled to at the time of his death, notwithstanding that he may become entitled to the same subsequently to the execution of his will.

AMENDMENTS
Repealed, in relation to Northern Ireland, by Wills and Administration Proceedings (NI) Order 1994, SI 1994/1899, art 38, Sch 3.

First and third words omitted repealed by the Statute Law Revision (No 2) Act 1888; second and fourth words omitted repealed by the Statute Law (Repeals) Act 1969.

4–6 ...

AMENDMENTS
Repealed by the Statute Law (Repeals) Act 1969.

7 NO WILL OF A PERSON UNDER AGE VALID

... no will made by any person under the age of [eighteen years] shall be valid.

AMENDMENTS
Repealed, in relation to Northern Ireland, by Wills and Administration Proceedings (NI) Order 1994, SI 1994/1899, art 38, Sch 3.

Words omitted repealed by the Statute Law Revision (No 2) Act 1888; Words "eighteen years" in square brackets substituted by the Family Law Reform Act 1969, s 3(1)(a).

8 ...

AMENDMENTS
Repealed by the Statute Law (Repeals) Act 1969.

[9 SIGNING AND ATTESTATION OF WILLS]

[No will shall be valid unless—

(a) it is in writing, and signed by the testator, or by some other person in his presence and by his direction; and
(b) it appears that the testator intended by his signature to give effect to the will; and
(c) the signature is made or acknowledged by the testator in the presence of two or more witnesses present at the same time; and
(d) each witness either—

   (i) attests and signs the will; or
   (ii) acknowledges his signature, in the presence of the testator (but not necessarily in the presence of any other witness),

but no form of attestation shall be necessary.]

AMENDMENTS
Repealed, in relation to Northern Ireland, by Wills and Administration Proceedings (NI) Order 1994, SI 1994/1899, art 38, Sch 3.
Substituted by the Administration of Justice Act 1982, s 17.

10 APPOINTMENTS BY WILL TO BE EXECUTED LIKE OTHER WILLS, AND TO BE VALID, ALTHOUGH OTHER REQUIRED SOLEMNITIES ARE NOT OBSERVED

... no appointment made by will, in exercise of any power, shall be valid, unless the same be executed in manner herein-before required; and every will executed in manner herein-before required shall, so far as respects the execution and attestation thereof, be a valid execution of a power of appointment by will, notwithstanding it shall have been expressly required that a will made in exercise of such power should be executed with some additional or other form of execution or solemnity.

AMENDMENTS
Repealed, in relation to Northern Ireland, by Wills and Administration Proceedings (NI) Order 1994, SI 1994/1899, art 38, Sch 3.
Words omitted repealed by the Statute Law Revision (No 2) Act 1888.

11 SAVING AS TO WILLS OF SOLDIERS AND MARINERS

Provided always… that any soldier being in actual military service, or any mariner or seaman being at sea, may dispose of his personal estate as he might have done before the making of this Act.

AMENDMENTS
Words omitted repealed by the Statute Law Revision (No 2) Act 1888.

12 …

AMENDMENTS
Repealed by the Admiralty, &c Acts Repeal Act 1865, s 1.

13 PUBLICATION OF WILL NOT REQUISITE

… every will executed in manner herein-before required shall be valid without any other publication thereof.

AMENDMENTS
Repealed, in relation to Northern Ireland, by Wills and Administration Proceedings (NI) Order 1994, SI 1994/1899, art 38, Sch 3.
Words omitted repealed by the Statute Law Revision (No 2) Act 1888.

14 WILL NOT TO BE VOID ON ACCOUNT OF INCOMPETENCY OF ATTESTING WITNESS

… if any person who shall attest the execution of a will shall at the time of the execution thereof or at any time afterwards be incompetent to be admitted a witness to prove the execution thereof, such will shall not on that account be invalid.

AMENDMENTS
Repealed, in relation to Northern Ireland, by Wills and Administration Proceedings (NI) Order 1994, SI 1994/1899, art 38, Sch 3.
Words omitted repealed by the Statute Law Revision (No 2) Act 1888.

15 GIFTS TO AN ATTESTING WITNESS, OR HIS OR HER WIFE OR HUSBAND, TO BE VOID

… if any person shall attest the execution of any will to whom or to whose wife or husband any beneficial devise, legacy, estate, interest, gift, or appointment, of or affecting any real or personal estate (other than and except charges and directions for the payment of any debt or debts), shall be thereby given or made, such devise, legacy, estate, interest, gift, or appointment shall, so far only as concerns such person attesting the execution of such will, or the wife or husband of such person, or any person claiming under such person or wife or husband, be utterly null and void, and such person so attesting shall be admitted as a witness to prove the execution of such will, or to prove the validity or invalidity thereof, notwithstanding such devise, legacy, estate, interest, gift, or appointment mentioned in such will.

AMENDMENTS
Repealed, in relation to Northern Ireland, by Wills and Administration Proceedings (NI) Order 1994, SI 1994/1899, art 38, Sch 3.
Words omitted repealed by the Statute Law Revision (No 2) Act 1888.

16 CREDITOR ATTESTING A WILL CHARGING ESTATE WITH DEBTS SHALL BE ADMITTED A WITNESS

… in case by any will any real or personal estate shall be charged with any debt or debts, and any creditor, or the wife or husband [or civil partner] of any creditor, whose debt is so charged, shall attest the execution of such will, such creditor notwithstanding such charge shall be admitted a witness to prove the execution of such will, or to prove the validity or invalidity thereof.

AMENDMENTS
Repealed, in relation to Northern Ireland, by Wills and Administration Proceedings (NI) Order 1994, SI 1994/1899, art 38, Sch 3.
Words omitted repealed by the Statute Law Revision (No 2) Act 1888.
Words "or civil partner" in square brackets inserted by the Civil Partnership Act 2004, s 71, Sch 4, Pt 1, paras 1, 4, 5.

17 EXECUTOR SHALL BE ADMITTED A WITNESS

… no person shall, on account of his being an executor of a will, be incompetent to be admitted a witness to prove the execution of such will, or a witness to prove the validity or invalidity thereof.

AMENDMENTS
Repealed, in relation to Northern Ireland, by Wills and Administration Proceedings (NI) Order 1994, SI 1994/1899, art 38, Sch 3.
Words omitted repealed by the Statute Law Revision (No 2) Act 1888.

[18 WILL TO BE REVOKED BY MARRIAGE]

[(1) Subject to subsections (2) to (4) below, a will shall be revoked by the testator's marriage.
(2) A disposition in a will in exercise of a power of appointment shall take effect notwithstanding the testator's subsequent marriage unless the property so appointed would in default of appointment pass to his personal representatives.

(3) Where it appears from a will that at the time it was made the testator was expecting to be married to a particular person and that he intended that the will should not be revoked by the marriage, the will shall not be revoked by his marriage to that person.

(4) Where it appears from a will that at the time it was made the testator was expecting to be married to a particular person and that he intended that a disposition in the will should not be revoked by his marriage to that person,—

   (a) that disposition shall take effect notwithstanding the marriage; and
   (b) any other disposition in the will shall take effect also, unless it appears from the will that the testator intended the disposition to be revoked by the marriage.]

AMENDMENTS

Repealed, in relation to Northern Ireland, by Wills and Administration Proceedings (NI) Order 1994, SI 1994/1899, art 38, Sch 3.

Substituted, in relation to England and Wales, by the Administration of Justice Act 1982, s 18(1).

[18A EFFECT OF DISSOLUTION OR ANNULMENT OF MARRIAGE ON WILLS]

[(1) Where, after a testator has made a will, *a decree* [an order or decree] of a court [of civil jurisdiction in England and Wales] dissolves or annuls his marriage [or his marriage is dissolved or annulled and the divorce or annulment is entitled to recognition in England and Wales by virtue of Part II of the Family Law Act 1986],—

   [(a) provisions of the will appointing executors or trustees or conferring a power of appointment, if they appoint or confer the power on the former spouse, shall take effect as if the former spouse had died on the date on which the marriage is dissolved or annulled, and
   (b) any property which, or an interest in which, is devised or bequeathed to the former spouse shall pass as if the former spouse had died on that date,]

   except in so far as a contrary intention appears by the will.

(2) Subsection (1)(b) above is without prejudice to any right of the former spouse to apply for financial provision under the Inheritance (Provision for Family and Dependants) Act 1975.

(3) ...]

AMENDMENTS

Inserted by the Administration of Justice Act 1982, s 18(2).

Section 18A(1): first words in italics prospectively repealed with savings and subsequent words in square brackets prospectively substituted with savings by the Family Law Act 1996, s 66(1), Sch 8, para 1, (and s 66(2), Sch 9, para 5); second words in square brackets inserted, and third words in square brackets substituted, by the Family Law

Act 1986, s 53; Section 18A(1)(a), (b) substituted by the Law Reform (Succession) Act 1995, s 3.
Section 18A(3) repealed by the Law Reform (Succession) Act 1995, s 5, Sch.

[18B WILL TO BE REVOKED BY CIVIL PARTNERSHIP]

[(1) Subject to subsections (2) to (6), a will is revoked by the formation of a civil partnership between the testator and another person.
(2) A disposition in a will in exercise of a power of appointment takes effect despite the formation of a subsequent civil partnership between the testator and another person unless the property so appointed would in default of appointment pass to the testator's personal representatives.
(3) If it appears from a will—

  (a) that at the time it was made the testator was expecting to form a civil partnership with a particular person, and
  (b) that he intended that the will should not be revoked by the formation of the civil partnership,

the will is not revoked by its formation.

(4) Subsections (5) and (6) apply if it appears from a will—

  (a) that at the time it was made the testator was expecting to form a civil partnership with a particular person, and
  (b) that he intended that a disposition in the will should not be revoked by the formation of the civil partnership.

(5) The disposition takes effect despite the formation of the civil partnership.
(6) Any other disposition in the will also takes effect, unless it appears from the will that the testator intended the disposition to be revoked by the formation of the civil partnership.]

AMENDMENTS
Inserted by the Civil Partnership Act 2004, s 71, Sch 4, Pt 1, paras 1, 2, 5.

[18C EFFECT OF DISSOLUTION OR ANNULMENT OF CIVIL PARTNERSHIP ON WILLS]

[(1) This section applies if, after a testator has made a will—

  (a) a court of civil jurisdiction in England and Wales dissolves his civil partnership or makes a nullity order in respect of it, or
  (b) his civil partnership is dissolved or annulled and the dissolution or annulment is entitled to recognition in England and Wales by virtue of Chapter 3 of Part 5 of the Civil Partnership Act 2004.

(2) Except in so far as a contrary intention appears by the will—

    (a) provisions of the will appointing executors or trustees or conferring a power of appointment, if they appoint or confer the power on the former civil partner, take effect as if the former civil partner had died on the date on which the civil partnership is dissolved or annulled, and

    (b) any property which, or an interest in which, is devised or bequeathed to the former civil partner shall pass as if the former civil partner had died on that date.

(3) Subsection (2)(b) does not affect any right of the former civil partner to apply for financial provision under the Inheritance (Provision for Family and Dependants) Act 1975.]

AMENDMENTS
Inserted by the Civil Partnership Act 2004, s 71, Sch 4, Pt 1, paras 1, 2, 5.

19 NO WILL TO BE REVOKED BY PRESUMPTION FROM ALTERED CIRCUMSTANCES

… no will shall be revoked by any presumption of an intention on the ground of an alteration in circumstances.

AMENDMENTS
Repealed, in relation to Northern Ireland, by Wills and Administration Proceedings (NI) Order 1994, SI 1994/1899, art 38, Sch 3.
Words omitted repealed by the Statute Law Revision (No 2) Act 1888.

20 NO WILL TO BE REVOKED OTHERWISE THAN AS AFORESAID OR BY ANOTHER WILL OR CODICIL, OR BY DESTRUCTION THEREOF

…no will or codicil, or any part thereof, shall be revoked otherwise than as aforesaid, or by another will or codicil executed in manner herein-before required, or by some writing declaring an intention to revoke the same, and executed in the manner in which a will is herein-before required to be executed, or by the burning, tearing, or otherwise destroying the same by the testator, or by some person in his presence and by his direction, with the intention of revoking the same.

AMENDMENTS
Repealed, in relation to Northern Ireland, by the Wills and Administration Proceedings (NI) Order 1994, SI 1994/1899, art 38, Sch 3.
Words omitted repealed by the Statute Law Revision (No 2) Act 1888.

21 NO ALTERATION IN A WILL AFTER EXECUTION EXCEPT IN CERTAIN CASES, SHALL HAVE ANY EFFECT UNLESS EXECUTED AS A WILL

...no obliteration, interlineation, or other alteration made in any will after the execution thereof shall be valid or have any effect, except so far as the words or effect of the will before such alteration shall not be apparent, unless such alteration shall be executed in like manner as herein-before is required for the execution of the will; but the will, with such alteration as part thereof, shall be deemed to be duly executed if the signature of the testator and the subscription of the witnesses be made in the margin or on some other part of the will opposite or near to such alteration, or at the foot or end of or opposite to a memorandum referring to such alteration, and written at the end or some other part of the will.

AMENDMENTS
Repealed, in relation to Northern Ireland, by Wills and Administration Proceedings (NI) Order 1994, SI 1994/1899, art 38, Sch 3.
Words omitted repealed by the Statute Law Revision (No 2) Act 1888.

22 NO REVOKED WILL SHALL BE REVIVED OTHERWISE THAN BY RE-EXECUTION OR A CODICIL, &C

... no will or codicil, or any part thereof, which shall be in any manner revoked, shall be revived otherwise than by the re-execution thereof or by a codicil executed in manner herein-before required and showing an intention to revive the same; and when any will or codicil which shall be partly revoked, and afterwards wholly revoked, shall be revived, such revival shall not extend to so much thereof as shall have been revoked before the revocation of the whole thereof, unless an intention to the contrary shall be shown.

AMENDMENTS
Repealed, in relation to Northern Ireland, by Wills and Administration Proceedings (NI) Order 1994, SI 1994/1899, art 38, Sch 3.
Words omitted repealed by the Statute Law Revision (No 2) Act 1888.

23 SUBSEQUENT CONVEYANCE OR OTHER ACT NOT TO PREVENT OPERATION OF WILL

... no conveyance or other Act made or done subsequently to the execution of a will of or relating to any real or personal estate therein comprised, except an act by which such will shall be revoked as aforesaid, shall prevent the operation of the will with respect to such estate or interest in such real or personal estate as the testator shall have power to dispose of by will at the time of his death.

AMENDMENTS
Repealed, in relation to Northern Ireland, by Wills and Administration Proceedings (NI) Order 1994, SI 1994/1899, art 38, Sch 3.
Words omitted repealed by the Statute Law Revision (No 2) Act 1888.

24 WILLS SHALL BE CONSTRUED, AS TO THE ESTATE COMPRISED, TO SPEAK FROM THE DEATH OF THE TESTATOR

Every will shall be construed, with reference to the real estate and personal estate comprised in it, to speak and take effect as if it had been executed immediately before the death of the testator, unless a contrary intention shall appear by the will.

AMENDMENTS
Repealed, in relation to Northern Ireland, by Wills and Administration Proceedings (NI) Order 1994, SI 1994/1899, art 38, Sch 3.
Words omitted repealed by the Statute Law Revision (No 2) Act 1888.

25 RESIDUARY DEVISES SHALL INCLUDE ESTATES COMPRISED IN LAPSED AND VOID DEVISES

… unless a contrary intention shall appear by the will, such real estate or interest therein as shall be comprised or intended to be comprised in any devise in such will contained, which shall fail or be void by reason of the death of the devisee in the lifetime of the testator, or by reason of such devise being contrary to law or otherwise incapable of taking effect shall be included in the residuary devise (if any) contained in such will.

AMENDMENTS
Repealed, in relation to Northern Ireland, by Wills and Administration Proceedings (NI) Order 1994, SI 1994/1899, art 38, Sch 3.
Words omitted repealed by the Statute Law Revision (No 2) Act 1888.

26 A GENERAL DEVISE OF THE TESTATOR'S LANDS SHALL INCLUDE COPYHOLD AND LEASEHOLD AS WELL AS FREEHOLD LANDS, IN THE ABSENCE OF A CONTRARY INTENTION

… a devise of the land of the testator, or of the land of the testator in any place or in the occupation of any person mentioned in his will, or otherwise described in a general manner, and any other general devise which would describe a … leasehold estate if the testator had no freehold estate which could be described by it, shall be construed to include the … leasehold estates of the testator, or his … leasehold estates, or any of them, to which such description shall extend, as the case may be, as well as freehold estates, unless a contrary intention shall appear by the will.

AMENDMENTS
Repealed, in relation to Northern Ireland, by Wills and Administration Proceedings (NI) Order 1994, SI 1994/1899, art 38, Sch 3.
First words omitted repealed by the Statute Law Revision (No 2) Act 1888; other words omitted repealed by the Statute Law (Repeals) Act 1969.

27 A GENERAL GIFT OF REALTY OR PERSONALTY SHALL INCLUDE PROPERTY OVER WHICH THE TESTATOR HAS A GENERAL POWER OF APPOINTMENT

... a general devise of the real estate of the testator, or of the real estate of the testator in any place or in the occupation of any person mentioned in his will, or otherwise described in a general manner, shall be construed to include any real estate, or any real estate to which such description shall extend (as the case may be), which he may have power to appoint in any manner he may think proper, and shall operate as an execution of such power, unless a contrary intention shall appear by the will; and in like manner a bequest of the personal estate of the testator, or any bequest of personal property described in a general manner, shall be construed to include any personal estate, or any personal estate to which such description shall extend (as the case may be), which he may have power to appoint in any manner he may think proper, and shall operate as an execution of such power, unless a contrary intention shall appear by the will.

AMENDMENTS
Repealed, in relation to Northern Ireland, by Wills and Administration Proceedings (NI) Order 1994, SI 1994/1899, art 38, Sch 3.
Words omitted repealed by the Statute Law Revision (No 2) Act 1888.

28 A DEVISE OF REAL ESTATE WITHOUT ANY WORDS OF LIMITATION SHALL PASS THE FEE, &C

... where any real estate shall be devised to any person without any words of limitation, such devise shall be construed to pass the fee simple, or other the whole estate or interest which the testator had power to dispose of by will in such real estate, unless a contrary intention shall appear by the will.

AMENDMENTS
Repealed, in relation to Northern Ireland, by Wills and Administration Proceedings (NI) Order 1994, SI 1994/1899, art 38, Sch 3.
Words omitted repealed by the Statute Law Revision (No 2) Act 1888.

29 THE WORDS "DIE WITHOUT ISSUE," OR "DIE WITHOUT LEAVING ISSUE," &C SHALL MEAN A WANT OR FAILURE OF ISSUE IN THE LIFETIME OR AT THE DEATH OF THE PERSON, EXCEPT IN CERTAIN CASES

... in any devise or bequest of real or personal estate the words "die without issue," or "die without leaving issue," or "have no issue," or any other words which may import either a want or failure of issue of any person in his lifetime or at the time of his death, or an indefinite failure of his issue, shall be construed to mean a want or failure of issue in the lifetime or at the time of the death of such person, and not an indefinite failure of his issue, unless a contrary intention shall appear by the will, by reason of such person having a prior estate tail, or of a preceding gift, being, without any implication arising from such words, a limitation of an estate tail to such person or issue, or otherwise:

Provided, that this Act shall not extend to cases where such words as aforesaid import if no issue described in a preceding gift shall be born, or if there shall be no issue who shall live to attain the age or otherwise answer the description required for obtaining a vested estate by a preceding gift to such issue.

AMENDMENTS
Repealed, in relation to Northern Ireland, by Wills and Administration Proceedings (NI) Order 1994, SI 1994/1899, art 38, Sch 3.
Words omitted repealed by the Statute Law Revision (No 2) Act 1888.

30 DEVISE OF REALTY TO TRUSTEES OR EXECUTORS SHALL PASS THE FEE, &C, EXCEPT IN CERTAIN CASES

... where any real estate (other than or not being a presentation to a church) shall be devised to any trustee or executor, such devise shall be construed to pass the fee simple or other the whole estate or interest which the testator had power to dispose of by will in such real estate, unless a definite term of years, absolute or determinable, or an estate of freehold, shall thereby be given to him expressly or by implication.

AMENDMENTS
Repealed, in relation to Northern Ireland, by Wills and Administration Proceedings (NI) Order 1994, SI 1994/1899, art 38, Sch 3.
Words omitted repealed by the Statute Law Revision (No 2) Act 1888.

31 TRUSTEES UNDER AN UNLIMITED DEVISE, WHERE THE TRUST MAY ENDURE BEYOND THE LIFE OF A PERSON BENEFICIALLY ENTITLED FOR LIFE, SHALL TAKE THE FEE, &C

... where any real estate shall be devised to a trustee, without any express limitation of the estate to be taken by such trustee, and the beneficial interest in such real estate, or in the surplus rents and profits thereof, shall not be given to any person for life, or such beneficial interest shall be given to any person for life, but the purposes of the trust may continue beyond the life of such person, such devise shall be construed to vest in such trustee the fee simple, or other the whole legal estate which the testator had power to dispose of by will in such real estate, and not an estate determinable when the purposes of the trust shall be satisfied.

AMENDMENTS
Repealed, in relation to Northern Ireland, by Wills and Administration Proceedings (NI) Order 1994, SI 1994/1899, art 38, Sch 3.
Words omitted repealed by the Statute Law Revision (No 2) Act 1888.

32 DEVISES OF ESTATES TAIL SHALL NOT LAPSE WHERE INHERITABLE ISSUE SURVIVES, &C

AMENDMENTS

Repealed, in relation to Northern Ireland, by Wills and Administration Proceedings (NI) Order 1994, SI 1994/1899, art 38, Sch 3.

Repealed by the Trusts of Land and Appointment of Trustees Act 1996, s 25(2), Sch 4 (with ss 24(2), 25(4)).

[33 GIFTS TO CHILDREN OR OTHER ISSUE WHO LEAVE ISSUE LIVING AT THE TESTATOR'S DEATH SHALL NOT LAPSE]

[(1) Where—

(a) a will contains a devise or bequest to a child or remoter descendant of the testator; and
(b) the intended beneficiary dies before the testator, leaving issue; and
(c) issue of the intended beneficiary are living at the testator's death,

then, unless a contrary intention appears by the will, the devise or bequest shall take effect as a devise or bequest to the issue living at the testator's death.

(2) Where—

(a) a will contains a devise or bequest to a class of persons consisting of children or remoter descendants of the testator; and
(b) a member of the class dies before the testator, leaving issue; and
(c) issue of that member are living at the testator's death,

then, unless a contrary intention appears by the will, the devise or bequest shall take effect as if the class included the issue of its deceased member living at the testator's death.

(3) Issue shall take under this section through all degrees, according to their stock, in equal shares if more than one, any gift or share which their parent would have taken and so that [(subject to section 33A)] no issue shall take whose parent is living at the testator's death and so capable of taking.

(4) For the purposes of this section—

(a) the illegitimacy of any person is to be disregarded; and
(b) a person conceived before the testator's death and born living thereafter is to be taken to have been living at the testator's death.]

AMENDMENTS

Repealed, in relation to Northern Ireland, by Wills and Administration Proceedings (NI) Order 1994, SI 1994/1899, art 38, Sch 3.

Substituted by the Administration of Justice Act 1982, s 19.

Section 33(3) words "(subject to section 33A)" in square brackets inserted by the Estates of Deceased Persons (Forfeiture Rule and Law of Succession) Act 2011, s 2(1), (3).

[33A DISCLAIMER OR FORFEITURE OF GIFT]

[(1) This section applies where a will contains a devise or bequest to a person who—

(a) disclaims it, or
(b) has been precluded by the forfeiture rule from acquiring it.

(2) The person is, unless a contrary intention appears by the will, to be treated for the purposes of this Act as having died immediately before the testator.
(3) But in a case within subsection (1)(b), subsection (2) does not affect the power conferred by section 2 of the Forfeiture Act 1982 (power of court to modify the forfeiture rule).
(4) In this section "forfeiture rule" has the same meaning as in the Forfeiture Act 1982.]

AMENDMENTS

Inserted by the Estates of Deceased Persons (Forfeiture Rule and Law of Succession) Act 2011, s 2(1), (2).

34 ACT NOT TO EXTEND TO WILLS MADE BEFORE 1838, NOR TO ESTATES PUR AUTRE VIE OF PERSONS WHO DIE BEFORE 1838

… this Act shall not extend to any will made before the first day of January one thousand eight hundred and thirty-eight, and every will re-executed or republished, or revived by any codicil, shall for the purposes of this Act be deemed to have been made at the time at which the same shall be so re-executed, republished or revived; and this Act shall not extend to any estate pur autre vie of any person who shall die before the first day of January one thousand eight hundred and thirty-eight.

AMENDMENTS

Repealed, in relation to Northern Ireland, by Wills and Administration Proceedings (NI) Order 1994, SI 1994/1899, art 38, Sch 3.
Words omitted repealed by the Statute Law Revision (No 2) Act 1888.

35 ACT NOT TO EXTEND TO SCOTLAND

… this Act shall not extend to Scotland.

AMENDMENTS

Repealed, in relation to Northern Ireland, by Wills and Administration Proceedings (NI) Order 1994, SI 1994/1899, art 38, Sch 3.
Words omitted repealed by the Statute Law Revision (No 2) Act 1888.

36 …

AMENDMENTS

Repealed by the Statute Law Revision Act 1874.

A2 Administration of Justice Act 1982 (extracts)

20 RECTIFICATION

(1) If a court is satisfied that a will is so expressed that it fails to carry out the testator's intentions, in consequence—

    (a) of a clerical error; or
    (b) of a failure to understand his instructions,

it may order that the will shall be rectified so as to carry out his intentions.

(2) An application for an order under this section shall not, except with the permission of the court, be made after the end of the period of six months from the date on which representation with respect to the estate of the deceased is first taken out.

(3) The provisions of this section shall not render the personal representatives of a deceased person liable for having distributed any part of the estate of the deceased, after the end of the period of six months from the date on which representation with respect to the estate of the deceased is first taken out, on the ground that they ought to have taken into account the possibility that the court might permit the making of an application for an order under this section after the end of that period; but this subsection shall not prejudice any power to recover, by reason of the making of an order under this section, any part of the estate so distributed.

(4) In considering for the purposes of this section when representation with respect to the estate of a deceased person was first taken out, a grant limited to settled land or to trust property shall be left out of account, and a grant limited to real estate or to personal estate shall be left out of account unless a grant limited to the remainder of the estate has previously been made or is made at the same time.

SCHEDULE 2

THE ANNEX TO THE CONVENTION ON INTERNATIONAL WILLS

UNIFORM LAW ON THE FORM OF AN INTERNATIONAL WILL

ARTICLE 1

1. A will shall be valid as regards form, irrespective particularly of the place where it is made, of the location of the assets and of the nationality, domicile or residence of

the testator, if it is made in the form of an international will complying with the provisions set out in Articles 2 to 5 hereinafter.
2. The invalidity of the will as an international will shall not affect its formal validity as a will of another kind.

Article 2

This law shall not apply to the form of testamentary dispositions made by two or more persons in one instrument.

Article 3

1. The will shall be made in writing.
2. It need not be written by the testator himself.
3. It may be written in any language, by hand or by any other means.

Article 4

1. The testator shall declare in the presence of two witnesses and of a person authorized to act in connection with international wills that the document is his will and that he knows the contents thereof.
2. The testator need not inform the witnesses, or the authorized person, of the contents of the will.

Article 5

1. In the presence of the witnesses and of the authorized person, the testator shall sign the will or, if he has previously signed it, shall acknowledge his signature.
2. When the testator is unable to sign, he shall indicate the reason therefor to the authorized person who shall make note of this on the will. Moreover, the testator may be authorized by the law under which the authorized person was designated to direct another person to sign on his behalf.
3. The witnesses and the authorized person shall there and then attest the will by signing in the presence of the testator.

Article 6

1. The signatures shall be placed at the end of the will.
2. If the will consists of several sheets, each sheet shall be signed by the testator or, if he is unable to sign, by the person signing on his behalf or, if there is no such person, by the authorized person. In addition, each sheet shall be numbered.

Article 7

1. The date of the will shall be the date of its signature by the authorized person.
2. This date shall be noted at the end of the will by the authorized person.

Article 8

In the absence of any mandatory rule pertaining to the safekeeping of the will, the authorized person shall ask the testator whether he wishes to make a declaration concerning the safekeeping of his will. If so and at the express request of the testator the place where he intends to have his will kept shall be mentioned in the certificate provided for in Article 9.

Article 9

The authorized person shall attach to the will a certificate in the form prescribed in Article 10 establishing that the obligations of this law have been complied with.

Article 10

The certificate drawn up by the authorized person shall be in the following form or in a substantially similar form:

CERTIFICATE

1. I, ... (name, address and capacity), a person authorized to act in connection with international wills

2. Certify that on .... (date) at .... (place)

3. (testator) .... (name, address, date and place of birth) in my presence and that of the witnesses

4.(*a*) .... (name, address, date and place of birth)

(*b*) .... (name, address, date and place of birth) has declared that the attached document is his will and that he knows the contents thereof.

5. I furthermore certify that:

6.(*a*) in my presence and in that of the witnesses]

    (1) the testator has signed the will or has acknowledged his signature previously affixed.

    *(2) following a declaration of the testator stating that he was unable to sign his will for the following reason ....

    —I have mentioned this declaration on the will

    *—the signature has been affixed by .... (name, address)

7.(*b*) the witnesses and I have signed the will;

8.*(*c*) each page of the will has been signed by .... and numbered:

9.(*d*) I have satisfied myself as to the identity of the testator and of the witnesses as designated above;

10.(*e*) the witnesses met the conditions requisite to act as such according to the law under which I am acting;

11.*(f) the testator has requested me to include the following statement concerning the safekeeping of his will:

12. Place

13. Date

14. Signature and, if necessary, Seal

*To be completed if appropriate.

ARTICLE 11

The authorized person shall keep a copy of the certificate and deliver another to the testator.

ARTICLE 12

In the absence of evidence to the contrary, the certificate of the authorized person shall be conclusive of the formal validity of the instrument as a will under this Law.

ARTICLE 13

The absence or irregularity of a certificate shall not affect the formal validity of a will under this Law.

ARTICLE 14

The international will shall be subject to the ordinary rules of revocation of wills.

ARTICLE 15

In interpreting and applying the provisions of this law, regard shall be had as to its international origin and to the need for uniformity in its interpretation.

B1 Non-Contentious Probate Rules 1987 (SI 1987/2024) First Schedule, Form 3 Caveat

FORM 3   RULE 44(2)

CAVEAT

In the High Court of Justice

Family Division

The Principal [*or* .... District Probate] Registry.

    Let no grant be sealed in the estate of (*full name and address*) deceased, who died on the ……. day of ……… 19 … without notice to (*name of party by whom or on whose behalf the caveat is entered*).

Dated this …………………. day of ……………………….. 19 … .

(*Signed*) (*to be signed by the caveator's solicitor or by the caveator if acting in person*)

whose address for service is: ……………………………………………………………

Solicitor for the said ……… (*If the caveator is acting in person, substitute "In person".*)

B2 Non-Contentious Probate Rules 1987 (SI 1987/2024) First Schedule, Form 4 Warning to Caveator

FORM 4
WARNING TO CAVEATOR

RULE 44(5)

In the High Court of Justice

Family Division

[*The Registry in which the caveat index is maintained*]

To …………. of ………………… a party who has entered a caveat in the estate of …………………… deceased.

You have eight days (starting with the day on which this warning was served on you):

(i) to enter an appearance either in person or by your solicitor, at the [*name and address of the registry in which the caveat index is maintained*] setting out what interest you have in the estate of the above-named …………………… of ……………… deceased contrary to that of the party at whose instance this warning is issued; or

(ii) if you have no contrary interest but wish to show cause against the sealing of a grant to such party, to issue and serve a summons for directions by a registrar of the Principal Registry or a district probate registry.

If you fail to do either of these, the court may proceed to issue a grant of probate or administration in the said estate notwithstanding your caveat.

Dated the ………………………. day of ……………………….. 19 …. .

Issued at the instance of ……………………………………………………………

[*Here set out the name and interest (including the date of the will, if any, under which the interest arises) of the party warning, the name of his solicitor and the address for service. If the party warning is acting in person, this must be stated.*]

Registrar

B3 Non-Contentious Probate Rules 1987 (SI 1987/2024) First Schedule, Form 5 Appearance to Warning

FORM 5   RULES 44(10), 46(6)
APPEARANCE TO WARNING OR CITATION

In the High Court of Justice

Family Division

The Principal [*or* …………………………….. District Probate] Registry

Caveat No. …………………. dated the ………………….. day of …………….. 19 ….

[Citation dated the ……………………………………..… day of …………….. 19 ....]

Full name and address of deceased: ……………………………………………………….

Full name and address of person warning [*or* citor]: …………………………………….....

(*Here set out the interest of the person warning, or citor, as shown in warning or citation.*)

Full name and address of person warning [*or* citor]: …………………………………….....

(*Here set out the interest of the caveator or person cited, stating the date of the will (if any) under which such interest arises.*)

Enter an appearance for the above-named caveator [*or* person cited] in this matter.

Dated the ……………………………………………. day of …………...…… 19 .… .

(*Signed*)

whose address for service is: ………………………….

                             Solicitor (or 'In person').

B4 Affidavit of Service of Warning and of Non-receipt of Summons for Directions

In the High Court of Justice

Family Division

[The Principal Registry]

or

[The ... District Registry]

In the Estate of XX Deceased

I Julius Swift of Lowell Cottage, Winding Hill, Beufort (*state name and either home or work address*), Solicitor at Messrs Swift & Co of 5 Crooked Way Beufort BN8 9SU (*set out professional address including postcode*) make oath and say as follows:

1. I have the conduct of the case on behalf of the executors of the deceased's estate. At about 2.30 pm on 9 November 2014 [*date and time of service*] I duly served [*insert name of caveator or his solicitors and address*] Messrs Slow & Co of [*address*], who are representing the caveator, with a true copy of the warning, now produced and marked 'JS1', by delivering it to and leaving the said copy with Mr Slow's personal assistant [*insert name of the person who was served and his/her status*] at their offices [*set out address*] the address for service of YY [*name of caveator*] the Caveator / [by sending the copy by prepaid [registered] [recorded delivery] [special delivery] post to their offices at [*set out address*] being the address for service given in the caveat] or [*if a DX box number is given for service*] [by leaving a letter enclosing the copy at the DX for box number XXXX at ... Exchange] / [at the ... Document Exchange for transmission to the ... Document Exchange No ...] [*set out details of the Document Exchange given for service*] given for service in the caveat.
2. No summons for directions under Rule 44 of the Non-Contentious Probate Rules 1987 has been received by my firm.

SWORN at [*address*]

On [*date*]

Before me [*name of Solicitor / Commissioner for Oaths*]

Signed [*Signature of Deponent*]

B5 Witness Statement/Affidavit about Testamentary Documents

In the High Court of Justice   Case No. ...

Chancery Division (Probate)

In the Estate of XX Deceased

BETWEEN

                        YY   Claimant

                        and

                        ZZ   Defendant

I [*name and address*] the claimant/defendant in this claim state / [*if it is a sworn statement*] on oath that I have no knowledge of any document:

(a) Being or purported to be or having the form or effect of a will or codicil of [*name of the deceased*] whose estate is the subject of this claim;
(b) Being or purported to be a draft or written instructions for any such will or codicil made by or at the request of or under the instructions of the deceased;
(c) Being or purported to be evidence of the contents or a copy of any such will or codicil which is alleged to have been lost or destroyed;

except as follows:

[*describe any testamentary document of the deceased which is in the deponent's possession or control or of which he has knowledge. If any document is not in the possession or control of the deponent, give the name and address of the person who the deponent believes has possession or control of it or state that he does not know the name and address of that person.*] e.g.

I believe that [*set out the name of any relevant person(s)*] of [*set out address if known or if not known state the same*] has in his/her/their possession or control the following documents: [*Set these out*]

[I believe that the facts stated in this witness statement are true] *or* [*if it is a sworn statement*]

SWORN at [*address*]

On [*date*]

Before me [*name of Solicitor / Commissioner for Oaths*]

Signed [*Signature of Deponent*]

Note: 'testamentary document' is defined in CPR rule 57.1.

B6 Some Examples of Undue Influence to Be Set Out in the Particulars of Claim

In the High Court of Justice   Case No. ...

Chancery Division (Probate)

In the Estate of XX Deceased

BETWEEN

                        YY   <u>Claimant</u>

                        and

                        ZZ   <u>Defendant</u>

PARTICULARS OF CLAIM

1. XX [*name of the deceased*] died on ... [*date*].
2. On ... [*date*] he had executed a Will ('the first Will') in which he had named the claimant as his executor and had divided his net estate between his four children in equal shares. The claimant is the deceased's son.
3. The defendant [*name*] has sought to obtain probate of a later Will ('the disputed Will') which allegedly was executed by the deceased on ... [*date*].
4. The disputed Will appoints the defendant sole executor and beneficiary of the whole of the net estate.
5. The disputed Will was procured by the defendant exerting undue influence on the deceased.
6. At the time of the disputed Will the deceased was ninety years of age and extremely frail. The defendant had been his next door neighbour and about three months prior to the deceased's death she had moved into the deceased's home purportedly to take care of him although the family had arranged professional carers to attend to the deceased's needs.

7. The defendant was known to be extremely domineering towards the deceased, and had repeatedly threatened to have him removed to a home unless he made a will leaving his estate to her. The deceased was fearful of her and believed that he would be removed. He had constantly asked his carers not to take him to a home.
8. Notwithstanding the fact that the family and the carers constantly assured him that we would not allow anyone to move him from his home he remained unsure and anxious because of what he was being told by the defendant.
9. On ... [*date*] when the disputed Will was executed the defendant had invited her sons to the home. She had presented the prepared will to the deceased and told him that he had to sign the document for his own safety otherwise he would be removed from his home. The disputed Will is in the hand of the defendant and has been witnessed by the defendant's sons.
10. On ... [*date*] when the carers arrived at the home they found the deceased in a collapsed state, distraught, visibly shaking and in a panic. They were able to elicit from him what had happened.
11. Although steps were taken to remove the defendant from entering the deceased's home and to reassure the deceased and to ascertain what exactly happened on ... [*date in paragraph 10*] the deceased died two days later.

The Claimant claims:

1. A declaration that the disputed Will is invalid.
2. That the defendant be refused a grant of probate in respect of the disputed Will.
3. That the court pronounce a grant in solemn form for the first Will dated ... [*date*].
4. Costs.

Date

Signed

B7 Defence Limited to Putting the Personal Representative to Proof of the Will

In the High Court of Justice   Case No. …

Chancery Division (Probate)

In the Estate of XX Deceased

BETWEEN

	YY	Claimant
	and	
	ZZ	Defendant

1. It is admitted that the deceased XX [*name of the deceased*] died on … [*date*].
2. The defendant puts the claimant to proof that:

    (a) The purported Will referred to in the claim was duly executed;
    (b) The deceased had testamentary capacity when it was made; and
    (c) The deceased knew and approved the contents of the said Will.

Dated

Signed, etc.

B8 Defence Alleging Want of Due Execution: Lack of Testamentary Capacity

In the High Court of Justice   Case No. …

Chancery Division (Probate)

In the Estate of XX Deceased

BETWEEN

	YY	<u>Claimant</u>
	and	
	ZZ	<u>Defendant</u>

1. It is admitted that the deceased XX [*name of the deceased*] died on … [*date*].
2. It is admitted that the claimant is named in the deceased's Will as the executor of the deceased's Will.
3. It is denied that at the time of the execution of the Will the deceased had testamentary capacity.

Particulars

At the time of the execution of the Will the deceased was ninety years of age and had been suffering from Alzheimer's disease and senile dementia [*set out details of the condition or circumstances which led to the incapacity*]. His mental capacity was impaired in that:

(1) He suffered from acute loss of memory [*set out examples*].
(2) He was known to be confused at all times over all matters and had lost all power of recall. He was unable to identify his children, members of his extended family and his closest friends.
(3) He was totally confused about his whereabouts, his finances and his property. He believed for instance, that he was homeless and that his home had been burned

down. [*set out details of the deceased's confusion or other examples of lack of capacity*]

(4) Further or in the alternative, at the time of execution of the Will the deceased did not know or approve of the contents of the Will by reason of the following facts:

    (a) The matters set out in paragraph (3) above.

    (b) The fact that the Will was prepared by the claimant who had total control over the deceased and was known to be overbearing.

    (c) The fact that the Will was made shortly before the deceased was taken to the nursing home where he died and the Will bequeaths the entire estate to the claimant whom the deceased had met only a few months before then. [*set out all matters of relevance relied on*]

Date

Signed, etc.

C1 ACTAPS Practice Guidance for the Resolution of Probate and Trust Disputes (ACTAPS Code)[1]

Paragraph 4 of the Practice Direction on Protocols has been substantially amended. It states that 'in cases not covered by any protocol, the court will expect the parties to act reasonably in exchanging information and documents relevant to their claim and in trying to avoid the necessity for the start of proceedings'.

Moreover, with effect from 1 April 2003, the 30th update to the CPR imposes on all parties to a dispute (whatever its nature) an obligation to comply with specified procedures designed to avoid litigation commencing.

Practitioners will no doubt remember the dicta of the Court of Appeal in *Carlson v Townsend* [2001] 3 All ER 663 where it stated the use of the protocol was not limited to fast track cases. The spirit if not the letter of the protocol was equally appropriate to some higher value claims. In accordance with the aims of the civil justice reforms, the courts expected to see the spirit of reasonable pre-action behaviour applied in all cases regardless of the existence of a specific protocol.

The Association of Contentious Trust & Probate Specialists 'ACTAPS' and the Trust Law Committee have, as many practitioners will be aware, given much thought to the possibility that a special Pre-Action Protocol ought to be developed for disputes within their area of expertise. Indeed a draft has for some time been on the ACTAPS website (www.actaps.com) and has since been the subject of extensive discussions with representatives of the judiciary concerned.

It is now clear that no special protocol will be adopted, despite a recognition that the draft contains useful elements. It will be seen that it deals in particular with the following matters:

---

[1] The ACTAPS Code is reproduced by kind permission of the Association of Contentious Trust and Probate Specialists (Henry Frydenson, Frydenson & Co, Chair ACTAPS, Central Court, 25 Southampton Buildings, London, WC2A 1AL).

(a) appointment of a representative to act on behalf of beneficiaries who cannot be ascertained or traced;
(b) requirement for a letter of claim setting out the basis of claim;
(c) early disclosure of documents;
(d) use of joint experts where possible;
(e) a joint letter of request for medical records;
(f) a joint *Larke v Nugus* letter; and
(g) a joint letter requesting details of deceased's capacity.

In these circumstances the committee of ACTAPS has concluded that it would be useful to encourage members to have regard to The ACTAPS Code as a means of developing best practices in areas where special problems may arise, for example the need to have representatives for persons who cannot speak for themselves in a context where others may feel that mediation would be desirable.

It is understood that the judges who have considered The ACTAPS Code have expressed no concerns that it is out of line with the CPR objectives or that to follow its principles would give rise to unnecessary problems in practice. In particular it is thought that CPR Rule 19.7(3)(b) gives the necessary scope for securing the appointment of representatives of those who are absent, unborn, or members of a large class, as well before as after the commencement of proceedings.

It is also hoped that in the context of probate issues the common difficulty of medical practitioners considering that they may as a matter of professional confidence be restricted in releasing records can be overcome by joint application (and following discussions between ACTAPS and the BMA the latter has confirmed that its future guidance will facilitate disclosure in accordance with The ACTAPS Code). The ACTAPS Code contains an outline for such a letter.

In these circumstances it is suggested that practitioners in the areas of trust and probate law should seek to follow the approaches indicated in The ACTAPS Code, approved by the Trust Law Committee and ACTAPS, on the basis that it may serve to amplify the basic principles of the general protocols and indicate considered methods of carrying the objectives of the general protocols into effect in areas which may be found to give rise to special difficulties with which the general protocols do not grapple. In putting forward this suggestion the committee of ACTAPS believes that it has the support of all who have been concerned to consider the draft protocol; the rejection of the proposal that it be adopted as a special protocol owes nothing (so far as is known) to any perception of defects and merely reflects the belief that the public interest is best served by seeking, where possible, to avoid specific protocols and to develop best practices in areas where general protocols have to be supplemented to meet the needs of special situations.

With that in mind the committee of ACTAPS encourages members and other users to help move the search for best practices forward by commenting on any defects, inadequacies or other difficulties which may be found to arise in carrying the terms of The ACTAPS Code into effect. Please make any such comments to the ACTAPS Chairman's or the ACTAPS Secretary's e-mail address.

Practitioners will wish to bear in mind the need for trustees and executors to consider the adequacy of their powers to enter into any particular course of conduct and the possibility that they may need eg Beddoes type directions if they propose a course of conduct to which their beneficiaries might wish to raise objection (as for example where the trustees wish voluntarily to disclose confidential documents to third parties) or which may involve material burdens of costs (as for example the institution of a lengthy mediation). But of course in circumstances where the aim is to explore ways of reaching agreement or otherwise saving costs any necessary order might be expected to be forthcoming (within the appropriate limits) without difficulty on the basis that the Court would be being asked to facilitate a course of action essentially in accordance with the overriding objective.

1. INTRODUCTION

The Scope of The Code

1.1 This Code is intended to apply to disputes about:

the devolution and administration of estates of deceased persons
the devolution and administration of trust funds ('probate and trust disputes'). It is not intended to displace other protocols if in the circumstances of the case they can be seen to be more appropriate.

The main types of disputes within the ambit of this Code can be expected to be:

- challenges to the validity of a will, for example on grounds of want of capacity or knowledge and approval, undue influence or forgery
- claims under the Inheritance (Provision for Family and Dependants) Act 1975 ('the Inheritance Act')
- actions for the removal of an administrator or executor or trustee or the appointment of a judicial trustee
- actions for the rectification of a will or other document
- disputes as to the meanings of provisions in a will or a trust
- administration actions
- allegations of breach of trust.

The ACTAPS Code may also apply to certain types of dispute where the provisions of a trust or the devolution of an estate are of the essence, for example where a claimant seeks in the alternative to set aside or overturn a trust or to take advantage of rights under a trust.

The Code has two aims; to encourage the resolution of disputes without hostile litigation; and even where litigation may be necessary to ensure that it is simplified as far as possible by maximizing the scope for the exchange of relevant information before the litigation process has commenced.

The Code is in general terms unlikely to be appropriate for disputes which involve:

- disputes as to the rights appertaining under rules of forced heirships under the law of some foreign jurisdiction
- the need for emergency injunctions
- (except in so far as concerns pre-action exchange of information) the need for a binding precedent or a declaration by the Court as to the true construction of some trust instrument or testamentary disposition.

The Code is formed in general terms to cover the broad range of trust and probate disputes; but it is recognised that the appropriate investigations and exchange of information will vary according to the circumstances of the dispute. However one of its primary purposes is to provide for a special feature of disputes in this area, namely that there may be beneficiaries who cannot speak for themselves but whose interests must be protected.

1.2 In cases where the express terms of The Code is not appropriate parties will be expected to follow the spirit of The Code and seek to achieve its aims so far as practicable in the particular case.

1.3 It is also to be borne in mind that there are certain cases in which a trust or probate dispute seeks to fulfil some non-contentious purpose, as for example where a question of difficulty is identified to which the parties are agreed that the best solution lies in inviting the Court to approve constructive proposals by way of compromise or where the objective is simply to find the cheapest way of protecting trustees or personal representatives against the risks involved in the existence of some theoretical doubt. In such cases The Code is unlikely to have any role to play.

1.4 One of the principal features of trust and probate disputes is that they may affect the interests of persons not of full capacity, as yet unborn or unascertained, or interested as members of a large class of persons who have similar beneficial interests. The Code is thus designed to make express provision for the need to find mechanisms that assist despite the absence of such persons (providing in particular an expedited process for Court approval of agreements reached in mediation). It is thus wrong in principle to regard a dispute as not amenable to the use of The Code just because there are persons concerned who cannot speak for themselves.

2. PRINCIPAL GUIDELINES

Parties

2.1 The parties to the probate or trust dispute will usually be trustees (or personal representatives or persons claiming to be entitled as such) and beneficiaries of the trust or estate who are of full capacity, though The Code is designed also to be capable of being used in exterior/third party disputes where appropriate.

2.2 In the case where interests of unascertained persons, minors, unborns, mentally incapacitated persons or members of a large class (such that it is not appropriate for all members of the class to be made parties to the dispute) will be affected, the procedure to be adopted will be an application to the Court (see Annex A) whether or not a claim has yet been instituted before the Court.

Status of Letters of Claim and Response

2.3 A letter of claim or of response is not intended to have the same status as pleadings. Matters may come to light as a result of investigation after the letter of claim has been sent or after the defendant has responded. These investigations could result in the pleaded case of a party differing in some respects from the case outlined in that party's letter of claim or response. It would not be consistent with the spirit of The Code for a party to complain about this difference provided that there was no indication of any intention to mislead.

Disclosure of Documents

2.4 The aim of the early disclosure of documents by the defendant is not to encourage 'fishing expeditions' by the claimant, but to promote an early exchange of relevant information to help in clarifying or resolving issues in dispute. The claimant's solicitors can assist by identifying in the letter of claim or in a subsequent letter the particular documents or categories of documents which they consider are relevant, and by providing copies of these where appropriate.

2.5 All documents are disclosed on the basis that they are not to be disclosed to third parties (other than legal advisers) or used for any purpose other than the resolution of the dispute, unless otherwise agreed in writing or permitted by the court.

Experts

2.6 Expert evidence appropriate to probate and trust disputes may include in particular medical evidence, handwriting evidence, valuation evidence, tax- related or actuarial evidence.

2.7 The Code encourages joint selection of, and access to, experts. However, it maintains the flexibility for each party to obtain their own expert's report. It is for the court to decide whether the costs of more than one expert's report should be recoverable.

Costs

2.8 Where The Code provides for the initial cost of obtaining information or reports to be borne by one party, it shall not restrict the court's discretion in relation to ultimate liability for such costs.

Negotiations/Mediation

2.9 Parties and their legal representatives are encouraged to enter into discussions and/or negotiations prior to starting proceedings. The parties should bear in mind that the courts increasingly take the view that litigation should be a last resort, and that claims should not be issued prematurely when a settlement is in reasonable prospect. Mediation of probate and trust disputes may assist in achieving a compromise, particularly in relation to disputes between family members. The form of the mediation will be set out in the mediation agreement between the mediator and the parties.

2.10 Mediation can be used to try to achieve a compromise whenever negotiation is appropriate and can be used at any stage in a trust dispute. Typically mediation may be considered:

(i) before proceedings have commenced but once the issues are fairly well defined and the parties affected by them are known;
(ii) even after proceedings have commenced and the statements of case have been served so that the parties have a better appreciation of the issues;
(iii) at any critical stage in the litigation such as after disclosure of documents, exchange of experts' reports, exchange of witness statements and in the lead up to the trial.

The parties should seek to conclude a mediation within 42 days of the appointment of the mediator.

2.11 Since mediation negotiations are treated by the Courts as without prejudice, points disclosed during an attempt to reach a settlement will be confidential between the parties and cannot be used as evidence in subsequent Court proceedings unless expressly agreed by the party who made the disclosure. The mediator will not divulge information without consent. Also he will not pass on such information to outside parties or act for either party to the dispute in subsequent proceedings.

2.12 A settlement reached pursuant to a mediation should be recorded in writing and signed by the parties or their authorised representative. In probate and trust disputes, if and insofar as the subject matter of the dispute requires the sanction and approval of the Court, any agreement achieved as a result of the mediation should be expressed to be subject to the approval of the Court.

2.13 In a probate or trust dispute where the position of the Inland Revenue may have some bearing on any compromise solution which may be reached, any agreement may be made conditional upon indications of the Inland Revenue's position or adjourned to enable clarification of its position to be sought.

3. THE CODE

Letters of Claim

3.1 The Claimant shall send a letter of claim to each of the deceased's personal representatives or to the trustees, as the case may be and, unless it is impractical (e.g. because there is a large class of beneficiaries or the beneficiaries are minors) to each beneficiary or potential beneficiary of the estate or trust fund likely to be adversely affected by the claim (referred to as 'the proposed Defendants'), as soon as sufficient information is available to substantiate a realistic claim which the Claimant has decided he is prepared to pursue.

3.2 The letter shall contain a clear summary of the claim and the facts upon which it is based and state the remedy sought by the claimant.

3.3 Solicitors are recommended to use a standard format for the claim letter. A sample letter is set out at Annex B; this can be amended to suit the particular case.

3.4 In claims under the Inheritance Act the claimant should give details to the best of his ability of the matters set out in Section 3 of the Inheritance Act as relevant to the exercise of the Court's discretion (see Annex B).

3.5 Copies of documents in the claimant's possession which he wishes to rely upon or which any other party is likely to wish to rely upon should be enclosed with the letter of claim. Examples of documents likely to be relevant in different types of dispute are set out at Annex C. These lists are not exhaustive. The letter of claim may specify classes of document considered relevant for early disclosure by the proposed defendants.

Letter of Response

3.6 Each of the proposed defendants should respond to the letter of claim within 21 days stating whether he admits or denies the claim, responding in outline to the matters of fact relied upon by the claimant and setting out any particular matters of fact upon which he relies. If a proposed defendant intends to make an answering claim on his own behalf, the letter of response should contain the same information and documents as a letter of claim in relation to the Part 20 claim. If a proposed defendant is unable to respond within the time limit on any particular matter, the letter of response should give the reasons for the absence of a full response and state when it will be available.

3.7 In claims under the Inheritance Act each proposed defendant should give details to the best of his ability of the matters set out in Section 3 of the Inheritance Act as relevant to the exercise of the Court's discretion (and set out in Annex B).

3.8 Copies of documents in the proposed defendant's possession which he wishes to rely upon or which any other party is likely to wish to rely upon should be enclosed with the letter of response. Examples of relevant documents in relation to different categories of disputes are set out at Annex C. These lists are not exhaustive.

Documents

3.9 In relation to the documents in Annex C, the personal representatives of the deceased (including executors named in the last alleged will of the deceased) or trustees as appropriate should provide copies of such documents (if available) to a party requesting a copy within 14 days of the date of a letter of request (or such other reasonable time as may be agreed between the parties) or, if a copy is only available from a third party with the consent of the personal representatives or trustees, provide to the party making the request written authority to the third party to provide a copy of the document to that party.

3.10 Trustees or personal representatives should not be inhibited from making full disclosure by the absence of litigation.

Applications for documents or information in control of third parties

3.11 In a probate dispute the release of medical notes may cast much light on the likely outcome and it should be assumed for the purposes of The Code that they ought to be disclosed at the outset absent special reason.

3.12 If so requested in writing by any party all parties shall (in the absence of good reason to withhold the relevant items) within 14 days of any such request (or such longer period as shall reasonably be agreed):

(1) Sign and return to the party making the request, a joint application for the provision of copies of the deceased's medical notes or social worker's reports to all parties. The notes and/or reports should be sent separately and directly to each party. A specimen joint application is at Annex D.
(2) Sign, and return to the party making the request, a joint application for a statement by the solicitor who prepared the will of the deceased setting out all the circumstances leading up to the preparation and making of the will. A specimen joint application is at Annex E.

3.13 The party making the request for a joint application for information or documents from a third party shall:

(1) Submit it to the third party within 7 days of receipt of the joint application completed by the other parties.
(2) on receipt of the information or documents from the third party check that they have been received by all other parties and, if not, provide them with copies within 7 days of receipt.

3.14 In cases where the mental capacity of a deceased at the date of a testamentary instrument is in issue, the party seeking to uphold the testamentary instrument should obtain a report as to the deceased's mental capacity from his GP as soon as possible after the issue is identified and send it to all other parties within 7 days of receipt. A specimen letter of request is at Annex F.

Experts

3.15 Parties should consider the use of jointly instructed experts so far as possible. Accordingly before any prospective party (the first party) instructs an expert he should (unless of the opinion that another party will want to instruct his own expert) give the other (second) party a list of the name(s) of one or more experts in the relevant discipline whom he considers are suitable to instruct.

3.16 Within 14 days the second party may indicate an objection to one or more of such experts and suggest alternatives. The first party should then instruct a mutually acceptable expert.

3.17 If an expert to be jointly instructed is not agreed, the parties may then instruct experts of their own choice. It would be for the court to decide subsequently, if proceedings are issued, whether either party had acted unreasonably. No party shall be entitled to instruct an expert proposed in a list of experts for joint instructions until it is clear that joint instructions cannot be agreed and thereafter the party who submitted the list of experts shall be entitled to nominate one of the experts on this list as his own chosen expert and no other party shall instruct any expert named on the list until such nomination has taken place.

3.18 If the second party does not object to an expert nominated, he shall not be entitled to rely on his own expert evidence within that particular discipline unless:

(1) the court so directs, or
(2) the first party's expert report has been amended and the first party is not prepared to disclose the original report.

3.19 Either party may send to the expert written questions on the report, relevant to the issues, via the first party's solicitors. The expert should send answers to the question separately and directly to each party.

3.20 The cost of the report from an agreed expert will usually be paid by the party first proposing that a joint expert be instructed. The costs of the expert replying to questions will usually be borne by the party asking the questions. The ultimate liability for costs will be determined by the Court.

ANNEX A

REPRESENTATION IN ESTATE OR TRUST DISPUTES OF INTERESTED PERSONS WHO CANNOT BE ASCERTAINED ETC.

(1) In any estate or trust dispute concerning:-
    (a) property comprised in an estate or subject to a trust or alleged to be subject to a trust; or
    (b) the construction of a written instrument; or
    (c) a situation where the interests of beneficiaries may require separate representation

the Court, if satisfied that it is expedient to do so, and that one or more of the conditions specified in paragraph (2) are satisfied, may appoint one or more persons to represent any person (including a person under a disability, a minor or an unborn person) or class who is or may be interested (whether presently or for any future, contingent or unascertained interest) in or affected by the dispute.

(2) The conditions for the exercise of the power conferred by paragraph (1) are as follows:-
    (a) that the person, the class or some member of the class cannot be ascertained or cannot be readily ascertained, or is not of full capacity; or
    (b) that the person, the class or some member of the class, though ascertained, cannot be found; or
    (c) that, though the person or the class and members thereof can be ascertained and found, it appears to the Court expedient (regard being had to all the circumstances, including the amount at stake and the degree of difficulty of the point to be determined) to exercise the power for the purposes of saving expense or for any other reason.

(3) Where, in any case to which paragraph 1 applies, the Court exercises the power conferred by that paragraph, a judgment or order of the Court given or made when the person or persons appointed in exercise of that power are before the Court shall be binding on the person or class represented by the person or persons so appointed.

(4) Where, in any such case, a compromise is proposed and some of the persons who are interested in, or who may be affected by the compromise have not been consulted (including persons under a disability, minors or unborn or unascertained persons) but
    (a) there is some other person in the same interest before the Court who assents to the compromise or on whose behalf the Court sanctions the compromise; or
    (b) the absent persons are represented by a person appointed under paragraph (1) who so assents, the Court, if satisfied that the compromise will be for the benefit of the absent persons and that it is expedient to exercise this power, may approve the compromise and order that it shall be binding on absent persons, and they shall be bound accordingly except where the order has been obtained by fraud or non-disclosure of material facts.

ANNEX B

To
Defendant

Dear

Re:

The estate of [name of deceased]
The Settlement made by [Settlor] on [date]

We are instructed on behalf of [claimant] [give details of relief sought eg to seek reasonable provision out of the estate of the above-named deceased; to set aside probate of the will of the above-named deceased dated [date]; to seek a declaration that upon a proper construction of the above settlement our client is entitled to ...]

The basis of our clients claim is: [brief outline]

The facts upon which our client relies are as follows:- [set out material facts with sufficient clarity and detail for the proposed defendants to make a preliminary assessment of the claim]

The details of matters to which the Court would have regard under Section 3 of the Inheritance (Provision for Family and Dependants) Act 1975 insofar as they are known to our client are:-

(a) Financial resources and needs of claimant;
(b) Financial resources and needs of any other claimant;
(c) Financial resources and needs of beneficiaries;
(d) Obligations and responsibilities of deceased towards claimants and beneficiaries;
(e) Size and nature of estate;
(f) Disabilities of claimants and beneficiaries;
(g) Any other matter; and if claimant spouse or co-habitee,
(h) age of claimant, length of marriage/co-habitation and contribution to family welfare.

We enclose the following documents which are relevant to the claim:- [list documents]

In accordance with The ACTAPS Code for probate and trust disputes, we look forward to receiving a letter of response, enclosing the documents in your possession and relevant to the claim within [21] days. We believe that the following documents relevant to the claim are likely to be in your possession:- (list documents)

Pursuant to The ACTAPS Code as [personal representatives of the deceased/trustees of the settlement] we invite you to furnish us within 14 days of the date of this letter with copies of the following documents or written authority, in the form enclosed, to obtain copies of such document(s):- [list asterisked documents required]

We have also sent a letter of claim to (name and address) and a copy of that letter is enclosed.

Yours faithfully

ANNEX C

All documents upon which you rely or upon which the other party is likely to wish to rely including but not limited to the following categories:

1. In disputes in which the assets of an estate/trust fund or the financial resources of an individual are relevant; eg claims under the Inheritance Act, breach of trust claims:
   - The Inland Revenue Account and any Corrective Account;
   - A schedule of the capital assets (with values, estimated where appropriate) and income of the estate, trust fund or individual as appropriate;
   - Trust or Estate Accounts.
2. In disputes in which the mental capacity or medical condition of an individual is relevant, eg challenges to testamentary capacity, Inheritance Act claims where disability is alleged:
   - A copy of the medical records of the individual or, if appropriate, the written authority of the personal representatives of a deceased to obtain his medical records together with an office copy of the grant of probate or letters of administration or other proof of their status.
3. In disputes as to the validity, construction or rectification of a will or other testamentary instrument of the deceased:
   - A statement setting out details of any testamentary script (now in CPR called testamentary document) within the knowledge of the claimant or proposed defendant and details of the name and address of the person who, to the best of his knowledge, has possession or control of such script.

Nb1: The provision of the statement in 3 above is of vital importance to all parties in a dispute since it ensures that the correct testamentary documents are being considered. This will prevent the problem of a dispute over a later testamentary document being allowed to overshadow the existence of an intermediate testamentary document which would be upheld if the later testamentary document fails.

Also it helps identify the correct parties to the existing disputes.

Nb2: Following from Nb1 above, it is most important that the fullest and most exhaustive search for all testamentary documents is made. Accordingly while the following list is not exhaustive it is incumbent upon all parties to check:-

(i) with all known solicitors of the deceased as to the existence of a testamentary document;
(ii) with all attesting witnesses to testamentary documents as to the existence of testamentary documents;
(iii) with all named executors of testamentary documents as to the existence of testamentary documents;
(iv) with immediate family members (brothers, sisters, parents and children of the deceased) as to the existence of testamentary documents.

Nb3: Definition of Testamentary Script (now in CPR called Testamentary document)

A will, a draft of a will, written instructions for a will made by or at the request of, or under the instructions of, the testator, and any document purporting to be evidence of the contents, or to be a copy, of a will which is alleged to have been lost or destroyed. The word 'will' includes a codicil.

ANNEX D

JOINT APPLICATION FOR MEDICAL NOTES OR SOCIAL WORKER'S REPORTS

To: The medical records officer/social services

Dear Sir

Re: (Name) Deceased of (address), (date of birth)

We the undersigned Messrs (firm's name) (ref) of (firm's address), Solicitors for (the Executors named in the Will of the late (deceased's name) of (deceased's address) who died on (date of death) and we, the undersigned Messrs (firm's name) of (firm's address), Solicitors for parties interested in his/her estate, hereby authorise you to forward [a full set of copies of the deceased's Medical Records] [all social workers reports and notes relating to the deceased] to each of the aforementioned firms.

We confirm that we will be responsible for your reasonable photocopying charges and your invoice in this regard should be sent to (firm's name) and marked for the attention of (ref.).

Dated [   ] 20[   ]

Signed
[   ]

Signed
[   ]

ANNEX E

JOINT APPLICATION LETTER TO SOLICITORS WHO PREPARED WILL REQUESTING LARKE v NUGUS STATEMENT

Dear Sirs

[Name of Deceased] deceased

We, the undersigned Messrs (firm's name) (ref:) of (firm's address), solicitors for the Executors named in the Will of (deceased's name) of (deceased's address) and we, the undersigned Messrs (firm's name) (ref:) of (firm's address), solicitors for parties interested in his/her estate regret to inform you that (deceased's name) died on (date of death).

We understand that you drafted the deceased's last will dated [ ].

You may be aware that in 1959 the Law Society recommended that in circumstances such as this the testator's solicitor should make available a statement of his or her evidence regarding instructions for the preparation and execution of the will and surrounding circumstances. This recommendation was endorsed by the Court of Appeal on 21st February 1979 in *Larke v Nugus*.

The practice is also recommended at paragraph 24.02 of the Law Society's *Guide to the Professional Conduct of Solicitors*, 7th edition (page 387).

Accordingly, we hereby request and authorise you to forward to each of the aforementioned firms statements from all appropriate members of your firm on the following points:

- How long had you known the deceased?
- Who introduced you to the deceased?
- On what date did you receive instructions from the deceased?
- Did you receive instructions by letter? If so, please provide copies of any correspondence.
- If instructions were taken at a meeting, please provide copies of your contemporaneous notes of the meeting including an indication of where the meeting took place and who else was present at the meeting.
- How were the instructions expressed?
- What indication did the deceased give to you that he knew he was making a will?
- Were you informed or otherwise aware of any medical history of the deceased that might bear upon the issue of his capacity?
- Did the deceased exhibit any signs of confusion or loss of memory? If so, please give details.
- To what extent were earlier wills discussed and what attempts were made to discuss departures from his earlier will-making pattern? What reasons, if any, did the testator give for making any such departures?
- When the will had been drafted, how were the provisions of the will explained to the deceased?
- Who, apart from the attesting witnesses, was present at the execution of the will? Where, when and how did this take place?
- Please provide copies of any other documents relating to your instructions for the preparation and execution of the will and surrounding circumstances or confirm that you have no objection to us inspecting your relevant file(s) on reasonable notice.

We confirm that we will be responsible for your reasonable photocopying charges in this connection and your invoice in this regard should be sent to (each firm's name etc) and marked for the attention of (each firm's ref.).

Dated this [ ] day of [ ] 20[ ]

Signed
[   ]

Signed
[   ]

ANNEX F

LETTER TO DECEASED'S GP REQUESTING REPORT AS TO MENTAL CAPACITY

To: Deceased's GP

Dear Dr [   ]

Re: (Name) Deceased of (address), (date of birth)

We the undersigned Messrs (firm's name) (ref) of (firm's address) are Solicitors for (the Executors named in the Will of the late (deceased's name) of (deceased's address) who died on (date of death)) and we, the undersigned Messrs (firm's name) of (firm's address), are Solicitors for parties interested in his/her estate.

We enclose a photocopy of the deceased's last Will. The clauses in the Will which cause particular concern are (clause numbers).

The question of the deceased's mental capacity at the time of the making of his/her last Will dated has now been raised.

The test of testamentary capacity remains that established in the case of *Banks -v- Goodfellow* where it was said:-

> 'It is essential that a testator (1) shall understand the nature of the act and its effects; (2) shall understand the extent of the property of which he is disposing; and (3) shall be able to comprehend and appreciate the claims to which he ought to give effect, and; with a view to the latter object, (4) that no disorder of mind shall poison his affections, pervert his sense of right or pervert the exercise of his natural faculties; (5) that no insane delusions shall influence his mind in disposing of his property and bring about a disposal of it which if his mind had been sound, would not have been made.' (We have added numbers for convenience).

(Set out the nature of the Estate if complex).

We would therefore be grateful if you would kindly provide us with a report setting out:-

1. Your medical qualifications and your experience in assessing mental states and capacity.
2. For how long you were the deceased's GP, how well you knew the deceased and a summary of his/her medical condition, insofar as it may have bearing upon the deceased's mental capacity.
3. Your findings as to the deceased's mental capacity at and around the time of the date of his/her last will.
4. Please also deal with any mental disorder from which the deceased may have been suffering at the relevant time, and any medication which could have affected his/her capacity as detailed above.
5. Please also consider any issues of vulnerability or suggestibility at or around the date of the deceased's last Will.

We confirm that we will be responsible for your reasonable fees in the preparation of your report which we look forward to receiving as soon as possible.

Dated this [   ] day of [   ] 20[   ]

Signed
[   ] (ref:)

Signed
[   ] (ref:)

Index

References are to page numbers.

Acknowledgement of service 185–186, 187
Adjournments 188
Adopted persons
    and I(PFD)A claims 167
    deceased, disposal of bodies 94–95
Age
    advanced, and testators 1–2, 45–46
    and the *Golden Rule* 31, 34–39, 45, 46, 47–50, 51–52
    and I(PFD)A claims 172
    minimum, for testators 19
    of witnesses to wills 29
Aircraft, wills executed on 17
Alteration, of wills 25
    see also Codicils; Revocation of wills
Alternative dispute resolution 162, 178, 183
Annulment of marriage or civil partnership
    and I(PFD)A claims 165–166, 171
    and revocation of wills 122, 125–126
Appointment, powers of 122, 125, 127, 175
Ashes, *see* Disposal of bodies
Attestation of wills 25–29, 186
    international wills 17
    see also Witnesses of wills

Beneficial interests, *see* Constructive trusts; Jointly owned assets
Beneficiaries
    ascertaining identity, *see* Construction of wills
    and I(PFD)A claims 172
    and preparation of wills 57–58, 59–61, 71–72
    and statutory wills 200, 201
    and undue influence, *see* Undue influence
    as witnesses of wills 15, 21, 29–30
    predeceasing testators 33
Bereavement, and testamentary capacity 37–38
Blindness
    of testators 20, 55, 61
    of witnesses to wills 28–29
Braille, wills in 20
Burden and standard of proof
    forgery 82–83
    fraud 187
    knowledge and approval 59–60, 61
    rectification of wills 117, 120
    revocation of wills 127, 129–130
    testamentary capacity 34, 50–51, 197

Burden and standard of proof *(continued)*
    undue influence 63–65, 66–67, 73–74, 187
Burial, *see* Disposal of bodies

Capital gains tax 201
Caveats 179–182, 185
Chambers, Kate 141
Chancery Guide 177, 183, 190, 192, 195
Charging clauses 30
Chattels
    ascertaining identity, *see* Construction of wills
    outside England and Wales, *see* Foreign domicile or property
Children
    and I(PFD)A claims 164, 167–168, 173
    as persons under a disability 170, 184, 186
    as witnesses to wills 29
    deceased, disposal of bodies 88, 92–93, 94–95, 101–102
    parents' fiduciary relationship with 66, 74
    see also Age: minimum, for testators
Civil partners
    and I(PFD)A claims 164–165, 166, 171, 172
    and review of law 165
    and revocation of wills
        annulment or dissolution of union 126
        formation of union 124–125
    female, status of children 167
    of beneficiaries, witnessing wills 29–30
    see also Former spouses and former civil partners; Same sex marriage

Claim forms 184–185
Clerical error 24, 55, 107–113
Codicils 2, 29, 30, 127
    see also Wills
    see also other topics relating to wills
Cohabitants, and I(PFD)A claims 164, 166–167, 172–173
Common form probate, *see* Non-contentious probate, overview
Conditional revocation of wills 134
Confidential relationships, *see* Fiduciary relationships
Construction of wills 8–16, 126–131
    foreign domicile or property 16–17, 18
    see also Rectification of wills; Revocation of wills
Constructive trusts 147, 149, 156–162
    see also Jointly owned assets; Proprietary estoppel
Contracts to leave property by will 138–141
    see also Mutual wills; Proprietary estoppel
Costs, orders for 31, 53, 64, 162, 186, 192–195
Counterclaims 186–187
Court of Protection 43, 51, 197–202
Cremation, *see* Disposal of bodies
Criminal proceedings 77, 80–82
Curl, Joseph 81

Dates, and wills 7
    international wills 17
Deafness, of testators 55
    sign language 42, 47, 61
Defences (pleadings) 186–187
Delusions 39, 43–45
Dementia 37, 41, 45, 46
    see also Golden Rule, the

Dependants, financial provision for, *see* I(PFD)A claims
Dependent relative revocation   134
Destruction of wills   129, 131–134
   see also Missing wills
Disability
   and I(PFD)A claims   171, 172
   and testators
      knowledge and approval of will   55, 61
      physical inability to sign will   20, 21–22, 27, 61
      testamentary capacity, *see* Testamentary capacity
      undue influence   64, 65, 66–67, 74
   and witnesses of wills   28–29
   persons under (children and protected persons)   170, 184, 186
Disclosure of documents   188–191
Discontinuance of claims   188
Disposal of bodies   85–103
   and human rights law   85, 86, 91, 96–101
   background   85–86
   organ donation and medical research   86–90
   posthumous use of sperm   90
   responsibility for and disputes over   90–101
      litigation: procedure   101–103
Dissolution of marriage or civil partnership, *see* Former spouses and former civil partners
DIY wills   1, 112–113
Doctors
   and assessment of testamentary capacity   31, 34–39, 45, 46, 47–50, 51–52
   and statutory wills   200, 201
   fiduciary relationship with patients   66

Domicile, *see* Foreign domicile or property
Donatio mortis causa   149–150, 175
Drunkenness   46–47, 132
Dumont, Thomas   81

Elderly clients   1–2, 45–46
   and the *Golden Rule*   31, 34–39, 45, 46, 47–50, 51–52
En ventre sa mere, child   167
Execution of wills   19–30
   alteration of will after execution   25
   attestation   25–29, 186
      see also Witnesses of wills
   and Law Commission project   5, 30
   and pleadings in probate claims   184
   background   19
   date   7
   effect on existing will   127–131
   privileged wills   7, 19, 20
   of wrong will   23–24, 54–55, 105, 110–111, 114
   on ships or aircraft   17
   signature, by or for testator   20–25
      acknowledgement of prior signature   24–25
      on behalf of testator   20, 21–22, 27, 61
      form   20–21, 27, 46
      position   22–23, 27
   statutory wills   201
   writing, need for and form of   7, 20
   see also International wills; Knowledge and approval; Rectification of wills; Testamentary capacity; Undue influence

Executors
    and charging clauses   30
    and disposal of deceased's
        body   90–91, 99, 100
    appointment   20
    as parties to probate claims
        182–183
    ascertaining identity, *see*
        Construction of wills
    protection by limitation
        periods   106, 117
Extension of time
    for bringing I(PFD)A and
        rectification claims
        115–117, 155, 169–170
    for steps within probate
        claims   184–185, 188

Family and dependants, financial
    provision for, *see* I(PFD)A
    claims
Fiduciary relationships   29, 66–67,
    69–70, 74
Financial provision for family and
    dependants, *see* I(PFD)A
    claims
Floating trusts   147
    see also Constructive trusts
Foreign domicile or property   5, 7,
    16–18, 127–129
    and disposal of bodies   98–
        99, 100–101
Forgery   77–84
    see also Fraud
Former spouses and former civil
    partners
    and I(PFD)A claims   164,
        165–166, 171, 172–173
    dissolution of union and
        revocation of wills
        125–126
Fraud   63, 73, 75, 84, 184, 187
    see also Forgery
Funeral arrangements, *see* Disposal
    of bodies

Gifts, *see* Beneficiaries;
    Construction of wills;
    Lifetime agreements and gifts
Golden Rule, the   31, 34–39, 45,
    46, 47–50, 51–52

Hearing impairments, of testators
    55
    sign language   42, 47, 61
Home-made wills   1, 112–113
Hospitals, deaths in   91–92
Human rights law   85, 86, 91, 96–
    101

Illegitimate children   167
Illiteracy, of testators   20–21, 47,
    55, 61
Immovable property, *see* Foreign
    domicile or property
Income tax   201
Inheritance tax
    and I(PFD)A claims   156,
        174, 175
    and statutory wills   201
Inspection of documents   189,
    190, 191
Insurance policies   33, 152
Inter vivos dispositions, *see*
    Lifetime agreements and gifts
International wills   5, 7, 16–18
Intestacy, and disposal of
    deceased's body   90
I(PFD)A claims   163–175
    applicants   164–168
    background   3–4, 163–164,
        175
    costs   194
    definition of net estate   174–
        175
    and jointly owned assets
        154–156, 162, 175
    and lifetime dispositions
        140–141, 150, 163, 175
    grounds and relevant factors
        170–173

limitation period 115–117,
    155, 168–170, 175
  orders 173–174
  within probate claims 162,
    175, 179

Joinder of parties 182–183
Joint wills, *see* Mutual wills
Jointly owned assets 151–156,
    159–161, 162, 175
  see also Constructive trusts
Judicial separation, and I(PFD)A
    claims 165, 171

Knowledge and approval 53–62,
    105, 184
  see also Fraud; Testamentary
    capacity; Undue influence

Language and speech difficulties
    42, 47, 55
Law Commission project 5, 30,
    52, 120
Law Society, guidance on mental
    capacity 31, 35, 50
Lee, Annabel 43
Legitimated children 167
Lex situs 16
Life insurance 33, 152
Lifetime agreements and gifts 4–
    5, 137–150
  and I(PFD)A claims 140–
    141, 150, 163, 175
  and undue influence 63, 64,
    67, 68–70, 74
  taking effect on death
    background 137–138
    contracts to leave property by
      will 138–141
    donatio mortis causa 149–
      150, 175
    mutual wills 5, 137–138,
      147–149
    proprietary estoppel 141–
      146

    without valuable
      consideration 8
  see also Constructive trusts
Limitation periods
  I(PFD)A claims 115–117,
    155, 168–170, 175
  rectification of wills 106–
    107, 115–117, 169
  see also Time limits, for steps
    within probate claims
Litigation friends 184, 186
Local authorities, and disposal of
    bodies 92, 94

Mariners at sea, *see* Privileged wills
Marriage, and revocation of wills
  annulment or dissolution of
    marriage 122, 125–
    126
  formation of marriage 121–
    124, 125
  see also Former spouses and
    former civil partners;
    Spouses
Mathers, Wendy 81
Mediation 162, 183
  see also Alternative dispute
    resolution
Medical evidence, *see* Doctors
Medical research, use of bodies for
    86–90
Mental capacity
  and *donatio mortis causa* 150
  and taking part in litigation
    see protected persons
  and wills
    making, *see* Testamentary
      capacity; Statutory wills
    witnessing 28, 29
  Law Society guidance 31,
    35, 50
Minors, *see* Age: minimum, for
  testators; Children
Mirror wills 148
  see also Mutual wills

Missing wills   129–131
Mistake, *see* Rectification of wills
Moral claims, on testators   32, 33–34, 38–39, 43–45, 49, 61
   and I(PFD)A claims   4
   and mutual wills   147
   and statutory wills   199
Movable property, *see* Foreign domicile or property
Mutual wills   5, 137–138, 147–149

Neuberger, Lord (and STEP lecture)   68
Nominations   5, 175
Non-contentious probate, overview
   background   177
   proposed changes to rules   6
   venue   179
   see also individual topics
Non-marital children   167

Objections, *see* Caveats
Official Solicitor   200
Organ donation   86–90

Parental orders (surrogacy)   167
Parents
   and disposal of deceased child's body   88, 92–93, 94–95, 101–102
   fiduciary relationship with children   66, 74
Partial destruction of wills   133–134
Particulars of claim   184, 185, 186
Pension schemes   5, 33
Personal representatives, *see* Executors
Polygamous marriages   165
Powers of appointment   122, 125, 127, 175
Pre-action disclosure   188–189
Pre-action protocols   175, 177, 183, 190, 192, 195

Privileged wills   7, 19, 20
Probate claims   177–195
   background   1–2, 177
   procedure, overview
      and related I(PFD)A claims   162, 175, 179
      and related prosecutions   80, 82
      caveats   179–182, 185
      costs, overview   192–195
      other pre-action steps   182–183, 188–189
      overriding objective   177–179
      stages of an action   182–188, 189–191
      unopposed rectification claims   117–118, 191–192
   see also individual topics
Property
   details of, and statutory wills   201
   knowledge of, and testamentary capacity   33
   net estate under I(PFD)A, defined   174–175
   see also Construction of wills; Foreign domicile or property; Jointly owned assets
Proprietary estoppel   141–146, 161
   see also Constructive trusts; Contracts to leave property by will; Mutual wills
Protected persons   170, 184, 186

Rectification of wills   105–120
   and Law Commission project   5, 120
   background   54, 105–107, 117, 120
   clerical error   24, 55, 107–113

limitation period   106–107, 115–117, 169
misunderstanding testator's instructions   113–115
procedure   117–120, 191–192
wrong will executed   23–24, 54–55, 105, 110–111, 114
see also Construction of wills
Reproductive treatment, and status of children   167
Resulting trusts   158, 159
see also Constructive trusts
Revocation of wills   121–135
and destruction   129, 131–134
and later wills   18, 126–129
and marriage or civil partnership   121–126
and missing wills   129–131
background   121, 134–135
conditional revocation   134
see also Mutual wills
Ruck Keene, Alex   43

Same sex marriage   122–124, 125, 126, 164–165
see also Civil partners; Former spouses and former civil partners; Spouses
Scotland   77, 99–100, 102
Seamen at sea, *see* Privileged wills
Senile dementia   37, 41, 45, 46
see also *Golden Rule*, the
Separation orders, and I(PFD)A claims   165, 171
Service, of probate claims   185, 187
Ships
wills executed on   17
wills of mariners and seamen at sea, *see* Privileged wills
Shorthand, wills in   20
Sign language   42, 47, 61

Signatures, and wills
by or for testators, *see* Execution of wills: signature, by or for testator
by witnesses, *see* Witnesses of wills
international wills   17
wrong will executed   23–24, 54–55, 105, 110–111, 114
Soldiers
deceased, disposal of bodies   91, 99–100
on actual military service, *see* Privileged wills
Solicitors
and execution of wills   23–24, 105, 114
and late I(PFD)A claims   169
and probate claims   195
and testamentary capacity of clients   31, 34–40, 45, 47, 49–50, 51
and unrectifiable errors in wills   114
fiduciary relationship with clients   66
see also Rectification of wills
Speech difficulties, *see* Language and speech difficulties
Sperm, posthumous use of   90
Spouses
and I(PFD)A claims   164–165, 166, 171, 172
of beneficiaries, witnessing wills   29–30
see also Former spouses and former civil partners; Marriage, and revocation of wills
Standard of proof, *see* Burden and standard of proof
Statutory wills   197–202
Subpoenas   189, 190
Surrogacy, and parental orders   167

Tax
   and I(PFD)A claims   156, 174, 175
   and statutory wills   201
Testamentary capacity   31–52
   and Law Commission project   5, 52
   and pleadings in probate claims   184
   background   31–32
   burden and standard of proof   34, 50–51, 197
   fluctuation   40, 45, 46
   Golden Rule, the   31, 34–39, 45, 46, 47–50, 51–52
   Law Society guidance   31, 35, 50
   test   32–34, 40–47, 48–49, 52
   time at which assessment is relevant   39, 40, 41, 46, 55–56
   see also Knowledge and approval; Statutory wills; Undue influence
Testamentary documents, and procedure in probate claims   184, 185, 186, 189, 190, 191
Time limits
   for bringing proceedings, *see* Limitation periods
   for steps within probate claims   184, 185–186, 188
Tringham, Michael   77
Trusts
   and orders under I(PFD)A   174
   and statutory wills   201
   charging clauses in wills   30
   constructive   147, 149, 156–162
   secret, beneficiaries as witnesses of wills   29
   see also Fiduciary relationships; Jointly owned assets; Nominations; Powers of appointment; Proprietary estoppel

Uncertainty, *see* Construction of wills; Rectification of wills
Undue influence   63–75, 184, 187
   and pleadings in probate claims   184, 187
   burden of proof   63–65, 66–67, 73–74, 187
   lifetime dispositions   63, 64, 67, 68–70, 74
   see also Knowledge and approval; Testamentary capacity

Void marriages   165
Voidable marriages   122, 165

Warnings (to caveats)   180–181
Wills
   background   2, 7, 20, 32–33, 177
   international   5, 7, 16–18
   mirror   148
   missing   129–131
   mutual   5, 137–138, 147–149
   privileged   7, 19, 20
   statutory   197–202
   see also Codicils
   see also other topics relating to wills
Witness summonses   189, 190
Witnesses of wills   25–29, 186
   beneficiaries as   15, 21, 29–30
   competence   28–29
   doctors as   35, 51
   international wills   17